Database Programming with JDBC™ and Java™

THE JAVA™ SERIES

Sreeni. Inturi.

Database Programming with JDBC™ and Java™

Second Edition

George Reese

O'REILLY®

Beijing · Cambridge · Farnham · Köln · Paris · Sebastopol · Taipei · Tokyo

Database Programming with JDBC™ and Java™, Second Edition
by George Reese

Copyright © 2000, 1997 O'Reilly & Associates, Inc. All rights reserved.
Printed in the United States of America.

Published by O'Reilly & Associates, Inc., 101 Morris Street, Sebastopol, CA 95472.

Editor: Andy Oram

Production Editors: Ann Schirmer and Claire Cloutier

Cover Designer: Edie Freedman

Printing History:

June 1997:	First Edition.
August 2000:	Second Edition.

Library of Congress Cataloging-in-Publication Data

Reese, George.
   Database programming with JDBC and Java/George Reese.--2nd ed, p.cm.
   Includes index.
   ISBN 1-56592-616-1
   1. Database design 2. Java (Computer program language) I. Title.

QA76.9 D26 R44 2000
005.75'6--dc21   00-060605

For Baa and Nonie

Table of Contents

Preface

It is never too late to become reasonable and wise;
but if the insight comes late, there is always
more difficulty in starting the change.

—Immanuel Kant
Prolegomena to Any Future Metaphysics

I began writing the first edition of this book in May 1996 as Java™ celebrated one of its first major rites of passage, the inaugural JavaOne conference. The conference's underlying theme was Java's transition from an applet language to a hard-core computing environment. In the time since that conference, that promise has become a reality. This book captures a small piece of that reality: Java as a language for enterprise computing.

Enterprise computing, a vague term used mostly to sell business systems development products, traditionally refers to the mission-critical systems on which a business depends. It almost always includes a database. At the heart of Java's enterprise computing philosophy is the Java 2 Enterprise Edition (J2EE) platform and its two platforms by APIs: Enterprise JavaBeans (EJB) and Java Database Connectivity (JDBC). Older languages require third-party APIs to provide this kind of support. Java, on the other hand, includes these features in the central Java enterprise distribution that you will find on every Java platform. As a developer, you can write distributed applications that run against relational databases and know that those applications will run on any system on which you deploy them.

What exactly are these APIs? JDBC—the basic component of this book—enables you to write applications that access relational databases without any thought as to which particular database you are using. If you have ever had experience programming to more than one database API, you will definitely appreciate this aspect of

Java. When you write a Java database program, that same program will run against Oracle, MySQL, Sybase, Ingres, Informix, mSQL, PostgreSQL, or any other database that supports this API.

EJB, on the other hand, gives real meaning to the expression "the network is the computer." If you have written Internet applications in the past, you have probably been faced with the challenge of writing TCP/IP or UDP/IP sockets. While socket programming in Java is not nearly as hard as it is in other programming languages, the task of writing sockets is generally a side technical issue that takes time away from the writing of your main application code. By using distributed object technology, you can build Java objects that run on different machines but communicate with one another through simple Java method calls.

How do these APIs make Java more than a simple applet building language? Database access is the core requirement of the majority of mission-critical business applications that get developed. By giving Java database access combined with the development of GUI development tools, Sun has made Java a language that competes with established tools, such as VisualBasic and PowerBuilder. Java distributed object support goes a giant step beyond these tools by liberating Java components from the need to be located together in the same Java Virtual Machine.

Audience

If you have not yet read a book on Java, then this book should not be the first one you pick up. I assume that readers have a basic understanding of the Java programming language. Specifically, you should feel comfortable with the basic syntax of Java and central concepts such as classes, interfaces, and packages. If you are looking for a starter book for Java programming, I strongly recommend *Learning Java* by Patrick Niemeyer and Jonathan Knudsen (O'Reilly & Associates).

I also expect that you know some basic database concepts. You do not need the same solid foundation with database concepts that I assume for Java. Instead, you should have some minimal exposure to relational databases; you should know what tables, columns, and rows are and understand basic SQL syntax. I do provide a basic introduction to these concepts in Chapter 2, *Relational Databases and SQL*; however, this introduction is very quick and certainly skips a lot of important details. While Chapter 2 does not provide nearly enough knowledge to make you a database expert, it will serve you well if you intend to study databases while using this book. If you are truly green to the database world and really want to dive in, I suggest downloading a copy of the MySQL database at *http://www.mysql.com* and purchasing the book *MySQL and mSQL* by Randy Jay Yarger, Tim King, and myself (O'Reilly). MySQL is a simple, accessible database engine that serves as a perfect learning tool.

Using This Book

This book is divided into three very different sections. The first section focuses on the JDBC API. Its first two chapters set the stage by covering enterprise programming and an introduction to relational databases and SQL. Programmers skilled in database programming in other languages may skip on to Chapter 3, *Introduction to JDBC*, where I introduce JDBC in full. Section II applies everything you learn in the first section to real world database programming. Within the context of a concrete business example—a banking application—Section II describes issues you are likely to encounter in building your own database applications. The final section is a reference section for the JDBC Core and Optional Package APIs.

Throughout this book, I have made sure that the examples use `javadoc` commenting. If you are not familiar with `javadoc`, it is a utility that ships with the Sun JDK. By using the `javadoc` format, you can automatically generate web pages that document your Java classes. The persistence library that gets developed later in the book has web documentation at *http://www.oreilly.com/catalog/jdbc2*. Though using `javadoc` comments takes more space, I believe that it is good programming practice and that it also increases the readability of the examples in this book.

Software and Versions

In developing the examples in this book, I used JDK 1.2. I performed database access for all of the book except Chapter 4, *Advanced JDBC*, using the mSQL 1.0.16 database engine with the mSQL-JDBC 2.0a2 JDBC driver. I handled database access for Chapter 4 using PersonalOracle 7.2.2.3.1 with the WebLogic Oracle driver.

Conventions Used in This Book

Italic is used for:

- Pathnames, filenames, and program names
- Internet addresses, such as domain names and URLs
- New terms where they are defined

Boldface is used for:

- Names of servers

`Constant width` is used for:

- Anything that might appear in a Java program, including object names, keywords, method names, variable names, class names, and interface names
- Command lines and options that should be typed verbatim

- Tags that might appear in an HTML document
- Java package norms
- SQL commands

Constant-width italic is used for:

- Replaceable elements in code statements

Constant-width bold is used for:

- New JDK 1.2 methods in old JDK 1.1 classes

Examples of the programs in this book may be retrieved online from *ftp.oreilly.com* in */pub/examples/java/jdbc*. The files are on the site as *examples.tar.gz*.

Comments and Questions

The information in this book has been tested and verified, but you may find that features have changed (or you may even find mistakes!). You can send any errors you find, as well as suggestions for future editions, to:

O'Reilly & Associates, Inc.
101 Morris Street
Sebastopol, CA 95472
1-800-998-9938 (in the United States or Canada)
1-707-829-0515 (international/local)
1-707-829-0104 (Fax)

You can also send messages electronically. To be put on the mailing list or request a catalog, send email to:

info@oreilly.com

To ask technical questions or comment on the book, send email to:

bookquestions@oreilly.com

We have a web site for the book, where examples, errata, and any plans for future editions are listed. You can access this site at:

http://www.oreilly.com/catalog/jdbc2

For more information about this book and others, see the O'Reilly web site:

http://www.oreilly.com

About the Philosophers

If you read prefaces, it is even possible that you read author biographies as well. Mine notes that I came out of college with a degree in philosophy. The path from philosophy to Java programming is of course not a very common one; I nevertheless honestly believe that philosophy provides a very solid grounding for programming logic and object-oriented systems development.

During the first JavaOne conference, I attended an address given by Dr. John Gage of Sun. In that speech, he quoted a modern philosopher of language and metaphysics, Dr. Donald Davidson. If you do not have a background in philosophy, chances are that you do not recognize his name. I was so amazed at hearing his name mentioned, I went up and spoke to Dr. Gage after the address. We got into a discussion of philosophy and computing during which he suggested I work philosophy quotes into this book. I have taken his advice and started each chapter with a quote from a major philosopher.

I have tried to choose quotes that have direct relevance to the topic at hand. In some cases, however, the quotes are only indirectly relevant. The philosophers, in order of appearance in the book, are:

Immanuel Kant (Preface)

Immanuel Kant may be the most influential philosopher of the second millennium. He was a German philosopher who lived from 1724 until 1804. He emphasized a rational approach to all philosophical pursuits. This rationalism has had its greatest impact in the area of ethics, where moral principles are, according to Kant, derived entirely from reason.

Jacques Derrida (Chapter 1)

Derrida is a 20th century French philosopher born in Algeria in 1930. His most famous contribution to philosophy is the school of Deconstruction. Deconstruction is a way of examining meaning and being that seeks to "undo" the thing being examined, and, as a result, removes the myth of an essential nature of that thing.

René Descartes (Chapter 2)

Though he lived from 1596 until 1650, Descartes' writings mark the beginning of modern philosophy. He was a French philosopher who emphasized a solipsistic approach to epistemology. He is the author of the famous quote "Cogito, ergo sum," or "I think, therefore I am."

Noam Chomsky (Chapter 3)

Born in 1928, Noam Chomsky is perhaps the most famous living philosopher. While often known for his political activism—especially during the Vietnam era—his greatest contributions to philosophy lie in the philosophy of language.

Daniel Dennett (Chapters 4 and 6)

Dennett, who teaches at Tufts University, is probably my favorite philosopher. His books are actually well written, which is a rare quality among philosophy texts. His works run the spectrum of philosophy, but his greatest influence lies in the philosophies of mind and science. If you want a fun philosophy book to read that does not require you to be a philosopher, pick up his book *Elbow Room*. If you are looking for something more weighty, but equally accessible, read *Darwin's Dangerous Idea*.

Friedrich Nietzsche (Chapter 5)

Nietzsche, who lived in Germany from 1844 until 1900, is likely the most controversial "serious" philosopher. His writings have influenced nearly every kind of philosophy, but have had their greatest impact—both positive and negative—in the area of ethics.

Ludwig Wittgenstein (Chapters 7 and 9)

Ludwig Wittgenstein was an Austrian philosopher who lived from 1889 until 1951. His primary contributions to philosophy were in the philosophy of language. He once wrote that "philosophy is a battle against the bewitchment of our intelligence by means of language."

Martin Heidegger (Chapter 8)

Heidegger, another 20th century German philosopher, made popular the movement started by Edmund Husserl known as Phenomenology. Phenomenology attempts to understand things as they present themselves rather than attempt to appeal to some sort of essential nature hidden from us. This movement eventually led to the most popularly known philosophical movement, Existentialism.

Jean-Paul Sartre (Chapter 10)

Sartre was a novelist, a philosopher, and a member of the French Resistance during World War II. As a philosopher, he is best known as the force behind the Existentialism movement. Existentialism goes beyond Phenomenology in its claims about the essential nature of things. While Phenomenology claims that we should not appeal to an essential nature of a thing in order to understand it, Existentialism says that no such essential nature exists. A thing is exactly as it presents itself.

Acknowledgments

While my name is the one that appears on the cover, this book would not be the book it is without the help of Andy Oram, the editor. I cannot thank him enough for the difference he has made in each chapter of this book. His efforts have helped make the difference between this being any Java book and it being an O'Reilly Java book.

A host of other people have influenced me in ways that have affected the quality of this book both directly and indirectly. First, there are those who have taken a look at individual portions of the book: Monique Girgis, Ryan Olson, and Paul Wouters. Another group provided me with detailed feedback on the entirety of the first edition: Dave Andreasen, Leigh Caldwell, Jim Farley, Patrick Killelea, Howard Melman, John Viega, and Tim O'Reilly. Shadia Atiyeh provided feedback on the second edition. Jim Farley, Thomas Lukasik, and Greg Nyberg all gave me detailed technical commentary on the second edition. At O'Reilly, I would like to thank Tim O'Reilly for publishing what I believe are the best books in the business. Finally, Monique deserves a special thanks for suggesting that I write this book in the first place.

Oh, and as cheesy as it sounds, I can't forget to thank my cats, Misty, Gypsy, and Tia, just for being there.

Feedback for the Author

I have done everything in my power both to explain the JDBC and RMI APIs and to provide a practical infrastructure in which you might use them. I hope this book serves you well as you tackle database programming in Java. In that spirit, I would like very much to hear your comments, corrections, praise, or criticism. You can contact me at *george.reese@imaginary.com*.

I

THE JDBC API

The first section of this book takes you through the JDBC API from the basics of SQL to the more esoteric features of advanced JDBC and the JDBC Optional Package. The understanding of JDBC you gain in this first section can then be applied to the real-world programming model of distributed, three-tier database application programming in Part II.

1

Java in the Enterprise

> *Is it certain that to the word communication corresponds a concept that is unique, univocal, rigorously controllable, and transmittable: in a word, communicable? Thus, in accordance with a strange figure of discourse, one must first of all ask oneself whether or not the word or signifier "communication" communicates a determinate content, an identifiable meaning, or a describable value.*
>
> —Jacques Derrida
> *Limited Inc*

Two years ago when the first edition of this book was initially published, Java was attracting unprecedented attention from its early success in bringing dynamic content to web pages. The question "Is Java ready for serious development?" was on everyone's mind. Presenting pretty pictures is one thing, but supporting the complex needs of enterprise development is very much another thing. Could Java leverage the infrastructure of existing business environments and take it where existing tools could never imagine going?

Today, Java's power as a server language is taken for granted. Ironically, due to problems with the early versions of the AWT, people tend to question its stability on the client. APIs such as JNDI, the servlet API, the security API, and the suite of APIs collectively known as the Java Enterprise APIs—JDBC, RMI, and Java IDL—together make Java a formidable force on the server. The leap from being a good server development language to being a powerful enterprise development platform, however, is still far.

Unfortunately, the word "enterprise" most certainly does not communicate a determinate content, an identifiable meaning, or a describable value. Just about every technology product aimed at the business customer is sold with the tag—the buzzword—"enterprise." As with any technology industry buzzword, the marketing people have twisted it and made it into a meaningless term. If you pull the marketing fog away, however, you can find an important concept that the word "enterprise" once captured. Within that meaning, the power of Java is fully realized. Before you get into the heart of Java Enterprise's capabilities, you should first understand what the term "enterprise" means in the context of enterprise software.

The Enterprise

Buried within the term "enterprise" is the idea of a business taken wholistically. An enterprise solution identifies common problem domains within a business and provides a shared infrastructure for solving those problems. If your business is running a bank, your individual branches may have different business cultures, but those cultures do not alter the fact that they all deal with customers and accounts. Looking at this business from an enterprise perspective means abstracting away from irrelevant differences in the way the individual branches do things, and instead approaching the business from their common ground. It does not mean dismissing meaningful distinctions, such as the need for bilingual support in California branches.

Applying this view to software engineering, an enterprise system provides the proper abstractions for business concepts that are constant across a business so that they may be shared by all the different units within the company. In the Internet age, enterprise systems even go beyond sharing those business concepts within the company to sharing them with vendors, clients, and customers. A detailed look at an example of a manufacturing company can better illustrate how to look at a business from the enterprise perspective.

A Business in Need of an Enterprise Solution

For this example, the hypothetical manufacturing company, Wombles, Inc., makes all sorts of goods—toasters, blenders, tire irons, light bulbs, etc.—and has three major business units: North America, Europe, and Asia-Pacific. The company started out as an American company. As it grew, it acquired two other companies to gain a worldwide presence. All three business units have their own systems and are mostly ignorant about the issues involved in doing business in the other two regions. Marketing, however, has worked hard and successfully at creating a single, world-recognized brand.

As long as each unit works within its own realm, everything runs smoothly. From the perspective of each unit working within its own realm, however, they might as well be three separate companies. Certainly, moving beyond the distinct realms of each business unit in this environment is a formidable task. What do you do if

Asia-Pacific runs out of light bulbs but North America experiences a light-bulb glut? What do you do if your distributors want a single interface into your inventory system? What do you do if your customers, who do not care that you are divided into three separate business units, demand direct and immediate online access via the Web?

An enterprise system answers all of these questions. You have one single repository of inventory and pricing information—a single repository that enables the individual business units to customize, but share this pricing information. Your vendors are then presented with a single interface into your inventory management, and web-enabling access to those systems is nothing more than writing Java servlets.

NOTE   Throughout the book I make reference to software "systems." With the advent of distributed computing, the terms "system" and "application" have lost any clear definition. For the purposes of this book, when I refer to a system, I am talking about one or more backend processes that support one or more user interfaces. When I talk about an application, it is almost always in reference to one of those user interfaces.

Requirements for a True Enterprise System

In order to solve enterprise problems, an enterprise system must exhibit certain characteristics. The goal of an enterprise system is simply to be able to represent business concepts to any possible user whether that user is an application within your business, an XML interface for your vendors or clients, or a web interface for your customers. An enterprise system enables you to worry about the specific issue of providing an appropriate window into your business for each audience without duplicating the effort required to capture the rules of your business—the things that never change. An enterprise system must therefore meet these requirements:

An enterprise system must have minimal proprietary components.
    Avoiding proprietary components means, among other things, being platform- and database-independent. You cannot impose technical requirements on your vendors, clients, and customers. Do you think Amazon.com would sell any books if they required all visitors to run MacOS? This requirement, however, goes beyond simple platform requirements for your audiences. It also means being able to integrate new components into the system as technology evolves. It is much harder—and often impossible—to integrate new technologies with closed, proprietary components.

An enterprise system must be capable of supporting personalized user experience.
    Personalized user experience comes in many forms—internationalization, localization, accessibility, personalization, and customization. Meeting this

requirement means supporting the creation of user interfaces that can display content tailored to the language and cultural norms of the user interacting with the system. It also means supporting tools on the client that help make an application accessible to users with disabilities. Finally, an enterprise system needs to be able to study the way users interact with it so that it can better support each user's unique mode of interaction.

An enterprise system must be the authoritative, shared source for the business concepts it represents.

All applications using concepts common across the business should reference the objects that represent those concepts from the same shared system. This does not mean that they are referencing the exact same processes on exactly the same servers. It means that any given concept has an authoritative location that is transparent to the client from which it can be referenced.

Java as a Tool for Enterprise Development

Java is really the only language in widespread use that can easily be used to build systems that meet the requirements I just listed for an enterprise system. Java is a standards-based language that is platform-independent. It has support for accessibility and internationalization and localization, including a Unicode basic character type, built into the language. Finally, Java is an object-oriented language with database access and distributed computing at its core.

The Java APIs and Platform Independence

One important test of whether a component of your enterprise system is propri-etary is whether or not another vendor could, in principal, provide a black-box implementation of that component. The Java Virtual Machine (JVM), for exam-ple, is an open specification for which others can—and some do—write indepen-dent implementations. Java's suitability for this requirement, however, goes beyond the fact that it is a standardized language that is platform-independent. It also provides a host of APIs that you are guaranteed to find on any JVM for access-ing hardware and software resources traditionally blocked by expensive, propri-etary interfaces. For its original release, the Java specification prescribed what Sun termed the Java Core API—the basic objects required for a minimally viable language. The Java platform specification has since grown to encompass many other APIs. The following is an abridged list of some of the Java APIs:

JavaBeans™

In response to the Microsoft ActiveX threat, JavaSoft developed JavaBeans, a platform-neutral specification for creating software components. Part of the JavaBeans specification actually involves interfacing with ActiveX components.

Java Commerce

Java Commerce is an Internet-based API for providing secure economic transactions across an insecure network. This API includes Java Wallet, which is a framework for client-side credit card, debit card, and electronic cash transactions.

Java Core

Java Core consists of libraries that shipped with the JDK 1.0 release. It includes the `java.applet`, `java.awt`, `java.io`, `java.lang`, `java.net`, and `java.util` packages and provides the core level of functionality needed in order to build simple applets and applications in Java.

Java Embedded

The Java Embedded API enables devices such as cellular phones and toasters, which may not be capable of supporting the full range of Java Core functionality, to offer a subset of Java Core.

Java Enterprise

Java Enterprise actually consists of three separate libraries that provide access to an organization's resources and applications. The Java DataBase Connectivity API, or JDBC, provides database connectivity. Using JDBC, an application can perform database access independent of the actual database engine being used for data storage. The same application can be written once, compiled once, and run against any database engine with a JDBC driver.

The Interface Definition Language (IDL) enables Java applications to provide a language-neutral interface between Java objects and objects located across the network. It follows the Object Management Group (OMG) IDL specification.

Remote Method Invocation (RMI), is a Java-specific API that lets objects call methods in objects located across the network. Unlike IDL, RMI is a Java-only solution. Instead of writing complex communication protocols using sockets, an application can communicate with remote objects through simple Java method calls.

Java Management

Java Management lets an application perform network administration.

Java Media

Java Media creates a single API that enables developers to write rich multimedia applications interfacing with a variety of multimedia hardware devices. The Media Frameworks provides clocks for synchronizing audio, video, and MIDI.

The 2D and 3D libraries provide enhanced imaging classes. The Animation API enables applications to perform transformations on 2D images. Telephony provides an application with a single API for accessing a range of telephone devices.

Java Security

The Java Security API provides developers with a simple API for enhancing applet or application security, including the ability to add cryptography, encryption, and authentication.

Java Server

Java Server is Java's answer to CGI. This API allows developers to interface with and enhance Internet servers using *servlets*, executable programs that users upload to run on networks or servers.

As Sun develops specific APIs, it enlists the cooperation of major industry players in the area of the API in question. In developing the database access API (the subject of this book), Sun worked with a team of database leaders and listened to extensive public input. Some of the companies that have been actively involved with database API development are shown in the following list. These companies are not simply paying lip service to the technology. They have committed time and money to make sure the level of support is intense enough to lend substance to the hype.

BEA WebLogic Enterprise	Intersoft	Recital Corporation
Borland International, Inc.	Intersolv	RogueWave Software
Bulletproof	Object Design	SAS Institute Inc.
Cyber SQL Corporation	Open Horizon	SCO
DataRamp	OpenLink Software	Sybase
Dharma Systems Inc.	Oracle	Symantec
Gupta Corporation	Persistence Software	Thunderstone
IBM	Presence Information Design	XDB Systems, Inc.
Informix	Pro-C Ltd.	

Internationalization, Localization, and Accessibility

Java is the first major language with internationalization and localization built into it. The most fundamental evidence of this support lies in the Java character datatype (and the String class based on it). Java characters are two bytes, and Java strings are Unicode, not ASCII. This means that you can store in a single Java string a paragraph containing sentences in every language known without any programming tricks.

Internationalization and localization involve a lot more than character-set encoding issues, and Java recognizes that. Java provides client applications direct access to the locale information for the clients on which it runs. Java applications can automatically use this locale information to provide the proper display of locale-sensitive strings such as date, currency, and numeric strings. A Java developer does not have to know any of the issues surrounding localization for a particular locale—Java does the formatting automatically.

Accessibility is even simpler for developers. In fact, there is absolutely nothing a Java developer needs to do to make an application accessible other than follow good user-interface programming practices. Java uses the clues a well-developed user interface provides to make that user interface accessible.

There is a lot more to Java support for internationalization and localization. A full discussion of these issues is well beyond the scope of this book.

Sharing Business Concepts Across the Business

One of Java's most powerful features is built-in support for distributed computing. Java RMI, one of the Java Enterprise APIs, provides this support. By taking advantage of Java RMI, business objects created in Java can be exported and shared by multiple user interfaces. The same business object that represents a toaster you have in stock can be immediately referenced by an employee in Singapore, a distributor in Houston, and a customer shopping on the Web.

NOTE   A *business object* is not necessarily a business concept. It is simply a term used to represent any concept that is part of a nontechnical problem domain. For our manufacturing example, product would most likely be a business object. The concept, however, extends beyond business. In an online fantasy game like a mud, Sword, Monster, Player, and Bag may all be business objects. Business objects are basically distinguished from other kinds of objects in that they are shared objects and represent a concept within the problem domain.

The Database

The database is the heart of any enterprise system. The shared business objects that make up an enterprise need some way to make sure they are saved across time. The database provides that storage mechanism. Any language that is going to claim to be an enterprise language therefore needs to have strong, reliable database connectivity.

How Java Interacts with a Database

Several important database concepts form the core of this book's discussion. This book assumes some basic familiarity with Java and databases. You should have a basic understanding of SQL and transaction management. Building on this foundation, we will discuss JDBC and how it can be used to execute SQL against any potential database engine.

SQL

The Java database API, JDBC, requires that the database being used support ANSI SQL2 as the query language. The SQL language itself is worthy of a tiny mini-industry within the publishing field, so covering it is well beyond the scope of this book.* The SQL in this book, however, stays away from the more complex areas of the language and instead sticks with basic DELETE, INSERT, SELECT, and UPDATE statements. For a short overview of SQL, check out Chapter 2, *Relational Databases and SQL.*

The only additional level of complexity I use consists of stored procedures in the later chapters. Stored procedures are precompiled SQL stored on the database server and executed by naming the procedure and passing parameters to it. In other words, a stored procedure is much like a database server function. Stored procedures provide an easy mechanism for separating Java programmers from database issues and improving database performance.

JDBC

JDBC is in a SQL-level API that allows you to embed SQL statements as arguments to methods in JDBC interfaces. To enable you to do this in a database-independent fashion, JDBC requires database vendors (such as those mentioned earlier in this chapter) to furnish a runtime implementation of its interfaces. These implementations route your SQL calls to the database in the proprietary fashion it recognizes. As the programmer, though, you do not ever have to worry about how it is routing SQL statements. The façade provided by JDBC gives you complete freedom from any issues related to particular database issues; you can run the same code no matter what database is present.

Transaction management

Transaction management involves packaging related database transactions into a single unit and handling any error conditions that result. To get through this book, you need only to understand basic transaction management in the form of

---

* O'Reilly is publishing a SQL reference guide, *SQL in a Nutshell,* by Kevin Kline with Daniel Kline.

beginning a transaction and either committing it on success or aborting it on failure. JDBC provides you with the ability to auto-commit any transaction on the atomic level (that is, statement by statement) or wait until a series of statements have succeeded (or failed) and call the appropriate commit (or rollback) method.

Database Technologies

A Java application can use one of three major database architectures:

- Relational database
- Object database
- Object-relational database

The overwhelming majority of today's database applications use relational databases. The JDBC API is thus heavily biased toward relational databases and their standard query language, SQL. Relational databases find and provide relationships between data, so they collide head-on with object solutions such as Java, since object-oriented philosophy dictates that an object's behavior is inseparable from its data. In choosing the object-oriented reality of Java, you need to create a translation layer that maps the relational world into your object world. While JDBC provides you with access to relational databases, it leaves the issue of object-to-relational mapping up to you.

Object databases, on the other hand, do not attempt to separate object data from behavior. The best way to think of an object database is as a permanent store of objects with which your applications can interface. This object-oriented encapsulation of data, however, makes it difficult to relate data as well as relational databases do. Additionally, with JDBC so tightly bound to SQL, it is difficult to create JDBC drivers to run against an object database. As of the writing of this book, Sun, in cooperation with the Object Database Management Group (ODMG), is working on a specification for a Java object database API.

Object-relational databases enjoy a "best of both worlds" advantage by providing both object and relational means of accessing data. Until recently, object relational databases have relied almost entirely on C++ objects to act as their object store. With all of the excitement around Java, however, object-relational vendors are starting to enable their systems to support database objects written and extended in Java. In this realm, your Java objects do not need to map relational data into business objects. For the sake of easy, ad hoc querying, however, an object-relational database also provides complex relational queries; sometimes these queries can even be done in an ANSI SQL superset language.

Database Programming with Java

While the marriage of Java and database programming is beneficial to Java programmers, Java also helps database programmers. Specifically, Java provides database programmers with the following features they have traditionally lacked:

- Easy object to relational mapping

- Database independence

- Distributed computing

If you are interested in taking a pure object approach to systems development, you may have run into the cold reality that most of the world runs on relational databases into which companies have often placed hefty investments. This leaves you trying to map C++ and Smalltalk objects to relational entities. Java provides an alternative to these two tools that frees you from the proprietary interfaces associated with database programming. With the "write once, compile once, run anywhere" power that JDBC offers you, Java's database connectivity allows you to worry about the translation of relational data into objects instead of worrying about how you are getting that data.

A Java database application does not care what its database engine is. No matter how many times the database engine changes, the application itself need never change. In addition, a company can build a class library that maps its business objects to database entities in such a way that applications do not even know whether or not their objects are being stored in a database. Later in the book I discuss building a class library that allows you to map the data you retrieve through the JDBC API into Java objects.

Java affects the way you distribute and maintain an application. A traditional client/server application requires an administrator responsible for the deployment of the client program on users' desktops. That administrator takes great pains to assure that each desktop provides a similar operating environment so that the application may run as it was intended to run. When a change is made to the application, the administrator makes the rounds and installs the upgrade.

The Java language employs the idea of the zero-install client. The object code for the entire application, client and server, resides on the network. Since the JVM provides an application with a guaranteed runtime environment, no administration is needed for the configuration of that environment for individual applications. The users simply use a virtual machine interface such as HotJava to locate the desired application. By clicking on the application icon, a user can run it without even realizing the application was never stored on their local machine.

The traditional application makes a clear distinction between the locations where processing occurs. In traditional applications, database access occurs on the server, and GUI processing occurs on the client; the objects on the client machine talk to the database through a specialized database API. In other situations, the client might talk to the server through a set of TCP/IP or UDP/IP socket APIs. Either way, a wall of complex protocols divides the objects found on the client from those on the server. Java helps tear down this wall between client and server through another piece of its Enterprise platform, RMI.

RMI allows applications to call methods in objects on remote machines as if those objects were located on the same machine. Calling a method in another object in Java is of course as simple as the syntax `object.method(arg)`. If you want to call that method from a remote machine without RMI, however, you would have to write code that allows you to send an object handle, a method name, and arguments through a TCP/IP socket, translate it into an `object.method(arg)` call on the remote end, perform the method call, pass the return value back across the socket, and then write a bunch of code to handle network failures. That is a lot of work for a simple method call, and I did not even get into the issues you would have to deal with, such as passing object references as arguments and handling garbage collection on each end. Finally, since you have written this complex protocol to handle method calls across the network, you have serious rewriting to do if you decide that a given object needs to exist on the client instead of the server (or vice versa).

With RMI, any method call, whether on the same machine or across the network, uses the same Java method call syntax. This freedom to distribute objects across the network is called a *distributed object architecture*. Other languages use much more complex protocols like Common Object Request Broker Architecture (CORBA) and the Distributed Computing Environment (DCE). RMI, however, is a Java-specific API for enabling a distributed architecture. As such, it removes many of the complexities of those two solutions.

For a client/server database application, a distributed architecture allows the various parts of the application to refer to the same physical objects when referring to particular objects in the data model. For example, take an airline ticketing system that allows customers on the Internet to book flights. Current web applications would have a user download a bunch of flight information as an HTML page. If I book the last seat on a flight that you are viewing at the same time, you will not see my booking of that last seat. This is because on each client screen you simply see copies of data from the database.

If you reconstruct this web application so that it uses RMI to retrieve data from a single flight object on the server, you can allow any number of different customers to view the exact same plane objects at the same time. In this way, you can be certain that all viewers see any change made to the plane object simultaneously. When I book the last seat on that flight, the flight object makes an RMI call to all clients viewing it to let them know another seat was booked.

Putting It All Together

The pieces of the story are now in place. You will be using JDBC for your database access and RMI to distribute the objects that make up your application. This book covers the JDBC API in complete detail and discusses RMI as it pertains to the creation of distributed three-tier database applications. To better use these APIs once you have gone beyond this book, I strongly recommend further reading on these topics: object-oriented design methodologies, patterns in software development, and general database programming.

2

Relational Databases and SQL

Good sense is the most evenly shared thing in the world, for each of us thinks he is so well endowed with it that even those who are the hardest to please in all other respects are not in the habit of wanting more than they have. It is unlikely that everyone is mistaken in this. It indicates rather that the capacity to judge correctly and to distinguish true from false, which is properly what one calls common sense or reason, is naturally equal in all men, and consequently the diversity in our opinions does not spring from some of us being more able to reason than others, but only from our conducting our thoughts along different lines and not examining the same things.

—René Descartes
Discourse on the Method

Before you dive into the details of database programming in Java, I would like to take a chapter to provide a basic discussion of relational databases for those of you who might have little or no experience in this area. The subject of relational databases, however, is a huge topic that cannot possibly be covered fully in this chapter. It is only designed to provide you with the most basic introduction. Experienced database developers will find nothing new in this chapter; you will probably want to skip ahead to Chapter 3, *Introduction to JDBC*.

What Is a Relational Database?

Programming is all about data processing; data is central to everything you do with a computer. Databases—like filesystems—are nothing more than specialized tools for data storage. Filesystems are good for storing and retrieving a single volume of information associated with a single virtual location. In other words, when you want to save a WordPerfect document, a filesystem allows you to associate it with a location in a directory tree for easy retrieval later.

Databases provide applications with a more powerful data storage and retrieval system based on mathematical theories about data devised by Dr. E. F. Codd. Conceptually, a relational database can be pictured as a set of spreadsheets in which rows from one spreadsheet can be related to rows from another; in reality, however, the theory behind databases is much more complex. Each spreadsheet in a database is called a table. As with a spreadsheet, a table is made up of rows and columns.

A simple way to illustrate the structure of a relational database is through a CD catalog. Let's say that you have decided to create a database to keep track of your music collection. Not only do you want to be able to store a list of your albums, but you also want to use this data later to help you select music for parties. Your collection might look something like Table 2-1.

Table 2-1. A List of CDs from a Sample Music Collection

Artist	Title	Category	Year
The Cure	Pornography	Alternative	1983
Garbage	Garbage	Alternative	1996
Hole	Live Through This	Alternative	1994
Nine Inch Nails	The Downward Spiral	Industrial	1994
Public Image Limited	Compact Disc	Alternative	1985
The Sex Pistols	Never Mind the Bollocks, Here's the Sex Pistols	Punk	1977
Skinny Puppy	Last Rights	Industrial	1992
Wire	A Bell Is a Cup Until It Is Struck	Alternative	1989

Of course, you could simply keep this list in a spreadsheet. But what if you wanted to have Johnny Rotten night? Nothing in this list tells you which music in your catalog features him. You might have another spreadsheet that lists musicians and the bands to which they belong, but there is nothing about such a spreadsheet that can provide an easy programmatic answer to your question.

With a database, you could easily ask the question "Can you give me all compact discs in my collection with which Johnny Rotten was involved?" We will formally ask that question in a minute. To make asking that question easier, however, you have to design your database to store the information you need so that you can relate compact discs to individual musicians. You might create another table called *musicians* that stores a list of musicians. For your purposes, you will store only last names, first names, and nicknames in this list. However, you could store more information, such as birthdays. Table 2-2 shows a part of your list.

Databases and Database Engines

Developers new to database programming often run into problems under-standing just what a *database* is. In some contexts, it represents a collection of common data like the music database you are looking at in this chapter. In other contexts, however, it may mean the software used to support that collection of data, a process instance of that software, or even the server machine on which the process is running.

Technically speaking, a database really is the collection of related data and the relationships supporting the data. The database software is the software—such as Oracle, Sybase, MySQL, and UDB—that is used to access that data. A database engine, in turn, is a process instance of the software accessing your database. Finally, the database server is the computer on which the database engine is running.

I will continue to use the term database interchangeably to refer to any of these definitions. It is important, however, to database programming to understand this breakdown.

Table 2-2. The Data in the Musicians Table

Last Name	First Name	Nickname
Jourgenson	Al	
Lydon	John	Johnny Rotten
Reznor	Trent	
Smith	Robert	

Nothing in these two lists relates musicians to bands, much less musicians to com-pact discs. Another problem you can see in this list is that Robert Smith is a very common name, and there are likely multiple artists who have that name. How do you know which Robert Smith should be related to which compact disc? Database tables generally have one or more columns called *keys* that uniquely identify each row. The key of the *albums* table could be the CD title; it is not uncommon, however, for the same title to be used for different albums by different bands. The simplest thing to do is to add another column to serve as the key column—let's call it an album ID. This column will just be a sequential list of numbers. As you add new discs to the collection, increment the album ID by one and insert that information. Thus album 1 is The Cure's *Pornography*, album 2 is Garbage's *Garbage*, album 3 is Hole's *Live Through This*, etc. You can do the same thing with the musicians table so that you have a musician ID for each musician.

It will now be easier to relate specific musicians to specific album titles. You still need to provide sufficient data in the proper format for you to ask your question. Specifically, you need to create a *bands* table that stores information about bands. Furthermore, you should remove each band as a column in the *albums* table since that information is now stored in the *bands* table. You are up to three tables: *albums, musicians,* and *bands.* Each table has an ID field that serves only to uniquely identify each row. The result is the data model shown in Figure 2-1.

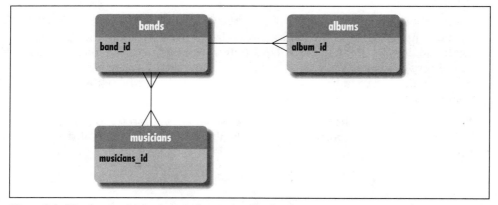

Figure 2-1. The data model for the sample compact disc database

A data model is a picture of your database tables—sometimes refered to as *entities*—and how they relate to one another. Your data model tells you the following things:

- Each band has one or more albums
- Each album belongs to exactly one band
- Each band contains one or more musicians
- Each musician is a member of one or more bands

This model is called a *logical data model.* A logical data model is a type of data model that tells you what you are modeling. You need to get from what you are modeling, to how you are going to model it to the physical data model. To implement this system, you need to take a few more steps. The first step is to add a column to the *albums* table representing the band ID for the band that produced that CD. This way, you are relating a row in the *albums* table to a row in the *bands* table.

The complex part of your data model is the many-to-many relationship between bands and musicians. You cannot simply stick a musician ID in the *bands* table nor can you stick a band ID in the *musicians* table. This relationship is traditionally captured through something called a *cross-reference table.* This table, which you will call *band_musician,* contains two columns: band ID and musician ID. Unlike your other tables, which represent database entities, the rows in this table represent relationships between rows in the *bands* and *musicians* tables. If John Lydon is represented by musician ID 2, Public Image Limited is band ID 5, and the Sex Pistols are band ID 6, the *band_musician* table would look like Table 2-3.

Table 2-3. A Portion of the band_musician Table

Band ID	Musician ID
5	2
6	2

An Introduction to SQL

> *NOTE*   SQL keywords are case-insensitive, meaning that SELECT and select are treated exactly the same. Depending on your database, however, table and column names may or may not be case-insensitive. In addition, the space between words in a SQL statement is unimportant. You can have a newline after each word, several spaces, or just a single space. Throughout this book I use the convention of placing SQL keywords in all capitals and separating single SQL statements across multiple lines for readability.

How do you get the data into the database? And how do you get it out once it is in there? All major databases support a standard query language called Structured Query Language (SQL). SQL is not much like any programming language you might be familiar with. Instead, it is more of a structured English for talking to a database. A SQL query to the album titles from your database would look like this:

```
SELECT title FROM albums
```

In fact, much of the simplest database access comes in the form of equally simple SQL statements. Most of what you will do in SQL boils down to four SQL commands: SELECT, INSERT, UPDATE, and DELETE. You can issue SQL statements in several ways. The simplest, quickest way is through a SQL command-line tool. Each database engine comes with its own. Throughout most of this book, however, you will send your SQL as Java strings to JDBC methods.

> *NOTE*   I should also make a couple of other syntactic notes. First, the single quotation mark (') is used to mark string constants, and double quotation marks (") are used to show significant space, such as in column names that contain spaces in them.

CREATE

Before you get into the four most common SQL statements, you need to actually create the tables in which your data will be stored. The major database engines provide GUI utilities that allow you to create tables without issuing any SQL. It is nevertheless good to know the SQL `CREATE` statement that handles the creation of database entities. Unfortunately, the exact syntax of this command is a little database dependent. The basic form is:

```
CREATE TABLE table_name (
    column_name column_type column_modifiers,
    ...,
    column_name column_type column_modifiers)
```

Using mSQL, the database engine used throughout much of this book, the *musicians* table might be created through the following statement:

```
CREATE TABLE musicians(
    musician_id INT,
    last_name CHAR(40),
    first_name CHAR(40),
    nickname CHAR(40))
```

The database-dependent part of the `CREATE` statement lies in the column modifiers. These might be modifiers such as `NOT NULL`, `PRIMARY KEY`, or other modifiers that say something specific about the column and the kind of data it can take. You should read the SQL manual that comes with your database for specific information about column modifiers.

INSERT

With the tables in place, you use the `INSERT` statement to add data to them. Its form is:

```
INSERT INTO table_name(column_name, ..., column_name)
VALUES (value, ..., value)
```

The first column name matches to the first value you specify, the second column name to the second value you specify, and so on for as many columns as you are inserting. If you fail to specify a value for a column that is marked as `NOT NULL`, you will get an error on insert.

You can now add Johnny Rotten into the database using the following SQL:

```
INSERT INTO musicians(musician_id, last_name, first_name, nickname)
VALUES(2, 'Lydon', 'John', 'Johnny Rotten')
```

You have to repeat this step for each row you wish to add to each table.

UPDATE

The UPDATE statement enables you to modify data that you previously inserted into the database. The UPDATE syntax looks like this:

```
UPDATE table_name
SET column_name = value,
    ...,
    column_name = value
WHERE column_name = value
```

This statement introduces the WHERE clause. It is used to help identify one or more rows in the database. For example, if you had made a mistake entering the year in which *The Downward Spiral* was released, you would issue the following statement:

```
UPDATE albums
SET year = 1994
WHERE album_id = 4
```

The WHERE column in this statement uniquely identifies the row where album_id is: the album ID for *The Downward Spiral*, which is 4. The UPDATE statement then sets the year column to 1994 for that one row.

The WHERE clause is not limited to identifying single rows. Perhaps you want to add another music category called "old music" and set all albums older than 1980 to that category. The appropriate SQL would look like this:

```
UPDATE albums
SET category = 'old music'
WHERE year < 1980
```

WARNING   You can leave out the WHERE clause of SQL commands that allow WHERE clauses. If you do this, however, your statement will operate on every relevant row. If you left out the WHERE year < 1980 in the old music example, you would make every album category change to "old music." Accidentally leaving out a WHERE clause can create disastrous results when you are using the DELETE command!

DELETE

The DELETE command looks a lot like the UPDATE statement. Its syntax is:

```
DELETE FROM table_name
WHERE column_name = value
```

Instead of changing particular values in the row, DELETE removes the entire row from the table. When you sell *The Downward Spiral*, you would issue the command:

```
DELETE from albums
WHERE album_id = 4
```

SELECT

The most common SQL command you will use is the `SELECT` statement. It allows you to select specific rows from the database based on search criteria. It takes the following form:

```
SELECT column_name, ..., column_name
FROM table_name
WHERE column_name = value
```

Retrieving all of the industrial albums from the *albums* table would thus appear as:

```
SELECT title
FROM albums
WHERE category = 'industrial'
```

Joins and Subqueries

I still have not answered the question of how you get all of the albums in which Johnny Rotten was involved. No simple `SELECT` statement following the syntax I outlined above will handle that. The `SELECT` statement allows you to perform some very complex queries; this is in fact the very power of a relational database. Among the most common complex `SELECT` statements is the *join*. A join enables you to create a sort of virtual table on the fly that contains data from two or more tables. In the CD collection, a simple join might take the form of a search for all alternative bands:

```
SELECT bands.band_name
FROM bands, albums
WHERE albums.category = 'alternative'
    AND bands.band_id = albums.band_id
```

The newest thing you will notice here is the prefixing of table names before the column names. You need to take this step since you relate the *albums* and *bands* tables through the `band_id` value in both tables. In this example, you selected the names of bands from the *bands* table whose band ID appears in the *albums* table with "alternative" as a category.

But your target query is trying to relate album titles to musicians, and your data provides no direct relationship between albums and musicians. To accomplish this task you need to formulate a *subquery**—a query within a query. You specifically need to select all of Johnny Rotten's bands and then get the album titles associated with those bands. Your first query is therefore the query that selects all bands associated with Johnny Rotten (musician ID 2). The main query, the one that

---

* Not all databases support subqueries. As of the writing of this book, for example, MySQL does not support subqueries, though the feature should be added soon.

provides you with the CD titles, uses the band IDs from the first query and selects all album titles for those band IDs:

```
SELECT title
FROM albums,
WHERE band_id IN
    (SELECT bands.band_id
     FROM bands, band_musician
     WHERE band_musician.musician_id = 2
         AND bands.band_id = band_musician.band_id)
```

Transaction Logic

Often you will want to issue many updates or inserts together as part of a single transaction. When adding a new band, for example, you will want to add all musicians in that band together at once. Unfortunately, as with many things in the computer world, individual SQL statements can fail for various reasons. The most common reason is a network problem. No matter what, you will find that errors do occur when issuing database statements, and an error in the middle of multiple related SQL statements can leave you with corrupt data.

SQL allows you to specify a set of SQL commands that are supposed to be executed together or not at all through transaction management. A *transaction* is one or more SQL statements that should be treated as a single unit of work. If one of the statements that form the transaction fails, then the whole transaction needs to be aborted, including any statements that were successfully executed up to the failure. If the whole series of statements that form the transaction succeeds, then a signal is sent to the database to make the effects of the transaction permanent.

An abort from a transaction is called a ROLLBACK, and the notification to make a transaction permanent is called a COMMIT. Some databases start off in something called *auto-commit mode*. In this mode, each statement is implicitly committed to the database as a complete transaction as it is sent to the database. If you are not in auto-commit mode, the database waits for you to send an explicit COMMIT or ROLLBACK. If you send a COMMIT, any changes you made are reflected in the database permanently. A ROLLBACK, however, returns the database to its state after the last COMMIT.

Transaction logic will be fully illustrated in Chapter 3 and Chapter 4, *Advanced JDBC*.

A Note on SQL Versions

This book deals almost exclusively with the current, widespread version of SQL, SQL2 (also called SQL/92). Part of the JDBC specification is that SQL2 is its supported SQL version. A newer and not universally supported SQL specification now exists, SQL3 (SQL/99). Among its most fundamental changes is support for abstract data types—an extremely useful change for developers programming in object-oriented languages like Java.

Newer versions of some databases—especially object-relational databases—now support some parts of the SQL3 specification. To take advantage of this important power in newer databases, the new JDBC 2.0 specification has added some extra features. I will note instances when you encounter SQL3-specific functionality, but you should be aware that these SQL calls are bleeding-edge SQL and thus unlikely to be supported by your particular database engine.

3

Introduction to JDBC

*These common thoughts are expressed in a shared public
language, consisting of shared signs...a sign has a
"sense" that fixes the reference and is "grasped by
everybody" who knows the language...*
—Noam Chomsky
Language and Thought

Database programming has traditionally been a technological Tower of Babel. You
are faced with dozens of available database products, and each one talks to your
applications in its own private language. If your application needs to talk to a new
database engine, you have to teach it (and yourself) a new language. As Java
programmers, however, you should not worry about such translation issues. Java is
supposed to bring you the ability to "write once, compile once, and run anywhere," so it should bring it to you with database programming, as well.

SQL was a key first step in simplifying database access. Java's JDBC API builds on
that foundation and provides you with a shared language through which your
applications can talk to database engines. Following in the tradition of its other
multi-platform APIs, such as the AWT, JDBC provides you with a set of interfaces
that create a common point at which database applications and database engines
can meet. This chapter will discuss the basic interfaces that JDBC provides.

What Is JDBC?

Working with leaders in the database field, Sun developed a single API for database access—JDBC. As part of this process, they kept three main goals in mind:

- JDBC should be a SQL-level API.

- JDBC should capitalize on the experience of existing database APIs.
- JDBC should be simple.

A SQL-level API means that JDBC allows you to construct SQL statements and embed them inside Java API calls. In short, you are basically using SQL. But JDBC lets you smoothly translate between the world of the database and the world of the Java application. Your results from the database, for instance, are returned as Java objects, and access problems get thrown as exceptions. Later in the book, you will go a step further and talk about how you can completely hide the existence of the database from a Java application using a database class library.

Because of the confusion caused by the proliferation of proprietary database access APIs, the idea of a universal database access API to solve this problem is not new. In fact, Sun drew upon the successful aspects of one such API, Open Data-Base Connectivity (ODBC). ODBC was developed to create a single standard for database access in the Windows environment. Although the industry has accepted ODBC as the primary means of talking to databases in Windows, it does not translate well into the Java world. First of all, ODBC is a C API that requires intermediate APIs for other languages. But even for C developers, ODBC has suffered from an overly complex design that has made its transition outside of the controlled Windows environment a failure. ODBC's complexity arises from the fact that complex, uncommon tasks are wrapped up in the API with its simpler and more common functionality. In other words, in order for you to understand a little of ODBC, you have to understand a lot.

In addition to ODBC, JDBC is heavily influenced by existing database programming APIs, such as X/OPEN SQL Call Level Interface (CLI). Sun wanted to reuse the key abstractions from these APIs, which would ease acceptance by database vendors and capitalize on the existing knowledge capital of ODBC and SQL CLI developers. In addition, Sun realized that deriving an API from existing ones can provide quick development of solutions for database engines that support the old protocols. Specifically, Sun worked in parallel with Intersolv to create an ODBC bridge that maps JDBC calls to ODBC calls, thus giving Java applications access to any database management system (DBMS) that supports ODBC.

NOTE   The JDBC-ODBC bridge is a great tool for developers who are interested in learning JDBC but may not want to invest in anything beyond the Microsoft Access database that comes with Microsoft Office. When developing for production sites, however, you almost certainly want to move to a JDBC driver that is native to your deployment database engine.

JDBC attempts to remain as simple as possible while providing developers with maximum flexibility. A key criterion employed by Sun is simply asking whether database access applications read well. The simple and common tasks use simple interfaces, while more uncommon or bizarre tasks are enabled through specialized interfaces. For example, three interfaces handle a vast majority of database access. JDBC nevertheless provides several other interfaces for handling more complex and unusual tasks.

The Structure of JDBC

JDBC accomplishes its goals through a set of Java interfaces, each implemented differently by individual vendors. The set of classes that implement the JDBC interfaces for a particular database engine is called a JDBC driver. In building a database application, you do not have to think about the implementation of these underlying classes at all; the whole point of JDBC is to hide the specifics of each database and let you worry about just your application. Figure 3-1 illustrates the JDBC architecture.

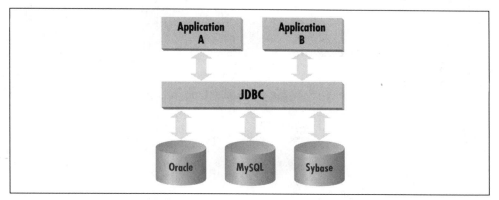

Figure 3-1. The JDBC architecture

If you think about a database query for any database engine, it requires you to connect to the database, issue your SELECT statement, and process the result set. In Example 3-1, you have the full code listing for a simple SELECT application from the Imaginary JDBC Driver for mSQL.* I wrote this driver for the Dasein Project (*http://www.dasein.org*). This application is a single class that gets all of the rows from a table in an mSQL database located on my Solaris box. First, it connects to

---

* mSQL stands for Mini-SQL. It is a small database that supports a subset of SQL and is ideal for systems that need a database that can operate with few system resources. You can get more information on it at *http://www.Hughes.com.au* or from the O'Reilly book *MySQL and mSQL*, which I coauthored with Randy Jay Yarger and Tim King.

the database by getting a database connection under my user id, **borg**, from the JDBC **DriverManager** class. It uses that database connection to create a **Statement** object that performs the SELECT query. A **ResultSet** object then provides the application with the **key** and **val** fields from the *test* table.

Example 3-1. Simple SELECT Application from the Imaginary mSQL-JDBC mSQL Driver

```
import java.sql.*;

public class Select {
  public static void main(String args[]) {
    String url = "jdbc:msql://carthage.imaginary.com/ora";
    Connection con = null;

    try {
      String driver = "com.imaginary.sql.msql.MsqlDriver";

      Class.forName(driver).newInstance();
    }
    catch( Exception e ) {
      System.out.println("Failed to load mSQL driver.");
      return;
    }
    try {
      con = DriverManager.getConnection(url, "borg", "");
      Statement select = con.createStatement();
      ResultSet result = select.executeQuery
                         ("SELECT test_id, test_val FROM test");

      System.out.println("Got results:");
      while(result.next()) { // process results one row at a time
        int key;
        String val;

        key = result.getInt(1);
        if( result.wasNull() ) {
            key = -1;
        }
        val = result.getString(2);
        if( result.wasNull() ) {
            val = null;
        }
        System.out.println("key = " + key);
        System.out.println("val = " + val);
      }
    }
    catch( Exception e ) {
      e.printStackTrace();
    }
```

Example 3-1. Simple SELECT Application from the Imaginary mSQL-JDBC mSQL Driver (continued)

```
    finally {
      if( con != null ) {
        try { con.close(); }
        catch( Exception e ) { e.printStackTrace(); }
      }
    }
  }
}
```

If you already have Java experience, you should be able to understand the flow of the code in Example 3-1 without knowing any JDBC. Other than the string that loads the mSQL-JDBC driver, there are no references to specific database engine classes. Instead, the code simply uses JDBC interfaces to provide a façade for the DBMS-specific implementation. The JDBC implementation, in turn, performs the actual database access somewhere behind the scenes. Figure 3-2 is a UML class diagram of the basic JDBC classes and interfaces.

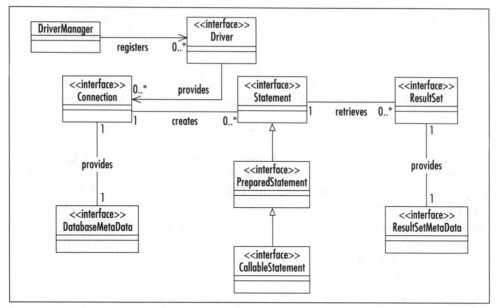

Figure 3-2. The basic classes and interfaces of the JDBC API

In the simple application presented in Example 3-1, the Select class asks the JDBC DriverManager to hand it the proper database implementation based on a database URL. The database URL looks similar to other Internet URLs. The actual content of the URL is loosely specified as jdbc:*subprotocol:subname*. The subprotocol identifies which driver to use, and the subname provides the driver with any required connection information. For the Imaginary JDBC Implementation for mSQL used to test Example 3-1, the URL is *jdbc:msql://carthage.-.imaginary.com/ora.* In other words, this URL says to use the mSQL-JDBC driver to connect to the database ora on the server running at the default port on *carthage.imaginary.com.* Each URL, however, is specific to the JDBC implementation being sought, so I can't say anything more explicit that will tell you exactly what the URL for your database will be. You should find the URL format for your driver in the documentation that comes with it. Whatever its format, the primary function of a database URL is to uniquely identify the driver needed by the application and pass that driver any information it needs to connect to the proper database.

Databases and Drivers

In putting together the examples in this book, I used both an mSQL database for the simple examples in this chapter and an Oracle database for the more complex examples in Chapter 4, *Advanced JDBC.* If you do not have a corporate pocketbook to back up your database purchase, mSQL or other free/cheap database solutions such as MySQL might prove more feasible. You should keep in mind, however, that mSQL does not allow you to abort transactions and does not support the stored procedures used in Chapter 4. Whatever your database choice, you must set up your database engine, create a database, and create the tables shown in the data model for each example before you can begin writing JDBC code. The examples for this book include scripts to create support tables for mSQL, MySQL, and Oracle.

Once your database engine is installed and your database is all set up, you will need a JDBC driver for that database engine. You can find an mSQL-JDBC driver at *http://www.imaginary.com/Java/mSQL-JDBC.* The more commercial database engines such as Oracle have commercial JDBC drivers. Most of them, however, allow you to have a free trial period for experimenting with the driver. Follow the install instructions for the driver you choose, and remember that some JDBC drivers require to you install native code on client machines. To help you understand what different drivers require, Sun has defined the driver-categorization system shown in Figure 3-3.

Type 1

> These drivers use a bridging technology to access a database. The JDBC-ODBC bridge that comes with JDK 1.2 is a good example of this kind of driver. It provides a gateway to the ODBC API. Implementations of this API in turn do the actual database access. Bridge solutions generally require software to be installed on client systems, meaning that they are not good solutions for applications that do not allow you to install software on the client.

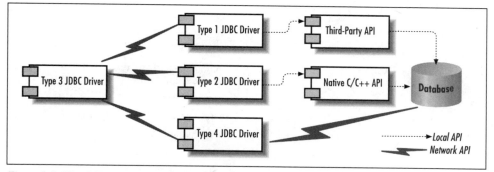

Figure 3-3. The different kinds of JDBC drivers

Type 2

Type 2 drivers are native API drivers. This means that the driver contains Java code that calls native C or C++ methods provided by the individual database vendors that perform the database access. Again, this solution requires software on the client system.

Type 3

Type 3 drivers provide a client with a generic network API that is then translated into database-specific access at the server level. In other words, the JDBC driver on the client uses sockets to call a middleware application on the server that translates the client requests into an API specific to the desired driver. As it turns out, this kind of driver is extremely flexible, since it requires no code installed on the client and a single driver can actually provide access to multiple databases.

Type 4

Using network protocols built into the database engine, type 4 drivers talk directly to the database using Java sockets. This is the most direct pure Java solution. Because these network protocols are almost never documented, this type of driver will almost always come only from the database vendor.

Table 3-1 lists the different drivers, along with their vendor and type, that were public at the time of this book's publication. As I write this chapter, most of these drivers exist only for JDBC 1.2 (JDK 1.1.x). By the time you read this, most drivers will hopefully have JDBC 2.0 (JDK 1.2/Java 2) versions. See *http://splash.javasoft. com/jdbc/jdbc.drivers.html* for a current list of JDBC drivers and the versions they support.

Table 3-1. A List of JDBC Driver Vendors

Vendor	Type	Supported Databases
Adabas D	4	ADABAS D
Agave Software Design	3	Oracle, Sybase, Informix, ODBC-supported databases
Altera Software	4	Altera SQL Server
Asgard Software	3	Unisys A series DMSII database
BEA WebLogic	2	Oracle, Sybase, MS SQL Server
BEA WebLogic	3	ODBC-supported databases
BEA WebLogic	4	MS SQL Server, Informix
Caribou Lake Software	3	Ingres, OpenIngres, Oracle
Centura Software	4	Centura SQLBase
Cloudscape	4	JBMS
Compaq	2, 3	Nonstop SQL/MP
Ensodex, Inc.	3	ODBC-supported databases
FormWeb, Inc.	4	FormWeb
GIE Dyade	-	RMI Bridge for remote JDBC access
GNU	4	MySQL
GWE Technologies	4	MySQL
Hit Software	4	DB2, DB2/400
HOB electronic GmbH & Co. KG	4	DB2, VSAM, IMS-DB, DL/1
IBM	2, 3, 4	DB2
IDS Software	3	Oracle, Sybase, MS SQL Server, MS Access, Informix, ODBC-supported databases
I-Kinetics	3	Oracle, Informix, Sybase, ODBC-supported databases
Imaginary	4	mSQL, MySQL
i-net software	4	MS SQL Server
Information Builders	3	ECB
Informix Corporation	4	Informix
InterBase	3	InterBase
InterSoft	3	Essentia
Intersolv	2	DB2, Ingres, Informix, Oracle, MS SQL Server, Sybase
JavaSoft	1	ODBC-supported databases
KonaSoft, Inc.	3, 4	Sybase, Oracle, Informix, SQL Anywhere
Liberty Integration Software	3	Most PICK flavors including VMARK, Unidata, General Automation, Pick systems
Lotus Development	2	Domino

Table 3-1. A List of JDBC Driver Vendors (continued)

Vendor	Type	Supported Databases
NetAway	3	DB2, Oracle, Informix, MS SQL Server, Sybase, ODBC-supported databases
Nogginware Corporation	3	ODBC-supported databases
OpenLink	3	CA-Ingres, Informix, MS SQL Server, Oracle, PostgreSQL, Progress, Unify, Solid, ODBC-supported databases
Oracle Corporation	2, 4	Oracle
Recital Corporation	3	DB2/6000, Informix, Ingres, Oracle, ODBC-supported databases
Recital Corporation	4	Recital, Xbase, CISAM, RMS
SAS Institute, Inc.	3, 4	SAS, and via SAS/ACCESS, Oracle, Informix, Ingres, and ADABAS
SCO	3	Informix, Oracle, Ingres, Sybase, InterBase
Simba Technologies, Inc.	3	Oracle, Sybase, MS SQL
Software AG	4	ADABAS D
Solid Information Technology	4	Solid Server
StarQuest Software	1	DB2/MVS, DB2/400, SQL/DS, DB2/CS, DB2 Universal Database
Sybase	3, 4	Sybase SQL Server, SQL Anywhere, Sybase IQ, Replication Server and Sybase OmniCONNECT-supported databases
Symantec	3	Oracle, Sybase, MS SQL Server, MS Access, SQL Anywhere, ODBC-supported databases
ThinWeb SoftWare	-	All JDBC and ODBC-supported databases
tjFM	4	MySQL
Trifox, Inc.	3	ADABAS, DB2, Informix, Ingres, Oracle, Rdb, MS SQL Server, Sybase, and legacy systems via GENESIS
Visigenic	3	ODBC-supported databases
XDB Systems, Inc.	1, 3	ODBC-supported databases
Yard Software GmbH	4	YARD-SQL Database

Alternatives to JDBC

Without JDBC, only disparate, proprietary database access solutions exist. These proprietary solutions force the developer to build a layer of abstraction on top of them in order to create database-independent code. Only after that abstraction layer is complete can the developer actually write the application. In addition, the experience you have with that abstraction layer does not translate immediately to other projects or other employers who are almost certainly using their own abstraction layers to provide access to a variety of database engines.

Of course, the ODBC specification exists to provide this universal abstraction layer for languages such as C and C++, as well as popular development tools such as Delphi, PowerBuilder, and VisualBasic. Unfortunately, ODBC does not enjoy the platform independence of Java. Using the JDBC interface design, however, your server application can pick the database at runtime based on which client is connecting. Imagine, for example, that you are building a new application against an Informix database to replace an old application running against an Oracle database. Because of the complexity of the system, you want to make the transition in phases. Once its data has been converted to Informix, all you have to do to run the application against the new database is provide it with different runtime configuration values—the JDBC URL and driver name. No new code needs to be written for the migration.

Many of the major database vendors have banded together to create an alternative solution to JDBC called SQLJ. SQLJ is a specification for writing embedded SQL in Java applications that a preprocessor can read and turn into JDBC calls. It is important to note that SQLJ is not an approved Java standard for database access, but instead an alternative based on old, outmoded forms of database access. The SQLJ paradigm is a familiar paradigm for C and COBOL programmers, but very much counter to the object-oriented nature of Java.

Of course, nothing forces you to use a relational database. Object and object-relational database engines are gaining acceptance every day. If you use an object database, JDBC is probably not the right database access solution for you. You should instead look to the forthcoming OMG-approved Java access protocol. For object-relational databases, the answer usually depends on the origins of your database engine. For relational database engines such as Oracle that use object extensions, JDBC is still probably the right answer. Object databases that have SQL frontends, however, may have a better Java approach.

Connecting to the Database

Now I am going to dive into the details about JDBC calls and how to use them. The examples in this book should run on your system regardless of the database or driver you use. The one phase when it is hard to achieve portability is the first step of connecting, because you have to specify a driver. I'll discuss that first to get it out of the way.

Figure 3-4 shows how an application uses JDBC to talk to one or more databases without knowing the details concerning the driver implementation for that database. An application uses JDBC as an interface through which it passes all its database requests.

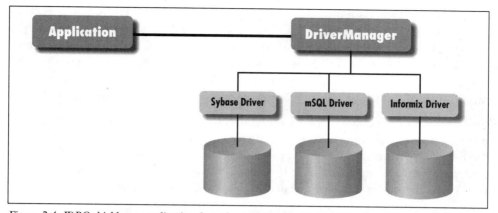

Figure 3-4. JDBC shields an application from the specifics of individual database implementations

When you write a Java database applet or application, the only driver-specific information JDBC requires from you is the database URL. You can even have your application derive the URL at runtime—based on user input or applet parameters.

Connection Troubles

The JDBC Connection process is the most difficult part of JDBC to get right. The API itself is fairly straightforward, but many "gotchas" hide right beneath the surface. The new JDBC Standard Extension discussed in Chapter 5, *The JDBC Optional Package,* will cover a simplified way of making database connections that avoids many of these problems. Unfortunately, few drivers support the JDBC Optional Package at this time. If you run into problems just making a connection, check if they match any of the following:

Connection fails with the message "Class not found"

This message usually results from not having the JDBC driver in your CLASSPATH. You should remember to enter *.zip* and *.jar* files explicitly into a CLASSPATH. If you put all your *.class* files and the *mSQL-JDBC.jar* file containing the mSQL-JDBC driver into *C:\lib,* your CLASSPATH should read *C:\lib; C:\lib\mSQL-JDBC.jar.*

Connection fails with the message "Driver not found"

You did not register your JDBC driver with the DriverManager class. This chapter describes several ways to register a JDBC driver. Sometimes developers using the Class.forName() method of registering a JDBC driver encounter an inconsistency between the JDBC specification and some JVM implementations. You should thus use the Class.forName().newInstance() method as a workaround.

Using the database URL and whatever properties your JDBC driver requires (generally a user ID and password), your application will first request a `java.sql.Connection` implementation from the `DriverManager`. The `DriverManager` in turn will search through all of the known `java.sql.Driver` implementations for the one that connects with the URL you provided. If it exhausts all the implementations without finding a match, it throws an exception back to your application.

Once a `Driver` recognizes your URL, it creates a database connection using the properties you specified. It then provides the `DriverManager` with a `java.sql.Connection` implementation representing that database connection. The `DriverManager` then passes that `Connection` object back to the application. In your code, the entire database connection process is handled by this one-liner:

```
Connection con = DriverManager.getConnection(url, uid, password);
```

Of course, you are probably wondering how the JDBC `DriverManager` learns about a new driver implementation. The `DriverManager` actually keeps a list of classes that implement the `java.sql.Driver` interface. Somehow, somewhere, something needs to register the `Driver` implementations for any potential database drivers it might require with the `DriverManager`. JDBC requires a `Driver` class to register itself with the `DriverManager` when it is instantiated. The act of instantiating a `Driver` class thus enters it in the `DriverManager`'s list. Instantiating the driver, however, is only one of several ways to register a driver:

Explicitly call new to load your driver's implementation of Driver
   In other words, you hardcode the loading of a `Driver` implementation in your application. This alternative is the least desirable since it requires a rewrite and recompile if your database or database driver changes.

Use the jdbc.drivers property
   The `DriverManager` will load all classes listed in this property automatically. This alternative works well for applications with a command-line interface, but might not be so useful in GUI applications and applets. This is because you can specify properties at the command line or in environment variables. While environment variables do work for GUI applications, you cannot rely on them in Java applets.

Load the class using Class.forName("DriverImplementationClass") newInstance( );
   This complex expression is a tool for dynamically creating an instance of a class when you have some variable representing the class name.* Because a

---

* Actually, `Class.forName("classname")` is supposed to be sufficient. Unfortunately, some Java virtual machines do not actually call the static initializer until an instance of a class is created. As a result, `newInstance()` should be called to guarantee that the static initializer is run for all virtual machines.

JDBC driver is required to register itself whenever its `static` initializer is called, this expression has the net effect of registering your driver for you.

I use the third alternative almost exclusively in the examples in the first half of this book since it does not require hardcoded class names and it runs well in all Java environments. In real-world applications, I use either this method along with a properties file from which I load the name of the driver or the method I describe in Chapter 5.

The JDBC Classes for Creating a Connection

As Example 3-2 illustrates, JDBC uses one class (`java.sql.DriverManager`) and two interfaces (`java.sql.Driver` and `java.sql.Connection`) for connecting to a database:

`java.sql.Driver`

> Unless you are writing your own custom JDBC implementation, you should never have to deal with this class from your application. It simply gives JDBC a launching point for database connectivity by responding to `DriverManager` connection requests and providing information about the implementation in question.

`java.sql.DriverManager`

> Unlike most other parts of JDBC, `DriverManager` is a class instead of an interface. Its main responsibility is to maintain a list of Driver implementations and present an application with one that matches a requested URL. The `DriverManager` provides `registerDriver()` and `deregisterDriver()` methods, which allow a Driver implementation to register itself with the `DriverManager` or remove itself from that list. You can get an enumeration of registered drivers through the `getDrivers()` method.

`java.sql.Connection`

> The `Connection` class represents a single logical database connection. In other words, you use the `Connection` class for sending a series of SQL statements to the database and managing the committing or aborting of those statements.

Example 3-2 puts the process of connecting to the database into a more concrete format.

Example 3-2. A Simple Database Connection

```
import java.sql.Connection;
import java.sql.DriverManager;
import java.sql.SQLException;
```

Example 3-2. A Simple Database Connection (continued)

```java
/**
 * The SimpleConnection class is a command line application that accepts
 * the following command line:
 * java SimpleConnection DRIVER URL UID PASSWORD
 * If the URL fits the specified driver, it will then load the driver and
 * get a connection.
 */
public class SimpleConnection {
  static public void main(String args[]) {
    Connection connection = null;

    // Process the command line
    if( args.length != 4 ) {
      System.out.println("Syntax: java SimpleConnection " +
                         "DRIVER URL UID PASSWORD");
      return;
    }
    try { // load the driver
      Class.forName(args[0]).newInstance();
    }
    catch( Exception e ) { // problem loading driver, class not exist?
      e.printStackTrace();
      return;
    }
    try {
      connection = DriverManager.getConnection(args[1], args[2], args[3]);
      System.out.println("Connection successful!");
      // Do whatever queries or updates you want here!!!
    }
    catch( SQLException e ) {
      e.printStackTrace();
    }
    finally {
      if( connection != null ) {
        try { connection.close(); }
        catch( SQLException e ) {
          e.printStackTrace();
        }
      }
    }
  }
}
```

In connecting to the database, this example catches a SQLException. This is a sort of catch-all exception for database errors. Just about any time something goes wrong between JDBC and the database, JDBC throws a SQLException. In addition to the information you commonly find in Java exceptions, SQLException provides database-specific error information, such as the SQLState value and vendor error code. In the event of multiple errors, the JDBC driver "chains" the exceptions together. In other words, you can ask any SQLException if another exception preceded it by calling getNextException().

Basic Database Access

Now that you are connected to the database, you can begin making updates and queries. The most basic kind of database access involves writing JDBC code when you know ahead of time whether the statements you are sending are updates (INSERT, UPDATE, or DELETE) or queries (SELECT). In the next chapter, you will discuss more complex database access that allows you to execute statements of unknown types.

Basic database access starts with the Connection object you created in the previous section. When this object first gets created, it is simply a direct link to the database. You use a Connection object to generate implementations of java.sql. Statement tied to the same database transaction. After you have used one or more Statement objects generated by your Connection, you can use it to commit or rollback the Statement objects associated with that Connection.

A Statement is very much what its name implies—a SQL statement. Once you get a Statement object from a Connection, you have what amounts to a blank check that you can write against the transaction represented by that Connection. You do not actually assign SQL to the Statement until you are ready to send the SQL to the database.

This is when it becomes important to know what type of SQL you are sending to the database, because JDBC uses a different method for sending queries than for sending updates. The key difference is the fact that the method for queries returns an instance of java.sql.ResultSet, while the method for nonqueries returns an integer. A ResultSet provides you with access to the data retrieved by a query.

Basic JDBC Database Access Classes

JDBC's most fundamental classes are the Connection, the Statement, and the ResultSet. You will use them everytime you write JDBC code. This book has already discussed the details of the Connection class.

java.sql.Statement

The Statement class is the most basic of three JDBC classes representing SQL statements. It performs all of the basic SQL statements the book has discussed so far. In general, a simple database transaction uses only one of the three statement execution methods in the Statement class. The first such method, executeQuery(), takes a SQL String as an argument and returns a ResultSet object. This method should be used for any SQL calls that expect to return data from the database. Update statements, on the other hand, are executed using the executeUpdate() method. This method returns the number of affected rows.

Finally, the Statement class provides an execute() method for situations in which you do not know whether the SQL being executed is a query or update. This usually happens when the application is executing dynamically created SQL statements. If the statement returns a row from the database, the method returns true. Otherwise it returns false. The application can then use the getResultSet() method to get the returned row.

java.sql.ResultSet

A ResultSet is one or more rows of data returned by a database query. The class simply provides a series of methods for retrieving columns from the results of a database query. The methods for getting a column all take the form:

```
type get type(int | String)
```

in which the argument represents either the column number or column name desired. A nice side effect of this design is that you can store values in the database as one type and retrieve them as a completely different type. For example, if you need a Date from the database as a String, you can get it as a String by calling result_set.getString(1) instead of result_set.getDate(1).

Because the ResultSet class handles only a single row from the database at any given time, the class provides the next() method for making it reference the next row of a result set. If next() returns true, you have another row to process and any subsequent calls you make to the ResultSet object will be in reference to that next row. If there are no rows left, it returns false.

JDBC 1.x allowed only one-way navigation through rows from a query. For JDBC 2.0, Sun added support for scrollable result sets. I discuss this new feature later in this chapter.

SQL NULL Versus Java null

SQL and Java have a serious mismatch in handling null values. Specifically, using methods like getInt(), a Java ResultSet has no way of representing a SQL NULL value for any numeric SQL column. After retrieving a value from a ResultSet, it is therefore necessary to ask the ResultSet if the retrieved value represents a SQL NULL. For Java object types, a SQL NULL will often map to Java null. To avoid running into database oddities, however, it is recommended that you always check for SQL NULL.

Checking for SQL NULL involves a single call to the wasNull() method in your ResultSet after you retrieve a value. The wasNull() method will return true if the last value read by a call to a getXXX() method was a SQL NULL. If, for example, your database allowed NULL values for PET_COUNT column because you do not know the number of pets of all your customers, a call to getInt() could return some driver attempt at representing NULL, most likely 0. So how do you know in Java who has 0 pets and who has an unknown number of pets? A call to wasNull() will tell you if 0 represents an actual 0 in the database or a NULL value in the database.

Clean Up

In the examples provided so far, you may have noticed many objects being closed through a close() method. The Connection, Statement, and ResultSet classes all have close(). A given JDBC implementation may or may not require you to close these objects before reuse. But some might require it, since they are likely to hold precious database resources. It is therefore always a good idea to close any instance of these objects when you are done with them. It is useful to remember that closing a Connection implicitly closes all Statement instances associated with the Connection.* Similarly, closing a Statement implicitly closes ResultSet instances associated with it. If you do manage to close a Connection before committing with auto-commit off, any uncommitted transactions will be lost.

Modifying the Database

In Example 3-1, you used JDBC to perform a simple SELECT query. Of course, you cannot really retrieve data from the database before you have put it there. Example 3-3 shows the simple Update class supplied with the mSQL-JDBC driver for mSQL.

Example 3-3. Update from the Imaginary mSQL-JDBC Driver for mSQL

```
import java.sql.*;

public class Update {
  public static void main(String args[]) {
    Connection connection = null;

    if( args.length != 2 ) {
      System.out.println("Syntax: <java Update [number] [string]>");
      return;
    }
```

---

* In practice, I have encountered buggy drivers in which calling close() in the Connection instance does not close associated statements or result set resources. specifically in IBM's native DB2 drivers. If you know you are working with a driver that fails to clean up properly, explicitly closing all connections, statements, and result sets will address the problem without affecting portability.

Example 3-3. Update from the Imaginary mSQL-JDBC Driver for mSQL (continued)

```
try {
  String driver = "com.imaginary.sql.msql.MsqlDriver";

  Class.forName(driver).newInstance();
  String url = "jdbc:msql://carthage.imaginary.com/ora";
  con = DriverManager.getConnection(url, "borg", "");
  Statement s = con.createStatement();
  String test_id = args[0];
  String test_val = args[1];
  int update_count =
    s.executeUpdate("INSERT INTO test (test_id, test_val) " +
                    "VALUES(" + test_id + ", '" + test_val + "')");

  System.out.println(update_count + " rows inserted.");
  s.close();
}
catch( Exception e ) {
  e.printStackTrace();
}
finally {
  if( con != null ) {
    try { con.close(); }
      catch( SQLException e ) { e.printStackTrace(); }
  }
}
```

Again, making a database call is nothing more than creating a `Statement` and passing it SQL via one of its execute methods. Unlike `executeQuery()`, however, `executeUpdate()` does not return a `ResultSet` (you should not be expecting any results). Instead, it returns the number of rows affected by the UPDATE, INSERT, or DELETE.

By default, JDBC commits each SQL statement as it is sent to the database; this is called *auto-commit*. However, for more robust error handling, you can set up a `Connection` object to issue a series of changes that have no effect on the database until you expressly send a commit. Each `Connection` is separate, and a commit on one has no effect on the statements on another. The `Connection` class provides the `setAutoCommit()` method so you can turn auto-commit off. Example 3-4 shows a simple application that turns auto-commit off and either commits two statements together or not at all.

Example 3-4. UpdateLogic Application That Commits Two Updates Together

```java
import java.sql.*;

public class UpdateLogic {
  public static void main(String args[]) {
    Connection connection = null;

    if( args.length != 2 ) {
      System.out.println("Syntax: <java UpdateLogic [number] [string]>");
      return;
    }
    try {
      String driver = "com.imaginary.sql.msql.MsqlDriver";

      Class.forName(driver).newInstance();
      String url = "jdbc:msql://carthage.imaginary.com/ora";
      Statement s;

      con = DriverManager.getConnection(url, "borg", "");
      con.setAutoCommit(false);   // make sure auto commit is off!
      s = con.createStatement();// create the first statement
      s.executeUpdate("INSERT INTO test (test_id, test_val) " +
                    "VALUES(" + args[0] + ", '" + args[1] + "')");
      s.close();                      // close the first statement
      s = con.createStatement();      // create the second statement
      s.executeUpdate("INSERT into test_desc (test_id, test_desc) " +
                    "VALUES(" + args[0] +
                    ", 'This describes the test.')");
      con.commit();                   // commit the two statements
      System.out.println("Insert succeeded.");
      s.close();                      // close the second statement
    }
    catch( SQLException e ) {
      if( con != null ) {
        try { con.rollback(); }         // rollback on error
        catch( SQLException e ) { }
      }
      e.printStackTrace();
    }
    finally {
      if( con != null ) {
        try { con.close(); }
        catch( SQLException e ) { e.printStackTrace(); }
      }
    }
  }
}
```

SQL Datatypes and Java Datatypes

Support for different datatypes in SQL2 is poor. Since Java is an object-oriented language, however, datatype support is extremely rich. Therefore a huge disconnect exists between what sits in the database and the way you want it represented in your Java application. The SQL concept of a variable width, single-byte character array, for example, is the VARCHAR datatype. Java actually has no concept of a variable width, single-byte character array; Java doesn't even have a single-byte character type.* The closest thing is the String class.

To make matters worse, many database engines internally support their own datatypes and loosely translate them to a SQL2 type. All Oracle numeric types, for example, map to the SQL NUMERIC type. JDBC, fortunately, lets you retrieve data in their Java forms defined by a JDBC-specified datatype mapping. You do not need to worry that a SQL LONG has a different representation in Sybase than it does in Oracle. You just call the ResultSet getLong() method to retrieve numbers you wish to treat as Java longs.

You do need to be somewhat concerned when designing the database, however. If you pull a 64-bit number into a Java application via getInt(), you risk getting bad data. Similarly, if you save a Java float into a numeric field with a scale of 0, you will lose data. The important rule of thumb for Java programming, however, is think and work in Java and use the database to support the Java application. Do not let the database drive Java. Table 3-2 shows the JDBC prescribed SQL to Java datatype mappings. Table 3-3 shows the reverse mappings. A full discussion of the SQL3 mappings will occur in Chapter 4.†

Table 3-2. JDBC Specification SQL to Java Datatype Mappings (SQL3 Types in Italic)

SQL Type (from java.sql.Types)	Java Type
BIT	boolean
TINYINT	byte
SMALLINT	short
INTEGER	int
BIGINT	long
REAL	float
FLOAT	double
DOUBLE	double

---

* This fact is actually important for people who believe in storing code values as character rather than numeric datatypes to save in memory overhead. Because Java characters are two bytes, a Java short works as well as a char.

† This type mapping is not strict, but suggested. Individual JDBC vendors may vary this type mapping.

Table 3-2. JDBC Specification SQL to Java Datatype Mappings (SQL3 Types in Italic) (continued)

SQL Type (from java.sql.Types)	Java Type
DECIMAL	java.math.BigDecimal
NUMERIC	java.math.BigDecimal
CHAR	java.lang.String
VARCHAR	java.lang.String
LONGVARCHAR	java.lang.String
DATE	java.sql.Date
TIME	java.sql.Time
TIMESTAMP	java.sql.Timestamp
BINARY	byte[]
VARBINARY	byte[]
LONGVARBINARY	byte[]
BLOB	java.sql.Blob
CLOB	java.sql.Clob
ARRAY	java.sql.Array
REF	java.sql.Ref
STRUCT	java.sql.Struct

Table 3-3. JDBC Specification Java to SQL Datatype Mappings

Java Type	SQL Type (from java.sql.Types)
boolean	BIT
byte	TINYINT
short	SMALLINT
int	INTEGER
long	BIGINT
float	REAL
double	DOUBLE
java.math.BigDecimal	NUMERIC
java.lang.String	VARCHAR or LONGVARCHAR
byte[]	VARBINARY or LONGVARBINARY
java.sql.Date	DATE
java.sql.Time	TIME
java.sql.Timestamp	TIMESTAMP
java.sql.Blob	BLOB
java.sql.Clob	CLOB
java.sql.Array	ARRAY
java.sql.Ref	REF
java.sql.Struct	STRUCT

These mappings are simply the JDBC specification for direct type mappings and not a law prescribing the format you must use in Java for your SQL data. In other words, you can retrieve an INTEGER column into Java as a long or put a Java Date object in a TIMESTAMP field. Some conversions are, nevertheless, nonsensical. You cannot save a Java boolean into a database DATE field.

Scrollable Result Sets

The single most visible addition to the JDBC API in its 2.0 specification is support for scrollable result sets. When the JDBC specification was first finalized, the specification contributors engaged in serious debate as to whether or not result sets should be scrollable. Those against scrollable result sets—and I was one of them— argued that they were antithetical to object-oriented programming and that they violated the rule that complex functionality should not encumber the most commonly used classes. In addition, requiring all driver vendors to implement scrollable result sets could adversely impact the performance of more mundane result set operations for some database engines. Scrollable result sets, on the other hand, are common in database vendor APIs, and the database vendors thus believed they should be present in JDBC.

Result Set Types

Using scrollable result sets starts with the way in which you create statements. Earlier in the chapter, you learned to create a statement using the createStatement() method. The Connection class actually has two versions of createStatement()—the zero parameter version you have used so far and a two parameter version that supports the creation of Statement instances that generate scrollable ResultSet objects. The default call translates to the following call:

```
conn.createStatement(ResultSet.TYPE_FORWARD_ONLY,
                ResultSet.CONCUR_READ_ONLY);
```

The first argument is the result set type. The value ResultSet.TYPE_FORWARD_ ONLY indicates that any ResultSet generated by the Statement returned from createStatement() only moves forward (the JDBC 1.x behavior). The second argument is the result set concurrency. The value ResultSet.CONCUR_READ_ ONLY specifies that each row from a ResultSet is read-only. As you will see in the next chapter, rows from a ResultSet can be modified in place if the concurrency specified in the createStatement() call allows it.

JDBC defines three types of result sets: TYPE_FORWARD_ONLY, TYPE_SCROLL_ SENSITIVE, and TYPE_SCROLL_INSENSITIVE. TYPE_FORWARD_ONLY is the only type that is not scrollable. The other two types are distinguished by how they reflect changes made to them. A TYPE_SCROLL_INSENSITIVE ResultSet is unaware of in-place edits made to modifiable instances. TYPE_SCROLL_ SENSITIVE, on the other hand, means that you can see changes made to the results if you scroll back to the modified row at a later time. You should keep in mind that this distinction remains only while you leave the result set open. If you close a TYPE_SCROLL_INSENSITIVE ResultSet and then requery, your new ResultSet reflects any changes made to the original.

Result Set Navigation

When ResultSet is first created, it is considered to be positioned before the first row. Positioning methods such as next() point a ResultSet to actual rows. Your first call to next(), for example, positions the cursor on the first row. Subsequent calls to next() move the ResultSet ahead one row at a time. With a scrollable ResultSet, however, a call to next() is not the only way to position a result set.

The method previous() works in an almost identical fashion to next(). While next() moves one row forward, previous() moves one row backward. If it moves back beyond the first row, it returns false. Otherwise, it returns true. Because a ResultSet is initially positioned before the first row, you need to move the ResultSet using some other method before you can call previous(). Example 3-5 shows how previous(), after a call to afterLast(), can be used to move backward through a ResultSet.

Example 3-5. Moving Backward Through a Result Set

```
import java.sql.*;
import java.util.*;

public class ReverseSelect {
  public static void main(String argv[]) {
    Connection con = null;

    try {
      String url = "jdbc:msql://carthage.imaginary.com/ora";
      String driver = "com.imaginary.sql.msql.MsqlDriver";
      Properties p = new Properties();
      Statement stmt;
      ResultSet rs;

      p.put("user", "borg");
      Class.forName(driver).newInstance();
      con = DriverManager.getConnection(url, "borg", "");
      stmt =
      con.createStatement(ResultSet.TYPE_SCROLL_INSENSITIVE,
                     ResultSet.CONCUR_READ_ONLY);
       rs = stmt.executeQuery("SELECT * from test ORDER BY test_id");
      // as a new ResultSet, rs is currently positioned
```

Example 3-5. Moving Backward Through a Result Set (continued)

```
      // before the first row
      System.out.println("Got results:");
      // position rs after the last row
      rs.afterLast();
      while(rs.previous()) {
        int a;
        String str;

        a = rs.getInt("test_id");
        if( rs.wasNull() ) {
          a = -1;
        }
        str = rs.getString("test_val");
        if( rs.wasNull() ) {
          str = null;
        }
        System.out.print("\ttest_id= " + a);
        System.out.println("/str= '" + str + "'");
      }
      System.out.println("Done.");
    }
    catch( Exception e ) {
      e.printStackTrace();
    }
    finally {
      if( con != null ) {
        try { con.close(); }
        catch( SQLException e ) { e.printStackTrace(); }
      }
    }
  }
}
```

This example is really no different than the SELECT example from earlier in the chapter. This example simply pulls the results out of the database backward.

Along with afterLast() and previous(), JDBC 2.0 provides new methods to navigate around rows in result sets: beforeFirst(), first(), last(), absolute(), and relative(). Except for absolute() and relative(), the names of the methods say exactly what they do. The beforeFirst() method positions the ResultSet before the first row—its initial state—and the first() and last() methods position the ResultSet on the first and last rows, respectively.

The methods absolute() and relative() each take integer arguments. For absolute(), the argument specifies a row to navigate to. A call to absolute(5) moves the ResultSet to row 5—unless there are four or fewer rows in the ResultSet. If the specified row is beyond the last row in the ResultSet, the

ResultSet is positioned after the last row. A call to absolute() with a row number beyond the last row is therefore identical to a call to afterLast().

You can also pass negative numbers to absolute(). A negative number specifies absolute navigation backwards from the last row. Where absolute(1) is identical to first(), absolute(-1) is identical to last(). Similarly, absolute(-3) is the third to last row in the ResultSet. If there are fewer than three rows in the ResultSet, then ResultSet is positioned before the first row.

The relative() method handles relative navigation through a ResultSet. In other words, it tells the ResultSet how many rows to move forward or backward. A value of 1 behaves just like next() and a value of -1 just like previous().

Determining Where You Are

It is hard to get where you want to go if you don't know where you are. Navigating through scrollable result sets is no different. Of course, you do know where a ResultSet is positioned when you first create it. While processing the ResultSet, however, you may find that you don't know where the ResultSet is positioned. The ResultSet class fortunately provides these methods to let you check the current ResultSet position: isFirst(), isLast(), isBeforeFirst(), isAfterLast(), and getRow(). All except getRow() return booleans; getRow() returns the current row number as an integer.

Helping Your Driver with Scrollable Result Sets

One of the drawbacks of scrollable result sets is that they can be inefficient for some database engines to implement. Specifically, a JDBC driver needs to process rows in an ad hoc fashion, rather than a single, unidirectional fashion. Before scrollable result sets, a JDBC driver can intelligently fetch rows from the database in a just-in-time fashion. While you are getting the first row, it is off retrieving the second and third rows.

JDBC 2.0 gives you the power to help your driver efficiently handle scrollable result sets—to help it avoid having to be ready for random navigation. The method setFetchDirection() lets you tell the driver the direction in which you intend to process a result set. It accepts the values ResultSet.FETCH_FORWARD, ResultSet.FETCH_REVERSE, or ResultSet.FETCH_UNKNOWN. Calling this method may mean absolutely nothing. If, however, the driver can take advantage of knowing the direction in which you intend to process results, then calling this method should improve your performance.

The setFetchSize() method is another method you can use to help the driver be more efficient. The default fetch size is 0 and ignored; the driver makes its best guess as to how many rows to prefetch. If, for example, you know you only want to grab the first row from a result set and no more, you can specify a fetch size of 1. If the driver can optimize based on this information, it can make sure it is not simply returning all the rows when you will only handle 1. By setting the value to 1, however, you do not limit yourself; this value is just a hint to the driver.

When writing a client that intends to use a subset of information in a result set at any given point, you should definitely take advantage of the ability to provide these hints. By indicating to a driver that uses this information that you intend to display only 50 rows at a time in a Swing JTable, you prevent it from sending all 1,000 rows of a result set to a client who will likely see at most 100 rows.

The JDBC Support Classes

JDBC provides a handful of other classes and interfaces that support JDBC's core functionality. Many of them are more SQL-friendly extensions of java.util classes like java.sql.Date and java.sql.Numeric. Others are exception classes that get thrown by JDBC calls.

java.sql.Types

The Types class provides constants that identify SQL datatypes. Each constant representing a SQL datatype that is mapped to an integer is defined by the XOPEN SQL specification. You will see this class used extensively in the next chapter.

java.sql.SQLException

The SQLException class extends the general java.lang.Exception class that provides extra information about a database error. The information provided by SQLException includes:

- The SQLState string describing the error according to the XOPEN SQLState conventions. The different values of this string are defined in the XOPEN SQL specification.

- The database-specific vendor error code. This code is usually a number you have to look up in the obscure reference section of your database's documentation. Fortunately, the error should be sufficiently described through the Java Exception class's getMessage() method.

- A chain of exceptions leading up to this one. This is one of the niftier features of this class. Specifically, if you get several errors during the execution of a transaction, they can be piggybacked in this class. This is frequently useful when you have exceptions that you want to inform the user of, but you do not want to stop processing:

```
try {
    Connection connection = DriverManager.getConnection(url, uid,
                              pass);
}
catch( SQLException e ) {
    while( e != null ) {
        System.err.println("SQLState: " + e.getSQLState());
        System.err.println("   Code: " + e.getErrorCode());
        System.err.println(" Message:");
        System.err.println(e.getMessage());
        e = e.getNextException();
    }
}
```

java.sql.SQLWarning and java.sql.DataTruncation

Depending on the driver you are using, nonfatal errors might occur that should not halt application processing. JDBC provides an extension to the SQLException class called SQLWarning. When a JDBC object, such as a ResultSet, encounters a warning situation internally, it creates a SQLWarning object and adds it to a list of warnings that it keeps. At any point, you can get the warnings for any JDBC object by repeatedly calling the getWarnings() method until it returns null.

The DataTruncation class is a special kind of warning that a JDBC implementation throws when JDBC unexpectedly truncates a data value. A DataTruncation object is chained as a warning on a read operation and thrown as an exception on a write.

java.sql.Date, java.sql.Time, and java.sql.Timestamp

Portable date handling among database engines can be complex; each relational database management system (RDBMS) seems to have its own unique way of representing date information. These three classes all extend the functionality of other Java objects to provide a portable representation of their SQL counterparts. The Date and Time classes represent different levels of granularity as well as different means of expressing information already found in the java.util.Date class. The java.sql.Date class, for example, provides methods to express just the date, month, and year, while the Time class works in terms of hours, minutes, and seconds. And finally, the Timestamp class takes the java.util.Date class down to nanosecond granularity.

A Database Servlet

This chapter has covered a lot of ground. Now it is time to put all the information together in a single, concrete example: a Java servlet that serves up dynamic

HTML content based on data in a database. This servlet will serve as a simple guest book. Visitors to the web page can enter their name, email address, and a few comments, as well as view a random list of other visitors to the site. This example assumes some level of familiarity with Java servlets, but you do not really need to have servlet knowledge to pick out the bits relevant to database access. For an excellent discussion of the Java Servlets API, see *Java Servlet Programming* by Jason Hunter with William Crawford (O'Reilly).

Getting Configuration Information

Before you can connect to a database, you need to have the information to make the connection. As the examples in this chapter have shown, and Example 3-2 in particular, you need a JDBC URL, the proper connection properties, and a way to register one or more JDBC drivers. For a servlet, the place to get this information is in the init() method. Like init() in applets, it is where a servlet does its initialization. It accepts the ServletConfig instance for this servlet from which you can grab initialization parameters. For this example, I have prefixed all initialization parameters with "gb.":

```
public void init(ServletConfig cfg) throws ServletException {
  super.init(cfg);
  driverName = cfg.getInitParameter("gb.driver");
  jdbcURL = cfg.getInitParameter("gb.jdbcURL");
  connectionProperties.put("user", cfg.getInitParameter("gb.user"));
  connectionProperties.put("password", cfg.getInitParameter("gb.pw"));
  try {
    driver = (Driver)Class.forName(driverName).newInstance();
  }
  catch( Exception e ) {
    throw new ServletException("Unable to load driver: " +
                               e.getMessage());
  }
}
```

Under the servlet API, the ServletConfig object holds runtime configuration information. Use this information to capture all JDBC runtime configuration and save it in the driverName, jdbcURL, and connectionProperties attributes. Finally, init() registers the driver.

Showing Random-Visitor Comments on an HTTP GET

When someone visits the page, you want to print out a form and show them random comments from other visitors. The doGet() method simply calls a series of other methods:

```
public void doGet(HttpServletRequest req, HttpServletResponse res)
throws ServletException, IOException {
  ServletOutputStream out = res.getOutputStream();
  String charset = getCharset(req);
  Locale l = getLocale(req);

  res.setContentType("text/html");
  printPageHeader(out, l, charset);
  printCommentForm(out, l, charset);
  printComments(out, l, charset);
  printPageFooter(out, l, charset);
}
```

The doGet() method gets the output stream and localization information and
then prints the top of the page, followed by a visitor comment entry form, a random set of visitor comments, and the bottom of the HTML page. The database
access for retrieving the user comments thus occurs in the printComments()
method:

```
private void printComments(ServletOutputStream out, Locale l, String cs)
throws IOException {
  Connection conn = null;

  try {
    // this is a DateFormat for the locale of the user
    // requesting the page
     DateFormat fmt = DateFormat.getDateInstance(DateFormat.FULL, l);
    ResultSet results;
    Statement stmt;
    int rows, count;

     conn = DriverManager.getConnection(jdbcURL, connectionProperties);
    stmt = conn.createStatement(ResultSet.TYPE_SCROLL_INSENSITIVE,
                                ResultSet.CONCUR_READ_ONLY);
    results = stmt.executeQuery("SELECT name, email, cmt_date, " +
                        "comment, comment_id " +
                        "FROM Comments " +
                        "ORDER BY cmt_date");
    out.println("<DL>");
    // move to the last row and get the row number
    // as a trick to get the number of rows
    results.last();
    rows = results.getRow();
    // pick a random row using the java.util.Random class
    rows = random.nextInt()%rows;
    if( rows < 4 ) {
      // if the random row is less than 4, print the first 4 rows
      results.afterLast();
    }
```

```
      else {
        // otherwise go to the specified row, print the prior 5 rows
        results.absolute(rows);
      }
      count = 0;
      // print up to 5 rows going backwards from the randomly
      // selected row
      while( results.previous() && (count < 5) ) {
        String name, email, cmt;
        Date date;

        count++;
        name = results.getString(1);
        // You should always check for NULL
        if( results.wasNull() ) {
          name = "Unknown User";
        }
        email = results.getString(2);
        if( results.wasNull() ) {
          email = "user@host";
        }
        date = results.getDate(3);
        if( results.wasNull() ) {
          date = new Date((new java.util.Date()).getTime());
        }
        cmt = results.getString(4);
        if( results.wasNull() ) {
          cmt = "No comment.";
        }
          out.println("<DT><B>" + name + "</B> (" + email + ") on " +
                     fmt.format(date));
        cmt = noHTML(cmt);
        out.println("<DD> <PRE>" + cmt + "</PRE>");
      }
      out.println("</DL>");
    }
    catch( SQLException e ) {
      out.println("A database error occurred: " + e.getMessage());
    }
    finally {
      if( conn != null ) {
        try { conn.close(); }
        catch( SQLException e ) { }
      }
    }
  }
```

Saving New Comments

The only task left is to save posted comments. The servlet doPost() method gets called whenever a visitor fills in the form from the doGet() method. In doPost(), you need to grab the values from the form and save them to the database. The update occurs in three pieces:

1. Get the parameter values from the form and validate them.

2. Generate a new, unique comment ID to serve as a primary key.

3. Insert the new comment into the database.

Getting parameter values

Getting parameter values and validating them is nothing more than an exercise in servlet programming. For each field in the form, get its value and make sure that the value makes sense. For example, you want to make sure the email field has a valid email address and that the comment field is not null.

Generating a new comment ID

Almost every database engine has its own proprietary mechanism for generating unique IDs for a database table. Some database engines call these auto-increment fields, others call them sequences. I am going to fudge that issue and provide a database-independent ID generation scheme that has the added value of demonstrating transaction logic.* Specifically, the database for the guest-book servlet contains a table called sys_gen that has two columns: id (VARCHAR) and next_id (BIGINT). The id column contains the name of the ID to be generated and the next_id field the value of the next ID. Your task, programmatically, is to retrieve the current value of next_id for the desired ID field, increment it, and write the incremented value back to the database:

```
conn = DriverManager.getConnection(jdbcURL, connectionProperties);
conn.setAutoCommit(false);
stmt = conn.createStatement();
// generate a new comment ID
result = stmt.executeQuery("SELECT next_id " +
                           "FROM sys_gen " +
                           "WHERE id = 'comment_id'");
if( !result.next() ) {
  throw new ServletException("Failed to generate id.");
}
id = result.getLong(1);
if( result.wasNull() ) {
  id = 0L;
}
```

---

* This code does not prevent dirty-writes, a condition we will cover in the second half of the book.

```
id++;
stmt.close();
// closing the statement closes the result
stmt = conn.createStatement();
stmt.executeUpdate("UPDATE sys_gen SET next_id = " + id +
                " WHERE id = 'comment_id'");
stmt.close();
stmt = conn.createStatement();
comment = fixComment(comment);
stmt.executeUpdate("INSERT into comments " +
                "(comment_id, email, name, comment, " +
                "cmt_date) "+
                "VALUES (" + id +", '" + email +
                "', '" + name + "', '" +
                comment + "', '" + date.getTime() +
                "')");
conn.commit();
```

Inserting a new comment

Finally, the doPost() method inserts the new comment using the generated unique ID and commits everything:

```
stmt = conn.createStatement();
// remove and quotes from the comment, as quotes
// would mess up the resulting SQL statement
comment = fixComment(comment);
stmt.executeUpdate("INSERT into comments " +
                "(comment_id, email, name, comment, " +
                "cmt_date) "+
                "VALUES (" + id +", '" + email +
                "', '" + name + "', '" +
                comment + "', '" + date.getTime() +
                "')");
conn.commit();
stmt.close();
```

The entire operational servlet is available with all other examples from this book at *ftp://ftp.oreilly.com/pub/examples/java/jdbc.*

4.

Advanced JDBC

> *The only thing that makes the device a quarter-detector*
> *rather than a slug detector or a quarter-or-slug detector is*
> *the shared intention of the device's designers, builders,*
> *owners, users. It is only in the environment or context of*
> *those users and their intentions that we can single out*
> *some of the occasions of state Q as "veridical" and others*
> *as "mistaken."*
>
> —Daniel C. Dennett
> *The Intentional Stance*

Chapter 3, *Introduction to JDBC*, provides all the JDBC you absolutely need to know to build database applications. If you understand all of it and then put this book away, you will probably never feel like anything is missing. That is exactly how JDBC's creators intended the API to feel. They wanted to provide a few simple interfaces to support the majority of what database programmers want to do. Extended and complex functionality appears in extra interfaces designed specifically to support that functionality.

Advanced JDBC programming supports advanced needs. These advanced needs break down into two categories: optimizations and extended functionality. This chapter dives into all of the extended functionality included in the JDBC Core API.

Prepared SQL

Each SQL statement you send to the database needs to be parsed by the database engine before it can actually be executed. When the database parses a SQL statement, it reads the SQL to determine what you want the database to do, and then it formulates a plan for carrying out your instructions. This processing is called building a query plan.

In Chapter 3, each SQL statement you sent to the database required the database to treat the statement as a brand-new query and thus build a new query plan for it. This processing is necessary only if each statement requires a distinct query plan. If you are executing statements over and over again that have the same query plan, you are wasting processing power. If, for example, your banking application uses the SQL UPDATE ACCOUNT SET BALANCE = *XXX* WHERE ACCOUNT_ID = *YYY*, you would force the database to rebuild the same query plan each time you changed the balance for the account. Databases enable you to optimize repeated calls through prepared SQL.

Databases provide two kinds of prepared SQL: prepared statements and stored procedures. Prepared SQL provides an advantage over the simple SQL statements you have covered so far; a database can get the SQL ahead of time and create a query plan while you are doing other application logic. This means that your SQL should execute faster and that you can have a generic reference to a statement for later reuse rather than repeatedly create new SQL statements for each new access to the database.

The optimization factor comes from the database knowing what you are about to do. When you create a Java instance of a prepared statement or stored procedure, you notify the database of what kind of SQL call that object represents. The database can then create a query plan for that SQL call before you ever actually execute it. When it comes time for you to execute the SQL, the database is ready for you. If you execute the same prepared SQL more than once, the database remains ready for your SQL without having to rebuild the query plan.

TIP   You could get more performance benefits by pooling your prepared
                 SQL resources. For example, if your code makes only a single call to
                 a specific SQL statement, but that call appears in different places
                 throughout the application, you could implement a prepared state-
                 ment pool that holds the JDBC representation of your prepared SQL
                 open for repeated use. This functionality may end up as a feature of
                 JDBC 3.0.

Prepared Statements

The PreparedStatement interface extends the Statement interface you used in Chapter 3. It enables a SQL statement to contain parameters like a function defini-tion, and you can execute a single statement repeatedly with different values for those parameters. The act of assigning values to parameters is called *binding param-eters.* You might want to use a prepared statement when updating a group of objects stored on the same table. For example, if you were updating many bank accounts at once, you might have a loop calling:

```
Statement statement = c.createStatement();
int i;

for(i=0; i<accounts.length; i++)
   statement.executeUpdate("UPDATE account " +
                       "SET balance = " + accounts[i].getBalance() +
                       "WHERE id = " + accounts[i].getId());
c.commit();
statement.close();
```

This statement creates the same query plan each time through the loop. Instead of calling this same statement repeatedly with different inputs, you can instead use a `PreparedStatement`:

```
PreparedStatement statement = c.prepareStatement(
                       "UPDATE account " +
                       "SET balance = ? " +
                       "WHERE id = ?");
int i;

for(i=0; i<accounts.length; i++) {
    statement.setFloat(1, accounts[i].getBalance());
    statement.setInt(2, accounts[i].getId());
    statement.execute();
    statement.clearParameters()
}
c.commit();
statement.close();
```

With a prepared statement, you send the actual SQL to the database when you get the `PreparedStatement` object through the `prepareStatement()` method in `java.sql.Connection`. Keep in mind that you have not yet actually executed any SQL. You execute that prepared SQL statement multiple times inside the `for()` loop, but you build the query plan only a single time.

Before each execution of the prepared statement, you tell JDBC which values to use as input for that execution of the statement. In order to bind the input parameters, `PreparedStatement` provides `setXXX()` methods (such as `setFloat()` and `setInt()`) that mirror the `getXXX()` methods you saw in `java.sql.ResultSet`. Just as the `getXXX()` methods read results according to the order in which you constructed your SQL, the `setXXX()` methods bind parameters from left to right in the order you placed them in the prepared statement. In the previous example, I bound parameter 1 as a float to the account balance that I retrieved from the account object. The first ? was thus associated with parameter 1.

Stored Procedures

While prepared statements let you access similar database queries through a single PreparedStatement object, stored procedures attempt to take the "black box" concept for database access one step further. A stored procedure is built inside the database before you run your application. You access that stored procedure by name at runtime. In other words, a stored procedure is almost like a method you call in the database. Stored procedures have the following advantages:

- Because the procedure is precompiled in the database for most database engines, it executes much faster than dynamic SQL, which needs to be re-interpreted each time it is issued. Even if your database does not compile the procedure before it runs, it will be precompiled for subsequent runs just like prepared statements.

- Syntax errors in the stored procedure can be caught at compile time rather than at runtime.

- Java developers need to know only the name of the procedure and its inputs and outputs. The way in which the procedure is implemented—the tables it accesses, the structure of those tables, etc.—is completely unimportant.

A stored procedure is written with variables as argument place holders, which are passed when the procedure is called through column binding. Column binding is a fancy way of specifying the parameters to a stored procedure. You will see exactly how this is done in the following examples. A Sybase stored procedure might look like this:

```
DROP PROCEDURE sp_select_min_bal
GO


CREATE PROCEDURE sp_select_min_bal
        @balance,
AS
SELECT account_id
FROM account
WHERE  balance > @balance


GO
```

The name of this stored procedure is sp_select_min_bal. It accepts a single argument identified by the @ sign. That single argument is the minimum balance. The stored procedure produces a result set containing all accounts with a balance greater than that minimum balance. While this stored procedure produces a result set, you can also have procedures that return output parameters. Here's an even more complex stored procedure, written in Oracle's stored procedure language, that calculates interest and returns the new balance:

```
CREATE OR REPLACE PROCEDURE sp_interest
(id IN INTEGER,
bal IN OUT FLOAT) IS
BEGIN
SELECT balance
INTO bal
FROM account
WHERE account_id = id;

bal := bal + bal * 0.03;

UPDATE account
SET balance = bal
WHERE account_id = id;

END;
```

This stored procedure accepts two arguments—the variables in the parentheses—and does complex processing that does not (and cannot) occur in the embedded SQL you have been using so far. It actually performs two SQL statements and a calculation all in one procedure. The first part grabs the current balance; the second part takes the balance and increases it by 3 percent; and the third part updates the balance. In your Java application, you could use it like this:

```
try {
    CallableStatement statement;
    int i;

    statement = c.prepareCall("{call sp_interest[(?,?)]}");

    statement.registerOutParameter(2, java.sql.Types.FLOAT);
    for(i=1; i<accounts.length; i++) {
        statement.setInt(1, accounts[i].getId());
        statement.execute();
        System.out.println("New balance: " + statement.getFloat(2));
    }
    c.commit();
    statement.close();
    c.close();
}
```

The CallableStatement class is very similar to the PreparedStatement class. Using prepareCall() instead of prepareStatement(), you indicate which procedure you want to call when you initialize your CallableStatement object. Unfortunately, this is one time when ANSI SQL2 simply is not enough for portability. Different database engines use different syntaxes for these calls. JDBC, however, does provide a database-independent, stored-procedure escape syntax in the form {call procedure_name[(?, ?)]}. For stored procedures with return values, the escape syntax is: {? = call *procedure_name*[(?,?)]}. In this escape syntax, each ? represents a place holder for either procedure inputs or return values. The JDBC driver then translates this escape syntax into the driver's own stored procedure syntax.

If your stored procedure has output parameters, you need to register their types using `registerOutParameter()` before executing the stored procedure. This step tells JDBC what datatype the parameter in question will be. The previous example did it like this:

```
CallableStatement statement;
int i;

statement = c.prepareCall("{call sp_interest[(?,?)]}");
statement.registerOutParameter(2, java.sql.Types.FLOAT);
```

The `prepareCall()` method creates a stored procedure object that will make a call to the specified stored procedure. This syntax sets up the order you will use in binding parameters. By calling `registerOutParameter()`, you tell the `CallableStatement` instance to expect the second parameter as output of type float. Once this is set up, you can bind the ID using `setInt()`, and then get the result using `getFloat()`.

Batch Processing

Complex systems often require both online and batch processing. Each kind of processing has very different requirements. Because online processing involves a user waiting on application processing order, the timing and performance of each statement execution in a process is important. Batch processing, on the other hand, occurs when a bunch of distinct transactions need to occur independently of user interaction. A bank's ATM machine is an example of a system of online processes. The monthly process that calculates and adds interest to your savings account is an example of a batch process.

JDBC 2.0 introduced new functionality to address the specific issues of batch processing. Using the JDBC 2.0 batch facilities, you can assign a series of SQL statements to a JDBC `Statement` (or one of its subclasses) to be submitted together for execution by the database. Using the techniques you have learned so far in this book, account interest-calculation processing occurs roughly in the following fashion:

1. Prepare statement.

2. Bind parameters.

3. Execute.

4. Repeat steps 2 and 3 for each account.

What Kind of Statement to Use?

This book presents you with three kinds of statement classes: `Statement`, `PreparedStatement`, and `CallableStatement`. You use the class that corresponds to the kind of SQL you intend to use. But how do you determine which kind is best for you? The plain SQL statements represented by the `Statement` class are almost never a good idea. Their only place is in quick and dirty coding. While it is true that you will get no performance benefits if each call to the database is unique, plain SQL statements are also more error prone (no automatic handling of data formatting, for example) and do not read as cleanly as prepared SQL. The harder decision therefore lies between prepared statements and stored procedures. The bottom line in this decision is portability versus speed and elegance. You should thus consider the following in making your decision:

- As you can see from the Oracle and Sybase stored procedures earlier in this chapter, different databases have wildly different syntaxes for their stored procedures. While JDBC makes sure that your Java code will remain portable, the code in your stored procedures will almost never be.

- While a stored procedure is generally faster than a prepared statement, there is no guarantee that you will see better performance in stored procedures. Different databases optimize in different ways. Some precompile both prepared statements and stored procedures; others precompile neither. The only thing you know for certain is that a prepared statement is very unlikely to be faster than its stored procedure counterpart and that the stored procedure counterpart is likely to be moderately faster than the prepared statement.

- Stored procedures are truer to the black-box concept than prepared statements. The JDBC programmer needs to know only stored procedure inputs and outputs—not the underlying table structure—for a stored procedure; the programmer needs to know the underlying table structure in addition to the inputs and outputs for prepared SQL.

- Stored procedures enable you to perform complex logic inside the database. Some people view this as an argument in favor of stored procedures. In three-tier distributed systems, however, you should never have any processing logic in the database. This feature should, therefore, be avoided by three-tier developers.

This style of processing requires a lot of "back and forth" between the Java application and the database. JDBC 2.0 batch processing provides a simpler, more efficient approach to this kind of processing:

1. Prepare statement.

2. Bind parameters.

3. Add to batch.

4. Repeat steps 2 and 3 until interest has been assigned for each account.

5. Execute.

Under batch processing, there is no "back and forth" between the database for each account. Instead, all Java-level processing—the binding of parameters— occurs before you send the statements to the database. Communication with the database occurs in one huge burst; the huge bottleneck of stop and go communication with the database is gone.

Statement and its children all support batch processing through an addBatch() method. For Statement, addBatch() accepts a String that is the SQL to be executed as part of the batch. The PreparedStatement and CallableStatement classes, on the other hand, use addBatch() to bundle a set of parameters together as part of a single element in the batch. The following code shows how to use a Statement object to batch process interest calculation:

```
Statement stmt = conn.createStatement();
int[] rows;

for(int i=0; i<accts.length; i++) {
    accts[i].calculateInterest();
    stmt.addBatch("UPDATE account " +
                "SET balance = " +
                accts[i].getBalance() +
                "WHERE acct_id = " + accts[i].getID());
}
rows = stmt.executeBatch();
```

The addBatch() method is basically nothing more than a tool for assigning a bunch of SQL statements to a JDBC Statement object for execution together. Because it makes no sense to manage results in batch processing, the statements you pass to addBatch() should be some form of an update: a CREATE, INSERT, UPDATE, or DELETE. Once you are done assigning SQL statements to the object, call executeBatch() to execute them. This method returns an array of row counts of modified rows. The first element, for example, contains the number of rows affected by the first statement in the batch. Upon completion, the list of SQL calls associated with the Statement instance is cleared.

This example uses the default auto-commit state in which each update is committed automatically.* If an error occurs somewhere in the batch, all accounts before the error will have their new balance stored in the database, and the subsequent accounts will not have had their interest calculated. The account where the error occurred will have an account object whose state is inconsistent with the database. You can use the getUpdateCounts() method in the BatchUpdateException thrown by executeBatch() to get the value executeBatch() should have otherwise returned. The size of this array tells you exactly how many statements executed successfully.

In a real-world batch process, you will not want to hold the execution of the batch until you are done with all accounts. If you do so, you will fill up the transaction log used by the database to manage its transactions and bog down database performance. You should therefore turn auto-commit off and commit changes every few rows while performing batch processing.

Using prepared statements and callable statements for batch processing is very similar to using regular statements. The main difference is that a batch prepared or callable statement represents a single SQL statement with a list of parameter groups, and the database should create a query plan only once. Calculating interest with a prepared statement would look like this:

```
PreparedStatement stmt = conn.prepareStatement(
    "UPDATE account SET balance = ? WHERE acct_id = ?");
int[] rows;

for(int i=0; i<accts.length; i++) {
    accts[i].calculateInterest();
    stmt.setDouble(1, accts[i].getBalance());
    stmt.setLong(2, accts[i].getID());
    stmt.addBatch();
}
rows = stmt.executeBatch();
```

Example 4-1 provides the full example of a batch program that runs a monthly password-cracking program on people's passwords. The program sets a flag in the database for each bad password so a system administrator can act appropriately.

Example 4-1. A Batch Process to Mark Users with Easy-to-Crack Passwords

```
import java.sql.*;
import java.util.ArrayList;
import java.util.Iterator;
```

---

* Doing batch processing using a Statement results in the same inefficiencies you have already seen in Statement objects because the database must repeatedly rebuild the same query plan.

Example 4-1. A Batch Process to Mark Users with Easy-to-Crack Passwords (continued)

```java
public class Batch {
    static public void main(String[] args) {
        Connection conn = null;

        try {
            // we will store the bad UIDs in this list
            ArrayList breakable = new ArrayList();
            PreparedStatement stmt;
            Iterator users;
            ResultSet rs;

            Class.forName(args[0]).newInstance();
            conn = DriverManager.getConnection(args[1],
                                               args[2],
                                               args[3]);
            stmt = conn.prepareStatement("SELECT user_id, password " +
                                         "FROM user");
            rs = stmt.executeQuery();
            while( rs.next() ) {
                String uid = rs.getString(1);
                String pw = rs.getString(2);

                // Assume PasswordCracker is some class that provides
                // a single static method called crack() that attempts
                // to run password cracking routines on the password
                if( PasswordCracker.crack(uid, pw) ) {
                    breakable.add(uid);
                }
            }
            stmt.close();
            if( breakable.size() < 1 ) {
                return;
            }
            stmt = conn.prepareStatement("UPDATE user " +
                                         "SET bad_password = 'Y' " +
                                         "WHERE uid = ?");
            users = breakable.iterator();
            // add each UID as a batch parameter
            while( users.hasNext() ) {
                String uid = (String)users.next();

                stmt.setString(1, uid);
                stmt.addBatch();
            }
            stmt.executeBatch();
        }
        catch( Exception e ) {
            e.printStackTrace();
```

Example 4-1. A Batch Process to Mark Users with Easy-to-Crack Passwords (continued)

```
        }
        finally {
            if( conn != null ) {
                try { conn.close(); }
                catch( Exception e ) { }
            }
        }
    }
}
```

Updatable Result Sets

If you remember scrollable result sets from Chapter 3, you may recall that one of the parameters you used to create a scrollable result set was something called the *result set concurrency*. So far, the statements in this book have used the default concurrency, `ResultSet.CONCUR_READ_ONLY`. In other words, you cannot make changes to data in the result sets you have seen without creating a new update statement based on the data from your result set. Along with scrollable result sets, JDBC 2.0 also introduces the concept of *updatable result sets*—result sets you can change.

An updatable result set enables you to perform in-place changes to a result set and have them take effect using the current transaction. I place this discussion after batch processing because the only place it really makes sense in an enterprise environment is in large-scale batch processing. An overnight interest-assignment process for a bank is an example of such a potential batch process. It would read in an accounts balance and interest rate and, while positioned at that row in the database, update the interest. You naturally gain efficiency in processing since you do everything at once. The downside is that you perform database access and business logic together.

JDBC 2.0 result sets have two types of concurrency: `ResultSet.CONCUR_READ_ ONLY` and `ResultSet.CONCUR_UPDATABLE`. You already know how to create an updatable result set from the discussion of scrollable result sets in Chapter 3. You pass the concurrency type `ResultSet.CONCUR_UPDATABLE` as the second argument to `createStatement()`, or the third argument to `prepareStatement()` or `prepareCall()`:

```
PreparedStatement stmt = conn.prepareStatement(
        "SELECT acct_id, balance FROM account",
        ResultSet.TYPE_SCROLL_SENSITIVE,
        ResultSet.CONCUR_UPDATABLE);
```

The most important thing to remember about updatable result sets is that you must always select from a single table and include the primary key columns. If you don't, the concept of the result set being updatable is nonsensical. After all, updatable result set only constructs a hidden UPDATE for you. If it does not know what the unique identifier for the row in question is, there is no way it can construct a valid update.

NOTE   JDBC drivers are not required to support updatable result sets. The driver is, however, required to let you create result sets of any type you like. If you request CONCUR_UPDATABLE and the driver does not support it, it issues a SQLWarning and assigns the result set to a type it can support. It will not throw an exception until you try to use a feature of an unsupported result set type. Later in the chapter, I discuss the DatabaseMetaData class and how you can use it to determine if a specific type of concurrency is supported.

Updates

JDBC 2.0 introduces a set of updateXXX() methods to match its getXXX() methods and enable you to update a result set. For example, updateString(1, "violet") enables your application to replace the current value for column 1 of the current row in the result set with a string that has the value violet. Once you are done modifying columns, call updateRow() to make the changes permanent in the database. You naturally cannot make changes to primary key columns. Updates look like this:

```
while( rs.next() ) {
    long acct_id = rs.getLong(1);
    double balance = rs.getDouble(2);

    balance = balance + (balance * 0.03)/12;
    rs.updateDouble(2, balance);
    rs.updateRow();
}
```

WARNING   While this code does look simpler than batch processing, you should remember that it is a poor approach to enterprise-class problems. Specifically, imagine that you have been running a bank using this simple script run once a month to manage interest accumulation. After two years, you find that your business processes change—perhaps because of growth or a merger. Your new business processes introduce complex business rules pertaining to the accumulation of interest and general rules regarding balance changes. If this code is the only place where you have done direct data access, implementing interest accumulation and managing balance adjustments—a highly unlikely bit of luck—you could migrate to a more robust solution. On the other hand, your bank is probably like most systems and has code like this all over the place. You now have a total mess on your hands when it comes to managing the evolution of your business processes.

Deletes

Deletes are naturally much simpler than updates. Rather than setting values, you just have to call deleteRow(). This method will delete the current row out from under you and out of the database.

Inserts

Inserting a new row into a result set is the most complex operation of updatable result sets because inserts introduce a few new steps into the process. The first step is to create a row for update via the method moveToInsertRow(). This method creates a row that is basically a scratchpad for you to work in. This new row becomes your current row. As with other rows, you can call getXXX() and updateXXX() methods on it to retrieve or modify its values. Once you are done making changes, call insertRow() to make the changes permanent. Any values you fail to set are assumed to be null. The following code demonstrates the insertion of a new row using an updatable result set:

```
rs.moveToInsertRow();
rs.updateString(1, "newuid");
rs.updateString(2, "newpass");
rs.insertRow();
rs.moveToCurrentRow();
```

The seemingly peculiar call to moveToCurrentRow() returns you to the row you were on before you attempted to insert the new row.

In addition to requiring the result set to represent a single table in the database with no joins and fetch all the primary keys of the rows to be changed, inserts require that the result set has fetched—for each matching row—all non-null columns and all columns without default values.

Visibility of Changes

Chapter 3 mentioned two different types of scrollable result sets without diving into the details surrounding their differences. I ignored those differences specifically because they deal with the visibility of changes in updatable result sets. They determine how sensitive a result set is to changes to its underlying data. In other words, if you go back and retrieve values from a modified column, will you see the changes or the initial values? ResultSet.TYPE_SCROLL_SENSITIVE result sets are sensitive to changes in the underlying data, while ResultSet.TYPE_SCROLL_INSENSITIVE result sets are not. This may sound straightforward, but the devil is truly in the details.

How these two result set types manifest themselves is first dependent on something called *transaction isolation*. Transaction isolation identifies the visibility of your changes at a transaction level. In other words, what visibility do the actions of one transaction have to another? Can another transaction read your uncommitted database changes? Or, if another transaction does a select in the middle of your update transaction, will it see the old data?

Transactional parlance talks of several visibility issues that JDBC transaction isolation is designed to address. These issues are *dirty reads, repeatable reads,* and *phantom reads.* A dirty read means that one transaction can see uncommitted changes from another transaction. If the uncommitted changes are rolled back, the other transaction is said to have "dirty data"—thus the term dirty read.

A repeatable read occurs when one transaction always reads the same data from the same query no matter how many times the query is made or how many changes other transactions make to the rows read by the first transaction. In other words, a transaction that mandates repeatable reads will not see the committed changes made by another transaction. Your application needs to start a new transaction to see those changes.

The final issue, phantom reads, deals with changes occurring in other transactions that would result in new rows matching your where clause. Consider the situation in which you have a transaction reading all accounts with a balance less than $100. Your application logic makes two reads of that data. Between the two reads, another transaction adds a new account to the database with a balance of $0. That account will now match your query. If your transaction isolation allows phantom reads, you will see that "phantom row." If it disallows phantom reads, then you will see the same result set you saw the first time.

The tradeoff in transaction isolations is performance versus consistency. Transaction isolation levels that avoid dirty, nonrepeatable, phantom reads will be consistent for the life of a transaction. Because the database has to worry about a lot of issues, however, transaction processing will be much slower. JDBC specifies the following transaction isolation levels:

TRANSACTION_NONE

    The database or the JDBC driver does not support transactions of any sort.

TRANSACTION_READ_UNCOMMITTED

    The transaction allows dirty reads, nonrepeatable reads, or phantom reads.

TRANSACTION_READ_COMMITTED

    Only data committed to the database can be read. It will, however, allow nonrepeatable reads and phantom reads.

TRANSACTION_REPEATABLE_READ

> Committed, repeatable reads as well as phantom reads are allowed. Nonrepeatable reads are not allowed.

TRANSACTION_SERIALIZABLE

> Only committed, repeatable reads are allowed. Phantom reads are specifically disallowed at this level.

You can find the transaction isolation of a connection by calling its getTransactionIsolation() method. This visibility applies to updatable result sets as it does to other transaction components. Transaction isolation does not address the issue of one result set reading changes made by itself or other result sets in the same transaction. That visibility is determined by the result set type.

A ResultSet.TYPE_SCROLL_INSENSITIVE result set does not see any changes made by other transactions or other elements of the same transaction. ResultSet.TYPE_SCROLL_SENSITIVE result sets, on the other hand, see all updates to data made by other elements of the same transaction. Inserts and deletes may or may not be visible. You should note that any update that might affect the order of the result set—such as an update that modifies a column in an ORDER BY clause—acts like a DELETE followed by an INSERT and thus may or may not be visible.

Refreshing Data from the Database

In addition to all of these visibility issues, JDBC 2.0 provides a mechanism for getting up-to-the-second changes from the database. Not even a TYPE_SCROLL_SENSITIVE result set sees changes made by other transactions after it reads from the database. To go to the database and get the latest data for the current row, call the refreshRow() method in your ResultSet instance.

Advanced Datatypes

JDBC 1.x supported the SQL2 datatypes. JDBC 2.0 introduces support for more advanced datatypes, including the SQL3 "object" types and direct persistence of Java objects. Except for the BLOB and CLOB datatypes, few of these advanced datatype features are likely to be relevant to most programmers for a few years. While they are important features for bridging the gap between the object and relational paradigms, they are light years ahead of where database vendors are with relational technology and how people use relational technology today.

Blobs and Clobs

Stars of a bad horror film? No. These are the two most important datatypes introduced by JDBC 2.0. A blob is a **B**inary **L**arge **O**bject, and a clob is a **C**haracter

Large Object. In other words, they are two datatypes designed to hold really large amounts of data. Blobs, represented by the BLOB datatype, hold large amounts of binary data. Similarly, clobs, represented by the CLOB datatype, hold large amounts of text data.

You may wonder why these two datatypes are so important when SQL2 already provides VARCHAR and VARBINARY datatypes. These two old datatypes have two important implementation problems that make them impractical for large amounts of data. First, they tend to have rather small maximum data sizes. Second, you retrieve them from the database all at once. While the first problem is more of a tactical issue (those maximum sizes are arbitrary), the second problem is more serious. Fields with sizes of 100 KB or more are better served through streaming than an all-at-once approach. In other words, instead of having your query wait to fetch the full data for each row in a result set containing a column of 1-MB data, it makes more sense to not send that data across the network until the instant you ask for it. The query runs faster using streaming, and your network will not be overburdened trying to shove 10 rows of 1 MB each at a client machine all at once. The BLOB and CLOB types support the streaming of large data elements.

JDBC 2.0 provides two Java types to correspond to SQL BLOB and CLOB types: `java.sql.Blob` and `java.sql.Clob`. You retrieve them from a result set in the same way you retrieve any other datatype, through a getter method:

```
Blob b = rs.getBlob(1);
```

Unlike other Java datatypes, when you call getBlob() or getClob() you are getting only an empty shell; the Blob or Clob instance contains none of the data from the database.* You can retrieve the actual data at your leisure using methods in the Blob and Clob interfaces as long as the transaction in which the value was retrieved is open. JDBC drivers can optionally implement alternate lifespans for Blob and Clob implementations to extend beyond the transaction.

The two interfaces enable your application to access the actual data either as a stream:

```
Blob b = rs.getBlob(1);
InputStream binstr = b.getBinaryStream();
Clob c = rs.getClob(2);
Reader charstr = c.getCharacterStream();
```

so you can read from the stream, or you can grab it in chunks:

```
Blob b = rs.getBlob(1);
```

---

* Some database engines may actually fudge Blob and Clob support because they cannot truly support blob or clob functionality. In other words, the JDBC driver for the database may support Blob and Clob types even though the database it supports does not. More often than not, it fudges this support by loading the data from the database into these objects in the same way that VARCHAR and VARBINARY are implemented.

```
byte[] data = b.getBytes(0, b.length());
Clob c = rs.getClob(2);
String text = c.getSubString(0, c.length());
```

The storage of blobs and clobs is a little different from their retrieval. While you can use the setBlob() and setClob() methods in the PreparedStatement and CallableStatement classes to bind Blob and Clob objects as parameters to a statement, the JDBC Blob and Clob interfaces provide no database-independent mechanism for constructing Blob and Clob instances.* You need to either write your own implementation or tie yourself to your driver vendor's implementation.

A more database-independent approach is to use the setBinaryStream() or setObject() methods for binary data or the setAsciiStream(), setUnicodeStream(), or setObject() methods for character data. Example 4-2 puts everything regarding blobs together into a program that looks for a binary file and either saves it to the database, if it exists, or retrieves it from the database and stores it in the named file if it does not exist.

Example 4-2. Storing and Retrieving Binary Data

```
import java.sql.*;
import java.io.*;

public class Blobs {
    public static void main(String args[]) {
        Connection con = null;

        if( args.length < 5 ) {
            System.err.println("Syntax: <java Blobs [driver] [url] " +
                               "[uid] [pass] [file]");
            return;
        }
        try {
            Class.forName(args[0]).newInstance();
            con = DriverManager.getConnection(args[1],
                                              args[2],
                                              args[3]);
            File f = new File(args[4]);
            PreparedStatement stmt;

            if( !f.exists() ) {
                // if the file does not exist
                // retrieve it from the database and write it
                // to the named file
                ResultSet rs;
```

---

* This topic should be addressed by JDBC 3.0.

Example 4-2. Storing and Retrieving Binary Data (continued)

```
                    stmt = con.prepareStatement("SELECT blobData " +
                                                "FROM BlobTest " +
                                                "WHERE fileName = ?");

            stmt.setString(1, args[4]);
            rs = stmt.executeQuery();
            if( !rs.next() ) {
                System.out.println("No such file stored.");
            }
            else {
                Blob b = rs.getBlob(1);
                BufferedOutputStream os;

                os = new BufferedOutputStream(new FileOutputStream(f));
                os.write(b.getBytes(0, (int)b.length()), 0,
                        (int)b.length());
                os.flush();
                os.close();
            }
        }
        else {
            // otherwise read it and save it to the database
            FileInputStream fis = new FileInputStream(f);
            byte[] tmp = new byte[1024]; // arbitrary size
            byte[] data = null;
            int sz, len = 0;

            while( (sz = fis.read(tmp)) != -1 ) {
                if( data == null ) {
                    len = sz;
                    data = tmp;
                }
                else {
                    byte[] narr;
                    int nlen;

                    nlen = len + sz;
                    narr = new byte[nlen];
                    System.arraycopy(data, 0, narr, 0, len);
                    System.arraycopy(tmp, 0, narr, len, sz);
                    data = narr;
                    len = nlen;
                }
            }
            if( len != data.length ) {
                byte[] narr = new byte[len];
```

Example 4-2. Storing and Retrieving Binary Data (continued)

```
                System.arraycopy(data, 0, narr, 0, len);
                data = narr;
            }
            stmt = con.prepareStatement(
                "INSERT INTO BlobTest " + (fileName, " +
                "blobData) VALUES(?, ?)");
            stmt.setString(1, args[4]);
            stmt.setObject(2, data);
            stmt.executeUpdate();
            f.delete();
        }
        con.close();
    }
    catch( Exception e ) {
        e.printStackTrace();
    }
    finally {
        if( con != null ) {
            try { con.close(); }
            catch( Exception e ) { }
        }
    }
}
}
```

Arrays

SQL arrays are much simpler and much less frequently used than blobs and clobs. JDBC represents a SQL array through the `java.sql.Array` interface. This interface provides the `getArray()` method to turn an `Array` object into a normal Java array. It also provides a `getResultSet()` method to treat the SQL array instead as a JDBC result set. If, for example, your database has a column that is an array of string values, your code to retrieve that data might look like this:

```
Array col = rs.getArray(1);
String[] data = (String[])col.getArray();
```

The default SQL to Java type mapping you saw in Chapter 3 determines the datatype of the array elements. You can, however, customize mapping of these values using something called a type mapping. You will cover more on type mappings later in the chapter.

Array storage faces the same difficulty as blob and clob storage: there is no driver-independent way to construct an `Array` instance for the `setArray()` methods. As an alternative, you can use `setObject()`.

Other SQL3 Types

JDBC 2.0 supports a few other SQL3 types that behave in much the same way as types you have already seen. These types include the SQL REF, DISTINCT, and STRUCT types. Support for the REF type works in exactly the same way as support for the ARRAY type. JDBC provides a `java.sql.Ref` class with a `getRef()` method in `ResultSet` and `setRef()` methods in `PreparedStatement` and `CallableStatement`. The `Ref` interface only enables your application to reference its associated object; it does not provide a dereferencing mechanism. Using a DISTINCT type works in exactly the same way as using its underlying datatype. For example,

```
CREATE TYPE FRUIT AS VARCHAR(10)
```

should be treated by JDBC code just as if the SQL type were `VARCHAR(10)`. You would thus use `getString()` and `setString()` to retrieve and store the data for any column of this type.

Structured types work through `getObject()` and `setObject()` even though JDBC provides a special interface—`java.sql.Struct`—to support them. The JDBC driver fetches the underlying data in the `Struct` before returning it to you. The result is that a `Struct` reference is valid beyond the transaction until it is removed by the garbage collector.

Java Types

Sun is pushing the concept of a "Java-relational DBMS" that extends the basic type system of the DBMS with Java object types. What a Java-relational DBMS will ultimately look like is unclear, and the success of this effort remains to be seen. JDBC 2.0 nevertheless introduces features necessary to support it. These features are optional for JDBC drivers, and it is very likely that the driver you are using does not support them at this time.[*]

Returning to the example of a bank application, you might have customer and account tables in a traditional database. The idea behind a Java-relational database is that you have Customer and Account types that correspond directly to Java Customer and Account classes. You could therefore issue the following SQL:

```
SELECT Customer FROM Account
```

This SQL would give you all the data associated with all customers who have accounts. Your Java code might look like this:

```
ResultSet rs = stmt.executeQuery("SELECT Customer " +
                                 "FROM Account");
ArrayList custs = new ArrayList();
```

---

[*] My discussion of the topic is very cursory because it is still unclear how this feature will play itself out.

```
while( rs.next() ) {
    Customer cust = (Customer)rs.getObject(1);

    custs.add(cust);
}
```

All the types I have mentioned so far in this book have a corresponding value in the java.sql.Types class. All Java object types, however, use a single value in java.sql.Types: JAVA_OBJECT.

Type Mapping

The new type support in JDBC 2.0 blurs the fine type mappings mentioned in Chapter 3. To help give the programmer more control over this type mapping, JDBC 2.0 introduces a type mapping system that lets you customize how you want SQL types mapped to Java objects. The central character of this new feature is a class from the Java Collections API, java.util.Map. You can pass JDBC an instance of this class that contains information on how to perform type mapping for user-defined types. This object is called the type-map object. The keys of the type-map object are strings that represent the name of the SQL type to be mapped. The values are the corresponding java.lang.Class objects. For example, you may have a Account string as a key that maps to a bank.Account class in your type map.

There are several levels of type mapping. The first is the default mapping. Until now, you have been working with the default type mapping. The default type mapping is used unless you provide an alternate type mapping. You can specify an alternate type mapping at the connection level by calling setTypeMap() in your Connection instance. For example, you might have the following code to handle your DISTINCT FRUIT type:

```
HashMap tm = new HashMap();

tm.put("FRUIT", Fruit.class);
conn.setTypeMap(tm);
```

JDBC also provides you with a tool for more fine-grained type mapping. Many getXXX() methods such as getObject() have signatures that accept a type map as an argument. If, for example, you wanted to retrieve FRUIT data in most cases as the underlying String type, but in one specific instance wanted to retrieve it as an instance of a Java Fruit class, you would leave the default type map in place and instead use the following call to handle the special case:

```
HashMap tm = new HashMap();

tm.put("FRUIT", Fruit.class);
rs.getObject(1, tm);
```

Of course, this type map provides no information on how to turn the String "orange" to an instance of the Fruit class that represents an Orange. Any class that appears in a type map must therefore implement the java.sql.SQLData interface. This interface prescribes methods that enable a driver to pass it the String "orange" from the database and initialize its data. These methods are readSQL(), writeSQL(), and getSQLTypeName(). Example 4-3 shows a full implementation for the Fruit class.

Example 4-3. Mapping a SQL DISTINCT Type to a Java Class

```
import java.sql.*;

public class Fruit implements SQLData {
    private String name;
    private String sqlTypeName;

    public Fruit() {
        super();
    }

    public Fruit(String nom) {
        super();
        name = nom;
    }

    public String getName() {
        return name;
    }

    public String getSQLTypeName() {
        return sqlTypeName;
    }

    public void readSQL(SQLInput is, String type) throws SQLException {
        sqlTypeName = type;
        name = is.readString();
    }

    public void writeSQL(SQLOutput os) throws SQLException {
        os.writeString(name);
    }
}
```

The readSQL() method reads the Fruit's data from the database. The writeSQL() method, conversely, writes the Fruit's state to the object stream. Finally, the getSQLTypeName() method says what SQL type represents this Java type. When using custom SQL3 object types that have an inheritance structure, your Java classes should call super.readSQL() and super.writeSQL() as the first order of business when implementing the readSQL() and writeSQL() methods in subclasses.

Meta-Data

Much of what you have done with JDBC so far requires you to know a lot about the database you are using, including the capabilities of the database engine and the data model against which you are operating. Requiring this level of knowledge may not bother you much, but JDBC does provide the tools to free you from these limitations. These tools come in the form of meta-data.

The term "meta" here means information about your data that does not interest the end users at all, but which you need to know in order to handle the data. JDBC provides two meta-data classes: java.sql.ResultSetMetaData and java.sql. DatabaseMetaData. The meta-data described by these classes was included in the original JDBC ResultSet and Connection classes. The team that developed the JDBC specification decided instead that it was better to keep the ResultSet and Connection classes small and simple to serve the most common database requirements. The extra functionality could be served by creating meta-data classes to provide the often esoteric information required by a minority of developers.

Result Set Meta-Data

As its name implies, the ResultSetMetaData class provides extra information about ResultSet objects returned from a database query. In the embedded queries you made earlier in the book, you hardcoded into your queries much of the information a ResultSetMetaData object gives you. This class provides you with answers to the following questions:

- How many columns are in the result set?
- Are column names case-sensitive?
- Can you search on a given column?
- Is NULL a valid value for a given column?
- How many characters is the maximum display size for a given column?
- What label should be used in a display header for the column?
- What is the name of a given column?
- What table did a given column come from?
- What is the datatype of a given column?

If you have a generic database class that blindly receives SQL to execute from other classes, this is the sort of information you need in order to process any result sets that are produced. Take a look at the following code, for example:

```
public ArrayList executeSQL(String sql) {
    ArrayList results = new ArrayList();

    try {
        Statement stmt = conn.createStatement();

        if( stmt.execute(sql) ) {
            ResultSet rs = stmt.getResultSet();
            ResultSetMetaData meta = rs.getMetaData();
            int count;

            count = meta.getColumnCount();
            while( rs.next() ) {
                HashMap cols = new Hashtable(count);
                int i;

                for(i=0; i<count; i++) {
                    Object ob = rs.getObject(i+1);

                    if( rs.wasNull() ) {
                        ob = null;
                    }
                    cols.put(meta.getColumnLabel(i+1), ob);
                }
                results.add(cols);
            }
            return results;
        }
        return null;
    }
    catch( SQLException e ) {
        e.printStackTrace();
        return null;
    }
}
```

This example introduces the execute() method in the Statement class (as well as its subclasses). This method is more generic than executeUpdate() or executeQuery() in that it will send any SQL you pass it without any preconception regarding what kind of SQL it is. If the SQL produced a result set—if it was a query—it will return true. For modifications that do not produce result sets, execute() returns false. If it did produce a result set, you can get that result set by calling the getResultSet() method.

For a given ResultSet object, an application can call the ResultSet's getMetaData() method in order to get its associated ResultSetMetaData object. You can then use this meta-data object to find out extra information about the result set and its columns. In the previous example, whenever the execute() method in the Statement class returns a true value, it gets the ResultSet object using the getResultSet() method and the ResultSetMetaData object for that result set using the getMetaData() method. For each row in the result set, the example figures out the column count using the meta-data method getColumnCount(). Knowing the column count, the application can then retrieve each column. Once it has a column, it again uses the meta-data to get a column label via getColumnLabel() and stick the column's value in a HashMap with the label as a key and the column's meta-data value as an element. The entire set of rows is then returned as an ArrayList.

Database Meta-Data

As the ResultSetMetaData class relates to the ResultSet class, the DatabaseMetaData class relates to the Connection class (in spite of the naming inconsistency). The DatabaseMetaData class provides methods that tell you about the database for a given Connection object, including:

- What tables exist in the database visible to the user?

- What username is being used by this connection?

- Is this database connection read-only?

- What keywords are used by the database that are not SQL2?

- Does the database support column aliasing?

- Are multiple result sets from a single execute() call supported?

- Are outer joins supported?

- What are the primary keys for a table?

The list of information provided by this class is way too long to list here, but you can check the reference section for the methods and what they do. The class has two primary uses:

- It provides methods that tell GUI applications and other general-purpose applications about the database being used.

- It provides methods that let application developers make their applications database-independent.

Driver Property Information

Though driver property information is not represented in JDBC by an official meta-data class, the class does represent extra information about your driver. Specifically, every database requires different information in order to make a connection. Some of this information is necessary for the connection; some of it is optional. The mSQL-JDBC driver I have been using for many of the examples in this book requires a username to make a connection, and it optionally will accept a character set encoding. Other drivers usually require a password. A tool designed to connect to any database therefore needs a way of finding out what properties a specific JDBC driver requires. The `DriverPropertyInfo` class provides this information.

The `Driver` class provides the method `getPropertyInfo()` that returns an array of `DriverPropertyInfo` objects. Each `DriverPropertyInfo` object represents a specific property. This class tells you:

- The name of the property
- A description of the property
- The current value of the property
- An array of possible choices the value can be taken from
- A flag that notes whether the property is required or optional

At the end of this chapter is an example that uses driver property information to prompt a user for property values required for a database connection.

A Generic Terminal Monitor

I will demonstrate the power of the meta-data classes with a simple, but widely useful, SQL terminal monitor application that provides a generic command-line interface to any potential database. The application should allow a user to enter SQL statements at the command line and view formatted results. This program shown in Example 4-4 requires only a single class with static methods. The `main()` method creates a user input loop when the user enters commands or SQL statements. Each input is interpreted as either a command or a SQL statement. If it is interpreted as a command, the command is executed immediately. If it is not interpreted as a command, it is assumed to be part of a SQL statement and thus appended to a buffer. The application supports the following commands:

commit
> Sends a commit to the database, committing any pending transactions.

go
> Sends anything currently in the buffer to the database for processing as a SQL statement. The SQL is parsed through the `executeStatement()` method.

quit
> Closes any database resources and exits the application.

reset

Clears the buffer without sending it to the database.

rollback

Aborts any uncommitted transactions.

show version

Displays version information on this program, the database, and the JDBC driver using the `DatabaseMetaData` interface implementation.

Example 4-4. The main( ) Method for a SQL Terminal Monitor Application

```
static public void main(String args[]) {
    DriverPropertyInfo[] required;
    StringBuffer buffer = new StringBuffer();
    Properties props = new Properties();
    boolean connected = false;
    Driver driver;
    String url;
    int line = 1; // Mark current input line

    if( args.length < 1 ) {
        System.out.println("Syntax: <java -Djdbc.drivers=DRIVER_NAME " +
                        "TerminalMonitor JDBC_URL>");
        return;
    }
    url = args[0];
    // We have to get a reference to the driver so we can
    // find out what values to prompt the user for in order
    // to make a connection.
    try {
        driver = DriverManager.getDriver(url);
    }
    catch( SQLException e ) {
        e.printStackTrace();
        System.err.println("Unable to find a driver for the specified " +
                        "URL.");
        System.err.println("Make sure you passed the jdbc.drivers " +
                        "property on the command line to specify " +
                        "the driver to be used.");
        return;
    }
    try {
        required = driver.getPropertyInfo(url, props);
    }
    catch( SQLException e ) {
        e.printStackTrace();
        System.err.println("Unable to get driver " +
                        "property information.");
        return;
```

Example 4-4. The main( ) Method for a SQL Terminal Monitor Application (continued)

```
    }
    input = new BufferedReader(new InputStreamReader(System.in));
    // Some drivers do not implement getProperty properly
    // If that is the case, prompt for user name and password
    try {
        if( required.length < 1 ) {
            props.put("user", prompt("user: "));
            props.put("password", prompt("password: "));
        }
        else {
            // for each required attribute in the driver property info
            // prompt the user for the value
            for(int i=0; i<required.length; i++) {
                if( !required[i].required ) {
                    continue;
                }
                props.put(required[i].name,
                prompt(required[i].name + ": "));
            }
        }
    }
    catch( IOException e ) {
        e.printStackTrace();
        System.err.println("Unable to read property info.");
        return;
    }
    // Make the connection.
    try {
        connection = DriverManager.getConnection(url, props);
    }
    catch( SQLException e ) {
        e.printStackTrace();
        System.err.println("Unable to connect to the database.");
        return;
    }
    connected = true;
    System.out.println("Connected to " + url);
    // Enter into a user input loop
    while( connected ) {
        String tmp, cmd;

        // Print a prompt
        if( line == 1 ) {
            System.out.print("TM > ");
        }
        else {
            System.out.print(line + " -> ");
        }
```

Example 4-4. The main( ) Method for a SQL Terminal Monitor Application (continued)

```java
System.out.flush();
// Get the next line of input
try {
    tmp = input.readLine();
}
catch( java.io.IOException e ) {
    e.printStackTrace();
    return;
}
// Get rid of extra space in the command
cmd = tmp.trim();
// The user wants to commit pending transactions
if( cmd.equals("commit") ) {
    try {
        connection.commit();
        System.out.println("Commit successful.");
    }
    catch( SQLException e ) {
        System.out.println("Error in commit: " +
                            e.getMessage());
    }
    buffer = new StringBuffer();
    line = 1;
}
// The user wants to execute the current buffer
else if( cmd.equals("go") ) {
    if( !buffer.equals("") ) {
        try { // processes results, if any
            executeStatement(buffer);
        }
        catch( SQLException e ) {
            System.out.println(e.getMessage());
        }
    }
    buffer = new StringBuffer();
    line = 1;
    continue;
}
// The user wants to quit
else if( cmd.equals("quit") ) {
    connected = false;
    continue;
}
// The user wants to clear the current buffer
else if( cmd.equals("reset") ) {
    buffer = new StringBuffer();
    line = 1;
    continue;
}
```

Example 4-4. The main( ) Method for a SQL Terminal Monitor Application (continued)

```java
        // The user wants to abort a pending transaction
        else if( cmd.equals("rollback") ) {
            try {
                connection.rollback();
                System.out.println("Rollback successful.");
            }
            catch( SQLException e ) {
                System.out.println("An error occurred during rollback: " +
                                    e.getMessage());
            }
            buffer = new StringBuffer();
            line = 1;
        }
        // The user wants version info
        else if( cmd.startsWith("show") ) {
            DatabaseMetaData meta;

            try {
                meta = connection.getMetaData();
                cmd = cmd.substring(5, cmd.length()).trim();
                if( cmd.equals("version") ) {
                    showVersion(meta);
                }
                else {
                    System.out.println("show version"); // Bad arg
                }
            }
            catch( SQLException e ) {
                System.out.println("Failed to load meta data: " +
                                    e.getMessage());
            }
            buffer = new StringBuffer();
            line = 1;
        }
        // The input that is not a keyword
        // it should appended be to the buffer
        else {
            buffer.append(" " + tmp);
            line++;
            continue;
        }
    }
    try {
        connection.close();
    }
    catch( SQLException e ) {
        System.out.println("Error closing connection: " +
```

Example 4-4. The main( ) Method for a SQL Terminal Monitor Application (continued)

```
                              e.getMessage());
    }
    System.out.println("Connection closed.");
}
```

In Example 4-4, the application expects the user to use the *jdbc.drivers* property to identify the JDBC driver being used and to pass the JDBC URL as the sole command line argument. The program will then query the specified driver for its driver property information, prompt the user to enter values for the required properties, and finally attempt to make a connection.

The meat of main() is the loop that accepts user input and acts on it. It first checks if any line of input matches one of the applications commands. If so, it executes the specified command. Otherwise it treats the input as part of a larger SQL statement and waits for further input.

The interesting parts of the application are in the executeStatement() and processResults() methods. In executeStatement(), the application blindly accepts any SQL the user sends it, creates a Statement, and executes it. At that point, several things might happen:

- The SQL could have errors. If it does, the application displays the errors to the user and returns to the main loop for more input.

- The SQL could have been a nonquery. If this is the case, that application lets the user know how many rows were affected by the query.

- The SQL could have been a query. If it is, the application grabs the result set and sends it to processResults() for display.

Example 4-5 shows the executeStatement() method, which takes a raw SQL string and executes it using the specified JDBC Connection object.

Example 4-5. The executeStatement( ) Method for the Terminal Monitor Application

```
static public void executeStatement(StringBuffer buff)
throws SQLException {
    String sql = buff.toString();
    Statement statement = null;

    try {
        statement = connection.createStatement();
        if( statement.execute(sql) ) {
            // true means the SQL was a SELECT
            processResults(statement.getResultSet());
        }
        else {
            // no result sets, see how many rows were affected
            int num;
```

Example 4-5. The executeStatement( ) Method for the Terminal Monitor Application (continued)

```
            switch(num = statement.getUpdateCount()) {
            case 0:
                System.out.println("No rows affected.");
                break;

            case 1:
                System.out.println(num + " row affected.");
                break;

            default:
                System.out.println(num + " rows affected.");
            }
        }
    }
    catch( SQLException e ) {
        throw e;
    }
    finally { // close out the statement
        if( statement != null ) {
            try { statement.close(); }
            catch( SQLException e ) { }
        }
    }
}
```

To handle dynamic result sets, use the `ResultSetMetaData` class. The `processResults()` method shown in Example 4-6 uses these methods:

`getColumnCount()`

Finds out how many columns are in the result set. You need to know how many columns there are so that you do not ask for a column that does not exist or miss one that does exist.

`getColumnType()`

Finds out the datatype for each column. You need to know the datatype when you retrieve it from the result set.

`getColumnLabel()`

Gives a display name to place at the top of each column.

`getColumnDisplaySize()`

Tells how wide the display of the columns should be.

Example 4-6. The processResults( ) Method from the Terminal Monitor Application

```
static public void processResults(ResultSet results)
throws SQLException {
    try {
        ResultSetMetaData meta = results.getMetaData();
```

Example 4-6. The processResults( ) Method from the Terminal Monitor Application (continued)

```
StringBuffer bar = new StringBuffer();
StringBuffer buffer = new StringBuffer();
int cols = meta.getColumnCount();
int row_count = 0;
int i, width = 0;

// Prepare headers for each of the columns
// The display should look like:
// ------------------------------------
// |    Column One    |   Column Two   |
// ------------------------------------
// |    Row 1 Value   |   Row 1 Value  |
// ------------------------------------

// create the bar that is as long as the total of all columns
for(i=1; i<=cols; i++) {
    width += meta.getColumnDisplaySize(i);
}
width += 1 + cols;
for(i=0; i<width; i++) {
    bar.append('-');
}
bar.append('\n');
buffer.append(bar.toString() + "|");
// After the first bar goes the column labels
for(i=1; i<=cols; i++) {
    StringBuffer filler = new StringBuffer();
    String label = meta.getColumnLabel(i);
    int size = meta.getColumnDisplaySize(i);
    int x;

    // If the label is longer than the column is wide,
    // then we truncate the column label
    if( label.length() > size ) {
        label = label.substring(0, size);
    }
    // If the label is shorter than the column,
    // pad it with spaces
    if( label.length() < size ) {
        int j;

        x = (size-label.length())/2;
        for(j=0; j<x; j++) {
            filler.append(' ');
        }
        label = filler + label + filler;
        if( label.length() > size ) {
            label = label.substring(0, size);
        }
```

Example 4-6. The processResults( ) Method from the Terminal Monitor Application (continued)

```
        else {
            while( label.length() < size ) {
                label += " ";
            }
        }
    }
    // Add the column header to the buffer
    buffer.append(label + "|");
}
// Add the lower bar
buffer.append("\n" + bar.toString());
// Format each row in the result set and add it on
while( results.next() ) {
    row_count++;

    buffer.append('|');
    // Format each column of the row
    for(i=1; i<=cols; i++) {
        StringBuffer filler = new StringBuffer();
        Object value = results.getObject(i);
        int size = meta.getColumnDisplaySize(i);
        String str;

        if( results.wasNull() ) {
            str = "NULL";
        }
        else {
            str = value.toString();
        }
        if( str.length() > size ) {
            str = str.substring(0, size);
        }
        if( str.length() < size ) {
            int j, x;

            x = (size-str.length())/2;
            for(j=0; j<x; j++) {
                filler.append(' ');
            }
            str = filler + str + filler;
            if( str.length() > size ) {
                str = str.substring(0, size);
            }
            else {
                while( str.length() < size ) {
                    str += " ";
                }
            }
```

Example 4-6. The processResults( ) Method from the Terminal Monitor Application (continued)

```
                }
            }
            buffer.append(str + "|");
        }
        buffer.append("\n");
    }
    // Stick a row count up at the top
    if( row_count == 0 ) {
        buffer = new StringBuffer("No rows selected.\n");
    }
    else if( row_count == 1 ) {
        buffer = new StringBuffer("1 row selected.\n" +
                                  buffer.toString() +
                                  bar.toString());
    }
    else {
        buffer = new StringBuffer(row_count + " rows selected.\n" +
                                  buffer.toString() +
                                  bar.toString());
    }
    System.out.print(buffer.toString());
    System.out.flush();
}
catch( SQLException e ) {
    throw e;
}
finally {
    try { results.close(); }
    catch( SQLException e ) { }
}
}
```

As a small demonstration of the workings of the DatabaseMetaData class, I have also added a showVersion() method that grabs database and driver version information from the DatabaseMetaData class:

```
static public void showVersion(DatabaseMetaData meta) {
    try {
        System.out.println("TerminalMonitor v2.0");
        System.out.println("DBMS: " + meta.getDatabaseProductName() +
                           " " + meta.getDatabaseProductVersion());
        System.out.println("JDBC Driver: " + meta.getDriverName() +
                           " " + meta.getDriverVersion());
    }
    catch( SQLException e ) {
        System.out.println("Failed to get version info: " +
                           e.getMessage());
    }
}
```

5

The JDBC Optional Package

Narrow souls I cannot abide;
there's almost no good or evil inside.
—Friedrich Nietzsche
The Gay Science

The JDBC API you have covered in this book is called the JDBC 2.0 Core API. The JDBC 2.0 Core API is a narrowly focused specification that supports the functionality required by applications to successfully access databases. With the JDBC 2.0 release, however, Sun added an API called the JDBC 2.0 Optional Package (formerly called the JDBC 2.0 Standard Extension) to support extended database access functionality. The JDBC 2.0 version of the Optional Package encompasses the following elements:

- Data source-oriented database access via the new JNDI API

- JDBC driver-based connection pooling

- Rowsets

- Distributed transactions

As I write this chapter, the JDBC 2.0 Optional Package has just been finalized. Very few drivers support any of this functionality. I will therefore cover as much of the JDBC 2.0 Optional Package in this chapter as possible, but I will not be able to do full justice to some topics due to the scarcity of available information at the time of writing.

Data Sources

In Chapter 3, *Introduction to JDBC,* we covered how to register a JDBC driver and make a connection using a JDBC URL. Perhaps you, like me and many others, found this to be a bit of an annoyance, especially if you are trying to write database-independent code. I am now about to tell you that all of that is completely unnecessary. You don't have to register drivers. You don't have to know anything about JDBC URLs. JDBC has discovered the marvels of naming and directory services.

Naming and Directory Services

Naming and directory services are basic to computing. Naming services are the tool through which programmatic things—files, printers, file servers, etc.—are matched to names. You do not print to your local printer by referencing its I/O port. You reference the printer by its name. A naming service inside your OS maps that printer name to an I/O port.

A directory service is an extension of a naming service that allows naming service entries to have attributes. Referring back to your printer, it might have certain properties such as being a color printer, being able to print two sided, and so on. All of these attributes are stored in the directory service and associated with a printer object. Common directory services include NIS, NIS+, Microsoft Active Directory, and LDAP-compliant directory services such as Netscape's LDAP Service and Novell's NDS.

The problem with the JDBC 2.0 Core API driver registration and connection process is that it requires you to somehow register a JDBC driver and figure out a URL. While you can do this in a database-independent manner as has been shown, it is much simpler to hardcode that information. In addition, learning the nuances of connecting for each JDBC driver—the driver's name, its URL, etc.—is an unnecessary burden.

The JDBC 2.0 Optional Package enables you to store a kind of connection factory in a directory service via JNDI. This connection factory, or, in JDBC terms, a data source, contains all of the information necessary to create JDBC `Connection` instances to a specific database. Just as a file in a filesystem enables you to reference file data via a filename, a data source enables you to reference a database by name. The details of database connectivity can be changed by simply changing the directory entry for the data source. The application is never aware of the change.

Under the JDBC 2.0 Optional Package, you need to know only the name of a data source in order to make a connection. You do not need to know the driver name, you do not need to register any drivers, and you do not need to know any driver URLs. In fact, it is expected that one day the `Driver` and `DriverManager` classes might be deprecated once the JDBC Optional Package gains acceptance.

The `DataSource` interface in JDBC represents the data source. A `DataSource` object stores the attributes that tell it how to connect to a database. Those attributes are assigned when you bind the `DataSource` instance to its JNDI directory. In the

second JNDI example that follows, I set a server name and database name for a
MsqlDataSource. This class needs only those two attributes to connect to an
mSQL database. A GUI designed for the administration of JNDI data sources, however, might provide you with a dialog box that asks for the DataSource implementation class name. Once you specify the MsqlDataSource class, it could use the
Java Reflection API to find what attributes it requires and then prompt you to enter
those attributes—in this case, the server name and database name—before it binds
the newly created data source to whatever JNDI name you specify. Knowing only
the name of the data source, your code just pulls this fully configured data source
out of the JNDI directory and uses it:

```
Context ctx = new InitialContext();
DataSource ds = (DataSource)ctx.lookup("jdbc/ora");
Connection con = ds.getConnection("borg", "");
```

Isn't that much simpler than the way you first learned to specify a driver? Unfortunately, it requires you to have an LDAP server or some other naming and directory service available for binding JDBC data sources. You also need a JNDI service
provider for that naming and directory service.

A JNDI service provider is to JNDI as a JDBC driver is to JDBC. Specifically, JNDI
provides a naming- and directory-service independent API to support potential
naming and directory service. Current JNDI service providers include support for
LDAP and NIS.

Sun provides a filesystem-based JNDI service provider that stores directory entries
in flat files. The mSQL-JDBC driver used for many of the examples in this book
comes with a JNDI sample application that registers its data source in this filesystem-based directory. Finally, the data source needs to be bound to the naming and
directory service under a data-source name—in this case, "jdbc/ora." Here is a
quick code for binding an mSQL-JDBC data source:

```
MsqlDataSource ds = new MsqlDataSource();
Context ctx = new InitialContext();

ds.setServerName("carthage.imaginary.com");
ds.setDatabaseName("ora");
ctx.bind("jdbc/ora", ds);
```

In general, however, you will have a GUI tool to configure your JDBC data sources
in a JNDI-enabled naming and directory service. It will probably want to know
such things as the name of the JDBC driver you are using, the user ID and password to use for the connection, and the location of the data store. You do not normally write code to bind JDBC data sources unless you are writing such a GUI tool.

Connection Pooling

Up to this point, you have created a connection, done your database business, and closed the connection. This process clearly works fine for the examples I have presented to this point in the book. Unfortunately, it does not work in real-world server applications. It does not work because the act of creating a database connection is a very expensive operation for most database engines. If you have a server application, such as a Java servlet or a middle-tier application server, that application is likely going back and forth between the database many times per minute. Suddenly, the "open connection, talk to the database, close connection" model of JDBC programming becomes a huge bottleneck.

The JDBC Optional Package provides a standardized solution to the problem—*connection pooling*.* Connection pooling is a mechanism through which open database connections are held in a cache for use and reuse by different parts of an application. In a Java servlet, for example, each user initiates the execution of the servlet's doGet() method, which grabs a Connection instance from the connection pool. When it is done serving that user, it returns the Connection instance to the pool. The Connection is never closed until the web server shuts down.

Unlike the parts of JDBC you have encountered so far, connection pooling is not necessarily implemented by driver vendors. While a connection pool can be implemented by driver vendors (the mSQL-JDBC driver comes with a JDBC 2.0 Optional Package connection pooling implementation), the connection pooling API can be implemented by third-party vendors to meet different optimization needs. As a result, even if your vendor does not provide a connection pooling implementation, chances are you can find a driver-independent connection pooling package designed against the JDBC 2.0 Optional Package connection pooling API.

The connection pooling API is an extension of the regular connection API. From a programmer's perspective, there is absolutely no API difference between regular connections and pooled connections. There really is not much for you, the database-application developer, to learn about connection pooling.

The JDBC Optional Package connection pooling works through the JNDI support discussed earlier in the chapter. Figure 5-1 shows an activity model describing how the JDBC Optional Package handles a connection pool.

As Figure 5-1 illustrates, a Java application talks only to a JDBC DataSource implementation. Internally, the DataSource implementation talks to a ConnectionPoolDataSource, which holds pooled database connections. When

---

* The lack of connection pooling was such a glaring hole in initial JDBC releases that most driver vendors support some sort of connection-pooling scheme. Connection pooling in the JDBC Optional Package helps provide a standardized approach to this problem.

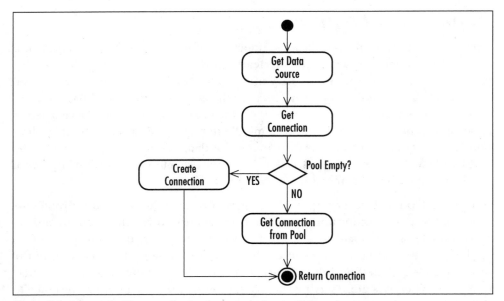

Figure 5-1. An activity diagram showing how connection pooling works

the application calls getConnection() in the DataSource instance, it pulls a Connection out of the connection pool. The application works with its Connection just like any other Connection until it is finished. It then closes the connection just as it normally would. Unknown to the application, the physical link to the database is not being closed. Its close() method returns it to the connection pool. If you try to use that Connection again without getting it from the connection pool, it will throw an exception.

Rowsets

JDBC predates the JavaBeans API. One place where JDBC could have made use of JavaBeans is in the ResultSet interface. Specifically, it would have been nice for simple two-tier applications to be able to map GUI widgets directly to a JavaBean representing data from the database. The JDBC Optional Package merges JavaBeans with result set management in a generalized fashion that is not limited to simple two-tier systems. This merger comes in the form of rowsets.

NOTE   In case you are not familiar with JavaBeans, it is Java's client-side component model. By writing your client-side components to the JavaBeans specification, you make it possible for them to plug into diverse applications. The specification dictates an event model for UI events and naming conventions for your components. JavaBeans, for example, enables you to write a component such as a RowSet and have other objects that know nothing about rowsets or the concept of a RowSet listen to that RowSet component for changes.

The rowset specification, like the connection pooling specification, is not necessarily provided by your JDBC driver. Instead, third parties can implement the rowset specification by providing different layers of result set encapsulation. The obvious use is the one I outlined previously—hiding a result set behind a JavaBeans-friendly interface. It is thus likely that driver vendors will provide a rowset implementation that supports direct access to their database. Because the rowset API does not require database-specific information, however, you can see rowset vendors providing implementations that encapsulate just about any sort of tabular data. Chapter 10, *The User Interface*, gives an example of a rowset in a Swing application.

Configuration

A rowset in JDBC is represented by the interface `javax.sql.RowSet`. It is an extension of the ResultSet interface that serves data up in accordance with the JavaBeans API. The first step of using a JDBC RowSet is configuring it. Here is a small code snippet that configures a RowSet to get the list of CDs from Chapter 2, *Relational Databases and SQL*:

```
RowSet rset = new ImaginaryRowSet();

rset.setDataSourceName("/tmp/jdbc/ora");
rset.setUsername("borg");
rset.setPassword("womble");
rset.setCommand("SELECT title FROM Album " +
                "WHERE album_id = ?");
```

In this code segment, you created an instance of the ImaginaryRowSet class, a database-independent rowset implementation that comes with the mSQL-JDBC driver. The RowSet is configured with four attributes: dataSourceName, username, password, and command. The dataSourceName attribute tells the RowSet what JDBC data source will provide a database connection for the RowSet. The password and username attributes specify the username and password to use for the database connection. Finally, the command attribute specifies what command to send to the data source. In this case, it is a SQL query.

Though you use a data source name in this example, you can use conventional JDBC connectivity by specifying a database URL via the RowSet setURL() method, in place of setDataSourceName(). Of course, the proper JDBC driver for the given URL must have been registered in the usual JDBC manner of registering drivers as described in Chapter 3.

Usage

Using a configured RowSet is very similar to using a PreparedStatement. You assign any input parameter, tell the RowSet to execute, and process the results. Unlike PreparedStatement, however, there is no ResultSet counterpart through which the results are processed. Instead, the RowSet itself provides the result set processing API. The following code segment shows the processing of the RowSet configured previously:

```
rset.setInt(1, 2);
rset.execute();
while( rset.next() ) {
  System.out.println("Album #1 is " + rset.getString(1) +
                        ".");
}
rset.close();
```

Rowset Events

So where does JavaBeans fit in? The RowSet class is a JavaBeans component whose input parameters serve as JavaBean setter calls and whose result set columns can be retrieved by JavaBeans getter calls. The real power of the JavaBeans support comes in the form of JavaBeans events. Through JavaBeans events, a RowSet can notify listener components when certain interesting things happen to it.

Components interested in rowset events implement the RowSetListener interface. By registering themselves with a RowSet, RowSetListener components get notified whenever anything happens to the RowSet. For example, a tabular GUI control that is displaying the results of a RowSet will certainly want to register itself as a RowSetListener for its RowSet. The RowSet will then notify it when any one of the following events occurs:

- Database cursor movement events that indicate the rowset's cursor has moved

- Row change events that indicate that a single row has been inserted, updated, or deleted

- Rowset change events that indicate the entire contents of a rowset have changed—as when execute() is called

What one does with this event is entirely up to the listener. The tabular GUI widget, for example, may want to remove a row from the display when a row-changed event indicates a row has been deleted.

Distributed Transactions

You have only one more element of JDBC to cover—distributed transactions. All database access you have dealt with so far involves transactions against a single database. In this environment, your DBMS manages the details of each transaction. This support is good enough for most database applications. As companies move increasingly towards an enterprise model of systems development, however, the need for supporting transactions against multiple databases grows. Where single data source transactions are the rule today, they will likely prove the exception in business computing in the future.

Distributed transactions are transactions that span two or more data sources. For example, you may have an Informix data source containing your corporate digital media assets and an Oracle database holding your corporate data. When you delete product information for an obsolete product line stored in the Oracle database, you need to know that the commercials and web images stored in Informix database have been deleted as well. Without support for distributed transactions, you are forced to handle the delete in two separate transactions: one against Oracle and the other against Informix. If the commit against Oracle succeeds but the Informix commit fails, you end up with inconsistent data.

Of course, you may simply avoid the issue by selecting either Oracle or Informix to store all of your corporate data. If you choose a nice supercomputer with terabytes of hard disk space and gigabytes of RAM, such a solution will most likely work for you. A more practical alternative, however, is to choose horizontal scalability and database engines that are well suited for the type of data being stored.

Because of the JDBC 2.0 Optional Package support for JNDI and connection pooling, your applications are freed from knowledge of the particulars of your implementation database. The specification's distributed transaction support builds on this independence to enable seamless access to distributed data sources. From the application developer's point of view, application code for access to distributed data sources is nearly identical to normal database code using data sources and connection pooling. The only real difference is that you never commit or rollback your code, and your distributed connections have auto-commit turned off by default. Any attempt to call `commit()`, `rollback()`, or `setAutoCommit(true)` results in a `SQLException`. Commits and rollbacks are managed by a complex transaction monitor in a mid-tier server.

I have marched through the concepts in this chapter without providing a full, concrete example. By now, I hope you see that the JDBC Optional Package is fairly trivial from the programmer's point of view. The DataSource interface greatly simplifies the connection process that you already understand. Connection pooling and distributed transactions are a features that you, the programmer, never actually see. Finally, the RowSet simply combines many features you have seen in other places into a single JavaBeans component. Example 5-1 puts all elements of the JDBC 2.0 Optional Package specification together in a single example.

Example 5-1. Calculating the Interest for Selected Bank Accounts

```
import java.sql.*;
import javax.naming.*;
import javax.sql.*;

public class Interest {
    static public void main(String[] args) {
        try {
            RowSet rs = new SomeRowSetClass(); // fictitious

            rs.setDataSourceName("jdbc/oraxa");
            rs.setUsername("borg");
            rs.setPassword("womble");
            rs.setCommand("SELECT acct_id, balance, cust_id " +
                        "FROM account");
            rs.execute();

            Context ctx = new InitialContext();
            // this data source is pooled and distributed
            // all distributed data sources are pooled data sources
            DataSource ds = (DataSource)ctx.lookup("jdbc/oraxa");
            Connection con = ds.getConnection("borg", "");
            PreparedStatement acct, cust;

            // the account and customer tables are in two different
            // databases, but this application does not need to care
            acct = con.prepareStatement("UPDATE account " +
                                    "SET balance = ? " +
                                    "WHERE acct_id = ?");
            cust = con.prepareStatement("UPDATE customer " +
                                    "SET last_interest = ? " +
                                    "WHERE cust_id = ?");
            while( rs.next() ) {
                long acct_id, cust_id;
                double balance, interest;

                acct.clearParameters();
                cust.clearParameters();
```

Example 5-1. Calculating the Interest for Selected Bank Accounts (continued)

```
                acct_id = rs.getLong(1);
                balance = rs.getDouble(2);
                cust_id = rs.getLong(3);
                interest = balance * (0.03/12);
                balance = balance + interest;
                acct.setDouble(1, balance);
                acct.setLong(2, acct_id);
                acct.executeUpdate();
                cust.setDouble(1, interest);
                cust.setLong(2, cust_id);
                cust.executeUpdate();
            }
            rs.close();
            con.close();
        }
        catch( Exception e ) {
            e.printStackTrace();
        }
    }
}
```

II

APPLIED JDBC

Now that you have covered the depths of the JDBC API, it is time to take this academic knowledge and apply it to real-world database programming. Database programming in Java, however, is vastly different from the kind of database programming required in the more common, non-OO environments. Java is an object-oriented language made for distributed systems programming and thus works in a new way with relational databases. This section introduces an architecture on which you can base object-oriented database applications and walks through an example-distributed database application.

6

Other Enterprise APIs

*If Life is a Tree, it could all have arisen from an
inexorable, automatic rebuilding process in which
designs would accumulate over time.*
—Daniel C. Dennett
Darwin's Dangerous Idea

I have already mentioned one of the Java mantras: "write once, compile once, run anywhere." You may have heard another very important one: "the network is the computer." The Web is based on the principle that information resources may be found all over the Internet. Your browser enables you to access all of this information as if it were on your desktop. "The network is the computer," however, refers to more than the ability to access information resources anywhere in the world. It means being able to access and utilize applications and computing resources anywhere in the world. It means forgetting about the barriers that separate machines and treating them as one huge computer.

JDBC is a key element in this equation, but it is far from the only element. Sun has defined an entire Java standard around those elements, the Java 2 Enterprise Edition (J2EE). Before you dive into the details of applying JDBC to real-world applications, you need to take a brief look at the other players in the world of enterprise systems—the J2EE APIs. I cannot possibly do full justice to these other players in a single chapter—each is worthy of a book of its own. I will nevertheless attempt to provide enough of an overview so that you have a clear picture of how they work with JDBC in real world enterprise systems.

Java Naming and Directory Interface

You touched on the Java Naming and Directory Interface (JNDI) in Chapter 5, *The JDBC Optional Package.* The JNDI API provides a single set of classes for accessing any kind of naming and directory service. If you intend to learn only one Java Enterprise API, learn JNDI because it is the door through which you will have to work to program in an enterprise environment.

Naming and Directory Services

JNDI is an API that provides a unified facade for diverse kinds of naming and directory services. Naming and directory services can be as simple as the filesystem on your OS or as complex as your corporate LDAP server. What they all have in common is the ability to associate technology components with names. The filesystem associates a chunk of data with a filename. You do not access the file by its physical location on the hard drive but instead by a name you have given it. The filesystem knows how to map the name you understand to a physical location on the hard drive.

A directory service is an extension of a naming service. It enables you to associate attributes as well as a name with the technology component. Your address book is an example of a directory service. It associates a person with a name and allows you to store attributes like a phone number, address, title, etc., with the person.

JNDI works much like JDBC in how it provides an independent view of naming and directory services. It specifies interfaces that must be implemented by service providers. Service providers are analogous to JDBC drivers. A vendor of an LDAP solution would likely provide an LDAP implementation of the JNDI API. Sun has provided a filesystem implementation as well as an NIS+ implementation. The examples in this book make use of the filesystem provider because everyone has access to a filesystem.

NOTE   JNDI is an extension package and does not ship with the standard
              JDK. It does come with J2EE versions of the JDK, or you can down-
              load it separately from the Sun web site at *http://java.sun.com/products/
              jndi*. The JNDI classes fall into the `javax.naming` namespace.

Object Binding

There are two key pieces to JNDI from a developer's perspective: binds and lookups. *Binding* is the process of registering a Java object with a JNDI-supported naming and directory service. If you think of a naming and directory service as the local phone book, binding is analogous to telling the phone company your phone number. Fortunately, the phone company often bundles up this notification when you get your phone line; you do not have to do the phone book registration yourself. The same is likely to be true whenever you work with JNDI. You will rarely actually write code to register a Java object with JNDI.

The first JNDI code you write in any JNDI application is code that creates an initial context. A *context* is simply a base from which everything is considered relative. In your local phone book, for example, the context is your country code and often an area code. The numbers in the phone book do not mention their country code or area code; you just assume those values from the context. A JNDI context performs the exact same function. The initial context is simply a special context to get you started with a particular naming and directory service. The simple form of initial context construction looks like this:

```
Context ctx = new InitialContext();
```

In this case, JNDI grabs its initialization information from your system properties. You can, however, specify your own initialization values by passing the properties to the `InitialContext` constructor:

```
Properties props = new Properties();
Context ctx;

// Specify the name of the class that will serve
// as the context factory
// this is analagous to the JDBC Driver class
props.put(Context.INITIAL_CONTEXT_FACTORY,
        "com.sun.jndi.fscontext.RefFSContextFactory");
ctx = new InitialContext(props);
```

This code creates an initial context for the filesystem provider. You can now use this context to bind Java objects to the filesystem.

Binding specifically occurs by calling the `bind()` method in your context object. This code binds an mSQL-JDBC data source object to the name */tmp/jdbc/jndiex*:

```
DataSource ds = new com.imaginary.sql.msql.MsqlDataSource();
Context ctx = new InitialContext(props);

ds.setServerName("carthage.imaginary.com");
ds.setDatabaseName("jndiex");
ctx.bind("/tmp/jdbc/jndiex", ds);
ctx.close();
```

The filesystem provider creates a hidden file in the directory */tmp/jdbc* called *.bindings*. This file holds all information about objects bound within the */tmp/jdbc* directory, including *jndiex*.

Object Lookup

Other than drawing on the cover, the thing you do most with a phone book is look up entries in it. The same principal applies to JNDI use. You spend most of your time looking up bound objects. The simplest lookup takes the following form:

```
DataSource ds = (DataSource)ctx.lookup("/tmp/jdbc/jndiex");
```

Using your JNDI context, you look up the desired object by name. JNDI then returns the desired object, and you can use it however you like. If the object is not found, JNDI will throw an exception.

Remote Method Invocation

The object is the center of the Java world. Distributed object technologies provide the infrastructure that lets you have two objects running on two different machines talk to one another using an object-oriented paradigm. Using traditional networking, you would have to write IP socket code to let two objects on different machines talk to each other. While this approach works, it is prone to error. The ideal solution is to let the Java virtual machine do the work. You call a method in an object, and the virtual machine determines where the object is located. If it is a remote object, it will do all the dirty network stuff automatically.

Several technologies like Common Object Request Broker Architecture (CORBA) already exist, enabling developers to provide a clean, distributed programming architecture. CORBA has a very wide reach and is wrought with complexities associated with its grandiose goals. For example, it supports applications whose distributed components are written in different languages. In order to support everything from writing an object interface in C to handling more traditional object languages such as Java and Smalltalk, it has built up an architecture with a very steep learning curve.

CORBA does its job very well, but it does a lot more than you need in a pure Java environment. This extra functionality has a cost in terms of programming complexity. Unlike other programming languages, Java has distributed support built into its core. Borrowing heavily from CORBA, Java supports a simpler pure Java distributed object solution called Remote Method Invocation (RMI).

The Structure of RMI

RMI is an API that lets you mostly ignore the fact that you have objects distributed all across a network. You write Java code that calls methods in remote objects almost identically to the way you treat local ones. The biggest problem with providing this sort of API is that you are dealing with two separate virtual machines existing in two separate address spaces. Take, for example, the situation in which you have a Bat object that calls hit() in a Ball instance. Located together on the same virtual machine, the method call looks like this:

```
ball.hit();
```

You want RMI to provide the exact same syntax when the Bat instance is on a client machine and the Ball on a server. The problem is that the Ball instance does not exist inside the client's memory. How can you possibly trigger an event in an object to which there is no reference? The first step is to get a reference.

Access to remote objects

I am going to coopt the term *server* for a minute and use it to refer to the virtual machine that holds the real copies of one or more distributed objects. In a distributed object system, you can have a single host (generally called an application server) act as an object server—a place from which clients get remote objects—or you can have all of the systems act as object servers. Clients simply need to be aware of where the object servers are located.* An object server has a single defining function: to make objects available to remote clients.

A special program that comes with the JDK called *rmiregistry* listens to a port on the object server's machine. The object server in turn binds object instances to that port using a special URL so it can be found by clients later. The format of the RMI URL is *rmi://server/object*. A client then uses that URL to find a desired object. For the previous ball example, the ball would be bound to the URL *rmi://athens.imaginary.com/Ball*. An object server binds an object to a URL by calling the static rebind() method of java.rmi.Naming:

```
Naming.rebind("rmi://athens.imaginary.com/Ball", new BallImpl());
```

The *rmi://athens.imaginary.com/* portion of the URL above is self-evident; you cannot bind an object instance to a URL on another machine in a secure environment. Naming allows you to rebind an object using only the object name for short:

```
Naming.rebind("Ball", new BallImpl());
```

NOTE   In RMI, binding is the process of associating an object with an RMI URL. The rebind() method specifically creates this association. At this point, the object is registered with the *rmiregistry* application and available to client systems. Reference by any system to its URL is thus specifically a reference to the bound object.

The rebind() methods make a specific object instance available to remote objects that do a lookup on the object's URL. This is where life gets complicated. When a client connects to the object URL, it cannot get the object bound to that URL. That object exists only in the memory of the server. The client needs a way to fool itself into thinking it has the object while routing all method calls in that object over to the real object. RMI uses Java interfaces to provide this sort of hocus pocus.

---

* Using JNDI, they do not even need to know where the server is. Clients just look up objects by name, and the naming and directory service knows where the server is. You will see this in practice later in the chapter when you read about Enterprise JavaBeans.

Remote interfaces

All Java objects that you intend to make available as distributed objects must implement an interface that extends the RMI interface `java.rmi.Remote`. You call this step making an object remote. You might do a quick double-take if you glance at the `java.rmi.Remote` source code. It looks like this:

```
package java.rmi;

public interface Remote {
}
```

No, there is no typo there. The interface specifies no methods to be implemented. It exists so that objects in the virtual machines on both the local and remote systems have a common base class they can use for deriving to all remote objects. They need this base class since the RMI methods look for subclasses of `Remote` as arguments.

When you write a remote object, you have to create an interface that extends `Remote` and specify all methods that can be called remotely. Each of these methods must throw a `RemoteException` in addition to any application-specific exceptions. In the bat and ball example, you might have had the following interface:

```
public interface Ball extends java.rmi.Remote {
    void hit() throws java.rmi.RemoteException;
    int getPosition() throws RemoteException;
}
```

The `BallImpl` class implements `Ball`. It might look like:

```
import java.rmi.RemoteException;
import java.rmi.server.UnicastRemoteObject;

public class BallImpl
extends UnicastRemoteObject implements Ball {
    private int position = 0;

    public Ball() throw RemoteException {
        super();
    }

    public int getPosition() {
        return position;
    }

    public void hit() {
        position += calculateDistance();
    }
```

```
    protected int calculateDistance() {
        return 10;
    }
}
```

The `java.rmi.server.UnicastRemoteObject` class that the `BallImpl` extends provides support for exporting the ball; that is, it allows the virtual machine to make it available to remote systems. This may look like what the `Naming` class does, but it has a different purpose. `Naming` ensures that the object is bound to a particular URL, while exporting an object enables it to be referenced across the network. This means that you can pass the object as a method argument or return it as a return value. It also means that you can use `Naming.rebind()` to make the object available through a URL lookup. A URL lookup looks like this:

```
ball = (Ball)Naming.lookup("rmi://athens.imaginary.com/Ball");
```

NOTE Because you have just read about JNDI, you might wonder why RMI forces you to know where the object is located instead of using a simple JNDI name. The answer is simple: RMI predates JNDI. JNDI now does, however, offer a service provider supporting RMI lookups.

Because you may not have the option of extending `UnicastRemoteObject`, you can export your objects another way using this syntax in the object constructor:

```
public BallImpl() throws RemoteException {
    super();
    UnicastRemoteObject.exportObject(this);
}
```

Both approaches are equally valid. The only difference is the structure of your inheritance tree.

After writing both classes, you compile them just like any other object. This will, of course, generate two *.class* files, *Ball.class* and *BallImpl.class*.

The final step in making the `BallImpl` class distributed is to run the RMI compiler, `rmic`, against it. In this case, run `rmic` using the following command line:

```
rmic BallImpl
```

Like the `java` command and unlike the `javac` command, `rmic` takes a fully qualified class name as an argument. This means that if you had the `Ball` class in a package called `baseball`, you would run `rmic` as:

```
rmic -d classdir baseball.Ball
```

In this case, *classdir* represents whatever the root directory for your `baseball` package class files is. This will likely be a directory in your CLASSPATH. The output of `rmic` will be two classes: `Ball_Skel.class` (the skeleton) and `Ball_Stub.class` (the stub). These classes will be placed relative to the *classdir* you specified on the command line.

Stubs and skeletons

I have introduced a couple of concepts, stub and skeleton, without any explana-
tion. They are two objects you should never have to concern yourself with, but they
perform all of the magic that makes a remote method call work. In Figure 6-1, I
show where these two objects fit in a remote method call.

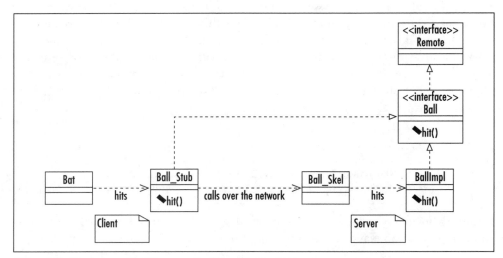

Figure 6-1. The process of calling a method in a remote object

The process of translating a remote method call into network format is called
marshaling; the reverse is called *unmarshaling*. When you run the rmic command
on your remote-enabled classes, it generates two classes that perform the tasks of
marshaling and unmarshaling. The first of these is the *stub object*, a special object
that implements all of the remote interfaces implemented by its remote object.
The difference is that where the remote object actually performs the business logic
associated with a method, the stub takes the arguments to the method and sends
them across the network to the *skeleton object* on the server. In other words, it mar-
shals the method parameters and sends them to the server. The skeleton object, in
turn, unmarshals those parameters; it takes the raw data from the network, translates it into Java objects, and then calls the proper method in the remote object.

The skeleton and stub perform the reverse roles for return values. The skeleton
takes the return value from the method and sends it across the network. The client
stub then takes the socket data and turns it into Java data, returning it to the calling method.

The special exception: java.rmi.RemoteException

All methods that can be called remotely and all constructors for remote objects must throw a special exception called `java.rmi.RemoteException`. The methods you write will never explicitly throw this exception. Instead, the local virtual machine will throw it when you encounter a network error during a remote method call. Examples of such situations include one of the machines crashing or a loss of connectivity between the two machines.

A `RemoteException` is unlike any other exception. When you write an application to be run on a single virtual machine, you know that if your code is solid, you can predict potential exception situations and where they might occur. You can count on no such thing with a `RemoteException`. It can happen at any time during the course of a remote method call, and you may have no way of knowing why it happened. You therefore need to write your application code with the knowledge that at any point your code can fail for no discernible reason and have contingencies to support such failures.

An Object Server

One of the things you cannot do through RMI is create a remote object on the object server at will; you cannot do a remote equivalent to new. Instead, you should need to rebind only one or two objects that give a client access to all other remote objects on the object server. Example 6-1 is an example of the classic factory pattern in the form of an `AppServer` object that makes itself available to clients for serving `Customer` objects. Each client can then use the `Customer` object to get all `Account` objects associated with the `Customer`.

Example 6-1. AppServer.Impl.java

```
import java.rmi.Naming;
import java.rmi.RemoteException;
import java.rmi.server.UnicastRemoteObject;

public class AppServerImpl
extends UnicastRemoteObject implements AppServer {
    static public void main(String[] args) {
        System.out.println("Installing the security manager...");
        try {
            AppServerImpl server;
            String url = args[0];

            System.out.println("Starting the application server...");
            Naming.rebind(url, new AppServerImpl());
            System.out.println("AppServer bound with url: " + url + "...");
        }
```

Example 6-1. AppServer.Impl.java (continued)

```
        catch( Exception e ) {
            e.printStackTrace();
        }
    }

    public AppServerImpl()
    throws RemoteException {
        super();
    }

    public Customer getCustomer(int id)
    throws RemoteException {
        return new CustomerImpl(id);
    }
}
```

After running `rmic` on the `AppServerImpl` and the other remote objects in the system, you need to run `rmiregistry` before running the application server. This program listens to port 1099 for client RMI requests. You can change this port number by specifying it at the command line. If you use an alternate port, however, your RMI URLs should reflect that port: for instance, *rmi://athens.imaginary. com:1500/AppServer.*

To connect with the application server, a client looks up the `AppServer` object:

```
AppServer server =
    (AppServer)Naming.lookup("rmi://athens.imaginary.com/AppServer");
```

The application server is responsible for serving all business objects. Each client shares this single `AppServer` instance from the application server. Using the `getCustomer()` method, a client can query the `AppServer` instance to find specific `Customer` objects. The important thing to note is that you can pass around objects—remote and otherwise—through return values and as parameters to methods once you have done a lookup on your first remote object. You just cannot create remote objects like you can local ones.

Object Serialization

Not all objects that you pass between virtual machines are remote. In fact, you need to be able to pass the primitive Java datatypes, as well as many basic Java objects, such as a `String` or a `HashMap`, that are not remote. When a nonremote object is passed across virtual machine boundaries, it gets passed by value using object serialization instead of the traditional Java RMI way of passing objects, by reference. Object serialization is a feature of the Java 1.1 release that allows objects to be turned into a data stream that you can use the way you use other Java streams— send it to a file, over a network, or to standard output. What is important about this method of passing objects across virtual machines is that changes you make to the object on one virtual machine are not reflected in the other virtual machine.

Most of the core Java classes are serializable. If you wish to build classes that are not remote but need to be passed across virtual machines, you need to make those classes serializable. A serializable class minimally needs to implement `java.io.Serializable`. For almost any kind of nonsensitive data you might want to serialize, just implementing `Serializable` is enough. You do not even have to write a method; `Object` already handles the serialization for you. It will, however, assume that you don't want the object to be serializable unless you implement `Serializable`. Example 6-2 provides a simple example of how object serialization works. When you run it, you will see the `SerialDemo` instance in the second block display the values of one created in the first block.

Example 6-2. A Simple Demonstration of Object Serialization

```java
import java.io.*;

public class SerialDemo implements Serializable {
    static public void main(String[] args) {
        try {
            { // Save a SerialDemo object with a value of 5.
                FileOutputStream f = new FileOutputStream("/tmp/testing");
                ObjectOutputStream s = new ObjectOutputStream(f);
                SerialDemo d= new SerialDemo(5);

                s.writeObject(d);
                s.flush();
            }
            { // Now restore it and look at the value.
                FileInputStream f = new FileInputStream("/tmp/testing");
                ObjectInputStream s = new ObjectInputStream(f);
                SerialDemo d = (SerialDemo)s.readObject();

                System.out.println("SerialDemo.getVal() is: " +
                        d.getVal());
            }
        }
        catch( Exception e ) {
            e.printStackTrace();
        }
    }

    int test_val= 7; // value defaults to 7

    public SerialDemo() {
        super();
    }
```

Example 6-2. A Simple Demonstration of Object Serialization (continued)

```
    public SerialDemo(int x) {
        super();
        test_val = x;
    }

    public int getVal() {
        return test_val;
    }
}
```

Enterprise JavaBeans

RMI is a distributed object API. It specifies how to write objects so that they can talk to each other no matter where on the network they are found. I could write dozens of business objects that can, in principal, talk to your business objects using RMI. At its core, however, RMI is nothing more than an API to which your distributed objects must conform. RMI says nothing about other characteristics normally required of an enterprise-class distributed environment. For example, it says nothing about how a client might perform a search for RMI objects matching some criteria. It also says nothing about how those objects might work together to construct a single transaction.

What is missing from the picture is a distributed component model. A component model is a standard that defines how components are written so that systems can be built from components by different authors with little or no customization. You may be familiar with the JavaBeans component model. It is a component model that defines how you write user interface components so that they may be plugged into third-party applications. The magic thing about JavaBeans is that there is very little API behind the specification; you neither implement nor extend any special classes and you need call no special methods. The force of JavaBeans is largely in conformance with an established naming convention.

Enterprise JavaBeans is a more complex extension of this concept. While there are API elements behind Enterprise JavaBeans, it is more than an API. It is a standard way of writing distributed components so that the written components can be used with the components you write in someone else's system. RMI does not support this ability for several reasons. Consider the following issues RMI does not address:

Security

RMI says nothing about security. RMI alone basically leaves your system wide open. Anybody who has access to your RMI interfaces can forge access to the underlying components. Unless you write complex security checks to authenticate clients and verify access, you will have no security. Your components are therefore unlikely to interoperate with my components unless you agree to share some sort of security model.

Searching

RMI provides the ability to do a lookup only for a specific, registry-bound object. It says nothing about how you find unbound objects or perform searches for a group of objects meeting certain requirements. Writing a banking application, you might want to support the ability to find all accounts with negative balances. In order to do this in an RMI environment, you would have to write your own search methods in bound objects. Your custom approach to handling searches won't work with someone else's custom approach to searching without forcing clients to deal with both search models.

Transactions

Perhaps the most important piece to a distributed component model is support for transactions. RMI says absolutely nothing about transactions. When you build an RMI-based application, you need to address how you will support transactions. In other words, you need to keep track of when a client begins a transaction, what RMI objects that client changes, and commit and roll back those changes when the client is done. This problem is compounded by the fact that most distributed object systems support more than one client at a time. Different transaction models are much more incompatible than different searching or security models. While client coders can get around differences in search and security models by being aware of those differences, transaction models can almost never be made to work together.

Persistence

RMI says nothing about how RMI objects persist across time. Later in this book, I will introduce a persistence utility that supports saving RMI objects to a database usign JDBC. Unfortunately, it will be difficult to integrate with RMI objects designed to use some other persistence model because the other persistence model may have very different persistence requirements.

Enterprise JavaBeans (EJB) addresses all of these points so that you can literally pick and choose the best designed business components from different vendors and make them work and play well with one another in the same environment. EJB is now the standard component model for capturing distributed business components. It hides from you the details you might have to worry about yourself if you were writing an RMI application. Beyond this chapter, you will deal with those details because EJB is not always going to be a feasible solution; the goal is therefore to understand the underlying elements of a distributed component model. The rest of this chapter, however, is designed to give you a strong understanding of what EJB brings you.

EJB Roles

One of the benefits of the EJB approach is that it separates different application development roles into distinct parts so that everything one role does is usable by possible players of any of the other roles. EJB specifically defines the following roles:*

The EJB provider

> The EJB provider is an expert in the problem domain in question and develops Java objects that capture the business concepts making up the problem domain. The EJB provider worries about nothing other than business logic programming.

The application assembler

> The application assembler is an expert in the processes that make up a business and in building user interfaces that employee the EJB provider's business components.

The deployer

> The deployer is an expert in a specific operating environment. The deployer takes an assembled application and configures it for deployment in the runtime environment.

The EJB server provider

> A server provider supports one or more services, such as a JDBC driver supporting database access.

The EJB container provider

> The container is where EJB components live. It is the runtime environment in which the beans operate. The container provider is a vendor that builds the EJB container.

The system administrator

> The system administrator manages the runtime environment in which EJB components operate.

An EJB provider captures each of the business components that model a business in Java code. The EJB specification breaks down each of these business components into three pieces: the home interface, the remote interface, and the bean implementation. Your job as the EJB provider is thus to write these three classes for each business component in your system.

---

* Any given role may be played by multiple players on a project. Similarly, one person may play multiple roles.

Kinds of Beans

EJB specifies two kinds of beans: entity beans and session beans. The distinction between the two is that entity beans are persistent and session beans are transient. In other words, entity beans save their states across time, while session beans do not. Most business concepts work best as entity beans; they are the entities that make up your business. Entity beans are shared by all clients.*

Session beans are unique to each client. They come to life only when requested by a client. When that client is done with them, they go away. An example of a session bean might be a `Registration` class that represents the registration of a person for an event. The `Registration` exists for a specific client to associate a person with an event. It manages the business logic associated with a registration but goes away once the registration is complete. The persistent data is in the `Person` and `Event` classes.

NOTE   The word *bean* is a heavily overloaded term in Java. Even within the EJB specification, bean has different meanings in different contexts. It can mean one of the three classes called the *bean implementation* or it can mean the business concept as a whole. I take the approach of using the term bean alone to mean the business component represented by the three EJB classes, and the term bean implementation to mean the one class that implements the business logic.

The home and remote interfaces for both kinds of beans are RMI remote interfaces. That is, they are indirectly derived from the `java.rmi.Remote` interface and are exported for remote access. The class extended by a remote interface is `EJBObject`. If, for example, you wanted to turn the `Ball` object from earlier in the chapter into an entity bean, you would create a `BallHome` interface, a `Ball` interface, and a `BallBean` implementation. The `Ball` interface would extend `javax.ejb.EJBObject`, which in turn extends `java.rmi.Remote`. The result might be a class that looks like this:

```
public interface Ball extends javax.ejb.EJBObject {
    void hit() throws java.rmi.RemoteException;
    int getPosition() throws RemoteException;
}
```

This interface looks a lot like the RMI example from earlier in the chapter. In fact, the only difference is that this one extends `Remote` via `EJBObject`. The interface specifies only those methods that should be made available to the rest of the world.

---

* This is not necessarily true of all environments. Specifically, EJB allows for a clustered environment in which multiple application servers work together to serve up beans. In such an environment, the same entity may appear on different servers and serve different clients. The containers are responsible in those situations for making the system appear as if the clients share the same entity reference.

The home interface is where you go to find or create instances of the bean. It specifies different versions of `create()` or `findXXX()`* methods that enable a client to create new instances of the bean or find existing instances. If you think about the problem of a banking system, they might have account beans, customer beans, and teller beans. When the bank attracts a new customer, its enterprise banking system needs to create a `Customer` bean to represent that customer. The bank manager's Windows application that enables the registration of new customers might have the following code for creating a new `Customer` bean:

```
InitialContext ctx = new InitialContext();
CustomerHome custhome;
Customer cust;

custhome = (CustomerHome)ctx.lookup("CustomerHome");
cust = custhome.create(ssn);
```

This code provides you with your first look at JNDI support in EJB. Using a JNDI initial context, you look up an implementation of the customer bean's home interface. That home interface, `CustomerHome`, provides a `create()` method that enables you to create a new `Customer` bean. In the previous case, the `create()` method accepts a `String` representing the customer's social security number.† The EJB specification requires that a home interface specify `create()` signatures for each way of creating a an implementation of that bean. The `CustomerHome` interface might look like this:

```
public interface CustomerHome extends EJBHome {
    Customer create() throws CreateException, RemoteException;

    Customer create(String ssn)
    throws CreateException, RemoteException;

    Customer findByPrimaryKey(CustomerKey pk)
    throws FinderException, RemoteException;

    Customer findBySocialSecurityNumber(String ssn)
    throws FinderException, RemoteException;
}
```

The finder methods provide ways to look up `Customer` objects. All except the `findByPrimaryKey()` method can be named anything you want, and they should return either a remote reference to the bean in question or an `Enumeration` of remote references to the bean. You should expect the EJB specification in the future to allow any kind of collection from the Java Collections API. Because the

---

* Only entity beans have finder methods.

† A social security number is a U.S. federal tax identifier.

EJB specification is based on Java 1.1, however, it supports only the `Enumeration` interface as a return value for collections.*

The `findByPrimaryKey()` method is a special finder for EJBs. Each entity bean instance has a primary key that uniquely identifies it. The primary key can be any serializable Java class you write. The only requirement is that the class must implement the `equals()` and `hashCode()` in an appropriate fashion. For example, if your beans have a unique numeric identifier, you might create your own `CustomerKey` class that stores the identifier as a long. If you do this, your `CustomerKey` class should look something like the following code:

```
public class CustomerKey implements Serializable {
    private long objectID = -1L;

    public CustomerKey(long l) {
        objectID = l;
    }

    public boolean equals(Object other) {
        if( other instanceof CustomerKey ) {
            return ((CustomerKey)other).objectID == objectID;
        }
        return false;
    }

    public int hashCode() {
        return (new Long(objectID)).hashCode();
    }
}
```

The EJB 1.1 specification even allows you to use primitive wrapper classes instead of custom primary key classes. The example below, for example, could just as easily have used the `Long` class for its primary keys.

You do not actually write the class that implements the `Customer` or `CustomerHome` interfaces; that is the task of the EJB container. Generally, the EJB container has tools that enable a deployer to automatically create and compile implementation classes for the home and remote interfaces. These automatically generated classes handle issues such as security and then delegate to your bean implementation class. The bean is where you write your business logic.

The bean class must implement the following methods:

- It must implement every method in the class it implements: `EntityBean` for entity beans and `SessionBean` for session beans.

---

* As of the most recent EJB specification, collections can be returned either in the form of an `Enumeration` or a JDK 1.2 `Collection`. Unless you must be compatible with JDK 1.1, I strongly suggest using a `Collection` for your return value.

- It must implement every method in the remote interface using the exact same signatures found in the remote interface, except the RemoteException.

- It must implement a variation of the methods in the home interface.* For create() methods, it must implement counterparts called ejbCreate(), each of which takes the same arguments but returns a primary key object. Similarly, the findXXX() counterparts for entities are ejbFindXXX() methods that each takes the same arguments and returns either a primary key object or an Enumeration or collection of primary keys.

Consider that the Customer remote interface for the earlier home interface looks like this:

```
public interface Customer extends EJBObject {
    String getSocialSecurityNumber() throws RemoteException;
}
```

A skeleton of the bean implementation might look something like this (minus the method bodies):

```
public class CustomerBean implements EntityBean {
    private transient EntityContext context = null;
    private         String         ssn    = null;

    public void ejbActivate() throws RemoteException {
        // you will mostly leave this method empty
        // activation of resources required by
        // an object of this type independent of the
        // customer it represents belong here
        // an example might be opening a file handle
        // for logging
    }

    public CustomerKey ejbCreate() throws CreateException {
        // this method creates a primary key for the
        // customer and inserts the customer into the
        // database
    }

    public CustomerKey ejbCreate(String ssn)
    throws CreateException {
        // this method works the same as the ejbCreate()
        // above
    }
```

---

* This applies only for beans using bean-managed persistence. For container-managed beans, the creates and finders are implemented by the container. I will touch on bean-managed persistence versus container-managed persistence later in the chapter.

```
public CustomerKey ejbFindByPrimaryKey(CustomerKey pk)
throws FinderException, RemoteException {
    // this method goes to the database and performs
    // a SELECT and returns the PK if it is in the
    // database
}


 public CustomerKey ejbFindBySocialSecurityNumber(String ssn)
throws FinderException {
    // this method goes to the database and performs
    // a SELECT and returns the PK of the row
    // with a matching SSN
}

public void ejbLoad() throws RemoteException {
    // this method goes to the database and selects
    // the row that has this object's primary key
    // and then populates this object's fields
}

public void ejbPassivate() throws RemoteException {
    // this method is generally empty
    // you should release any system resources held
    // by this object here
}

public void ejbPostCreate() {
    // this is called to let you do any initialization
    // for this object after ejbCreate() is called and
    // a primary key is assigned to the object
}

public void ejbRemove() throws RemoteException {
    // this method goes to the database and deletes
    // the record with a primary key matching this
    // object's primary key
}

public void ejbStore() throws RemoteException {
    // this method goes to the database and saves
    // the state of this bean
}

public String getSocialSecurityNumber() {
    // this method is from the Customer remote interface
    return ssn;
}
```

```
    public void setEntityContext(EntityContext ctx)
    throws RemoteException {
        // this method assigns an EntityContext to the
        // bean
        context = ctx;
    }

    public void unsetEntityContext()
    throws RemoteException {
        // this method removes the EntityContext assignment
        context = null;
    }
}
```

JDBC comes into play in the `ejbCreate()`, `ejbFindXXX()`, `ejbLoad()`, `ejbStore()`, and `ejbRemove()` methods. Though you will not use EJB, later in the book I will demonstrate exactly how these calls might look using a similar architecture. You may not even be writing your own database code in a EJB environment because the EJB specification allows container-managed persistence. Under container-managed persistence, you need not worry about any persistence issues.

While container-managed persistence sounds great, it does have some serious drawbacks:

- Most EJB servers provide only automated persistence against JDBC-supported database engines. If you use another data-storage product such as an object-oriented database or a specialized digital asset management data store, you will have to do the work yourself.

- Container-managed persistence demands that your persistent attributes have public visibility. Public attributes violate a key element of good OO design: encapsulation. As a result, container-managed beans make it very easy for people to make poor design choices that rely on the public nature of those attributes.

- Container-managed persistence makes it difficult to tweak your data model for maximum performance. For example, if you want to perform lazy-loading* of certain attributes, you must use bean-managed persistence.

- Container-managed persistence is incapable of supporting the complex class relationships common to enterprise system. For example, container-managed

---

* *Lazy-loading* is a technique through which certain attributes in an object are not restored from the database immediately but are instead restored in a background thread or when the system asks for that data. A Country object, for example, may be associated with quite a few cities—likely more cities than you want to load into memory when most clients are only looking for the name of the country. Using lazy-loading, you can put off loading all associated cities until a later time.

persistence cannot support most one-to-many or many-to-many relationships. If your analysis model requires those kinds of relationships, your architecture must specify bean-managed persistence or use a complex object-to-relational mapping tool such as TopLink.

In the remaining chapters of this book, I will not talk much more about EJB because it hides many issues important to real-world database programming with JDBC. If you are building an application that is using Enterprise JavaBeans, the remaining chapters of the book should give you a better appreciation of why the structure of EJB is the way it is and how to manage EJB programming issues such as bean-managed persistence. For developers who have to build their own Java database application environments, the remainder of the book should help you take care of all issues EJB handles for you. Ultimately, this book's goal—for either architecture—is to explain how to write enterprise-class database applications using the JDBC API as your foundation.

7

Distributed Application Architecture

Each thing is, as it were, in a space of possible
states of affair. This space I can imagine as empty,
but I cannot imagine the thing without the space.
—Ludwig Wittgenstein
Tractatus Logico Philosophicus

In isolation, your Java objects have no meaning, i.e., they do nothing. Java objects represent things outside the application: a customer, a savings account, and so on. Before getting into the details of individual objects, you truly need to understand the space in which you expect them to operate. Architecture is the space in which software objects operate.

In this chapter, I will lay the foundations for database development in the object-oriented world of Java by examining the architecture of an application you will be building over the rest of this book. You may find that these foundations span a broad spectrum of issues. I will not touch JDBC, EJB, or any of the other details required for the creation of individual objects. Instead, my goal is to help you cut down on the work you will need do over and over again each time you build a database application and to maximize the relevance of what you build to future needs. Many of the classes I show you in this chapter are common and generic, perhaps something that you could use to create a standard package for use in all kinds of applications.

One thing you may have noticed about Java or similar object-oriented languages such as Smalltalk or Python is that there are so many classes. You want to try to understand what class X does, but you find that it in turn extends class Z, which contains classes A and B. If you are totally comfortable with the object-oriented paradigm, this interweaving of classes may not faze you. On the other hand, it may easily seem confusing to people used to dealing with languages such as C. Unlike C, for which you may have a library function and perhaps an associated data structure, Java bundles up data and functions inside classes for manipulating that data. Java data never gets directly manipulated except by the class that owns the data.

I will, of course, continue operating in Java's object-oriented framework. Among other things, this means that whenever you need to represent a new concept, you will use new classes. You should approach each new class trying to understand what class it extends, which interfaces it implements, and what others it relates to in other ways. I will help you along graphically wherever possible by providing UML-standard* diagrams that illustrate the class relationships.

Architecture

The value of system architecture is only recently being recognized in the software industry. As I stated before, paraphrasing Wittgenstein, architecture is the space in which objects operate. It defines the contracts through which they interact with external system components and each other. The primary duty of a system architect is to ask the question, "What if . . . ?".

Strategic Versus Tactical

During most software development processes, each role in the process is responsible for some level of tactical thought and some level of strategic thought. By tactical thought, I mean thinking about the problem at hand and ignoring hypothetical issues. Strategic thought, on the other hand, means thinking about all possible worlds and weighing their probability. An example of a strategic decision might be to have your application design abstract to a generic concept of "product" when the only product your company sells is fuzzy dice. That strategic decision will let your company move into selling seat covers in the future without rewriting the system. Tactically speaking, however, the system only requires that you support fuzzy dice.

A good system architect is a heavily strategic thinker. The architect needs to understand these tactical issues and determine the best high-level solution that minimally addresses the tactical issues, while doing no harm to the ability to address strategic issues without good cause. In the previous example, it is certainly easier for everyone to think about the system in terms of fuzzy dice. The path of least resistance therefore would be to code a system made up of fuzzy dice objects. Everyone could agree that the business is about selling fuzzy dice, and everyone clearly understands what fuzzy dice are. Taking that path of least resistance, however, harms one important strategic question: What if the company decides to sell

---

* UML stands for Unified Modeling Language. It is a new standard for documenting object-oriented analysis and design.

other products? Furthermore, building the system as a system of fuzzy dice instead of a system of products provides absolutely no advantage to mitigate the harm done to the strategic question.

Architectural Questions

As odd as it may sound, development teams often unwittingly plan for failure instead of success. How often have you heard someone say, "I know that is the right way to do this, but you just need to be able to support . . . " or some variation thereof? That statement represents planning for failure. Any successful software project will see its software used in realms well beyond its original intentions. A poor piece of software, however, may minimally serve some short-term goals before it is eventually replaced. The job of an architect is to make sure no tactical decisions fall into the "planning for failure category." The architect assumes success and structures the system accordingly. Typical architectural questions are:

- How do I partition my system?
- Should I support diverse user bases?
- How do I enable the system to integrate with third-party applications?
- What standards should the design and development teams adhere to?
- What tools best meet these needs?

The first question is listed first for a reason: it is the first question any architect should address for a system. I will now present a high-level view of two distinct architectures and then introduce a very specific architecture that you will follow for the banking application you build in this book.

Common Architectures

There are basically two major kinds of modern architectures: two-tier client/server and three-tier—also commonly called n-tier. Each one has many variations. At a high level, these architectures focus on the partitioning system processing. They decide on what machine and in what process space a given bit of code executes.

Client/server is often a generic umbrella term for any application architecture that divides processing among two or more processes, often on two or more machines. Any database application is a client/server application if it handles data storage and retrieval in the database process and data manipulation and presentation somewhere else. The server is the database engine that stores the data, and the client is the process that gets or creates the data. The idea behind the client/server architecture in a database application is to provide multiple users with access to the same data.

Two-tier client/server

The simplest shape a client/server architecture takes is called a *two-tier* architecture. In fact, most client/server architectures are two-tier. The term "two-tier" describes the way in which application processing can be divided in a client/server application. A two-tier application ideally provides multiple workstations with a uniform presentation layer that communicates with a centralized data storage layer. The presentation layer is generally the client, and the data storage layer is the server. Some exceptional environments, such as the X Window System, shuffle the roles of client and server.

Most Internet applications—email, Telnet, FTP, gopher, and even the Web—are simple two-tier applications. Without providing a lot of data interpretation or processing, these applications provide a simple interface to access information across the Internet. When most application programmers write their own client/server applications, they tend to follow this two-tier structure.

Figure 7-1 shows how two-tier systems give clients access to centralized data. If you use the Web as an example, the web browser on the client side retrieves data stored at a web server.

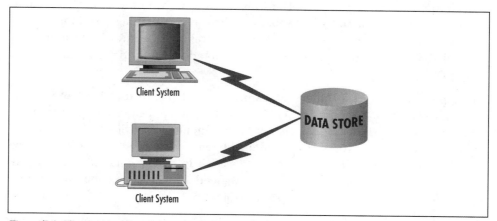

Figure 7-1. The two-tier client/server architecture

The architecture of a system depends on the application. For situations such as the display of simple web pages, you do not need anything more than a two-tier design has to offer. This is because the display of static HTML pages requires very little data manipulation, and thus there is very little to fight over. The server sends the page as a stream of text, and the client formats it based on the HTML tags. There are none of the complicating factors you will see in upcoming applications: choices between different tasks, redirecting of tasks to subordinate methods, searches through distributed databases, and so on.

Even when your application gets slightly more complex—such as a simple data-entry application like the many web-based contests that appeared in the early days of the Web—a two-tier architecture still makes sense. Let's look at how you might build such an application to see why additional complexity is unnecessary. Figure 7-2 shows this application in the context of a two-tier architecture that you saw in Figure 7-1.

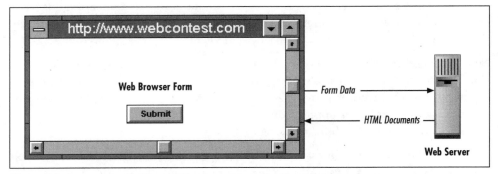

Figure 7-2. A contest registration application using a two-tier architecture

In addition to displaying the HTML forms you receive from the server, your client also accepts user input and sends it back to the server for storage. You might even build in some batch processing on the server to validate a contest entry and reject any ineligible ones. The application requires no additional processing in order to do its job.

The application can easily handle all its processing between the client and server; nothing calls for an additional layer. But what if the application were even more complex? Let's say that instead of waiting for ineligible entries to be submitted before rejecting them, you filter out ineligible entries on the client so people are not forced to fill out a form, only to be rejected. In place of handling entry processing in a separate application, you now need to write logic somewhere that rejects these rogue entries. Where are you going to do it?

Without Java, a client-side scripting language like JavaScript, or a peculiar browser plug-in, you can forget handling this processing on the client side. Processing in a web browser can happen using only one of those three solutions. The browser plug-in solution is unlikely since it requires the user to download and install a foreign application to simply fill out a one-time entry into a contest. Browser scripting languages, on the other hand, lack Java's portability and its ability to cleanly interface with server systems. The enterprise solution is Java.

Two-tier limitations

Using Java on the client, you can preserve the simple two-tier architecture. This solution is great if your processing is limited to simple data validation (Is your birthday a real date? Did you enter all the required fields?). But what if you add even more complexity? Now you require the application to be a generic contest entry application that you can sell to multiple companies running Internet contests. One of the implications of this generic design is that your application must be able to adapt to contests having different entry eligibility rules. If your eligibility rules are located in a Java applet on the client that is talking directly to the database, then changing eligibility rules essentially means rewriting the application! In addition, your direct database access ties your application to the same data model without regard for the individuality of the different contests the application is supposed to serve. Your needs have now outstripped the abilities of your two-tier architecture.

Fat clients. Perhaps you have seen the sort of scope-creep in a single application in the way I introduced new functions into the contest application. Ideally, the client/server architecture is supposed to let each machine do only the processing relevant to its specialization. Workstations are designed to provide users with a graphical interface, so they do data presentation. Servers are designed to handle complex data and networking management, so they serve as the data stores. But as systems get more complex, more needs appear that have no clear place in the two-tier model.

This evolution of application complexity has been paralleled by opposing trends in hardware. Client machines have grown larger and more powerful and server machines have scaled down and become less expensive. While client machines have been able to keep up with more complex user interface needs, servers have become less capable of handling more complex data storage needs. Whereas a single mainframe once handled a company's most complex databases, you might find today the same databases distributed across dozens of smaller servers. As odd as this sounds, companies do this because it is immensely cheaper to buy a dozen small workstations than one mainframe. Financial pressures have thus pushed new processing needs onto the client, leading to what is commonly called the problem of the "fat client."

Two-tier, fat-client systems are notorious for their inability to adapt to changing environments and scale with growing user and data volume. Even though a client's primary task is the presentation of data, a fat client is loaded with knowledge completely unrelated to that task. What happens if you need to distribute your data across multiple databases or multiple servers? What happens if some small bit of business logic changes? You have to modify, test, and redistribute a client program whose core functionality has nothing to do with the changes you made.

Object reuse. Object reuse is a very vague but central concept in object-oriented development.* You know it is a good thing, but you may have very different things in mind when you speak of it. In one common sense, object reuse is simply code reuse. You used the same code to build application X and application Y. But in another sense, object reuse means using exactly the same object instances in one application that you are using in another application. For instance, the customer account objects you likely built for an ATM system could be used by a new web interface you are building. While a two-tier system can contort to achieve the former sense of object reuse, it can almost never achieve the latter.

In the simplest form of object reuse, you would like to take code developed for one application, rewrite small bits of it, and have it run with minimal work. Two-tier solutions have had a nasty time doing this because they are so closely tied to the database. In PowerBuilder, for example, your GUI objects map directly to tables in a database! You need to throw away a large chunk of your GUI when moving from one environment to the next. Some very clever people—including a few I have worked with—have built complex class libraries to work around this problem. But my experience has been that such systems lack the flexibility you want in a toolkit of reusable objects.

Source code reuse is not the real object reuse you are looking for. You want to reuse actual object instances. If you look at building a system for viewing bank accounts both from the Web and an ATM, you really want the user's web browser and the ATM to look at the exact same data, especially if they are looking at that data at the same instant. Doing this with a two-tier system is nearly impossible since each client ends up with its own copy of the data. When one client changes some data, other clients end up with old data, resulting in a problem called *dirty writes*. A dirty write is a situation in which someone tries to modify data based on an old, out-of-date copy of the database. If my spouse makes a withdrawal at an ATM while I am paying bills at home, I want to see that change happen. If we each look at copies of the original data, however, I will end up paying a bill with money that my spouse just withdrew!

If a client, on the other hand, simply observes objects located in some centralized location, it always deals with the most recent information. When my spouse withdraws that last $100, my web browser is immediately notified so that I do not act on stale information.

---

* I am talking specifically about reuse in the development workflows of a project. The most effective reuse occurs in the analysis and design workflows of a project.

When to use a two-tier design

Two-tier solutions do have a place in application development. Simple applications with immediate deadlines that do not require a lot of maintenance are perfect for a two-tier architecture. The following checklist provides important questions to ask before committing yourself to a two-tier design. If you can answer "yes" to each of the questions in the checklist, then a two-tier architecture is likely your best solution. Otherwise you might consider a three-tier design.

- Does your application emphasize time-to-market over architecture?
- Does your application use a single database?
- Is your database engine located on a single host?
- Is your database likely to stay approximately the same size over time?
- Is your user base likely to stay approximately the same size over time?
- Are your requirements fixed with little or no possibility of change?
- Do you expect minimal maintenance after you deliver the application?

Three-tier

You can avoid the problems of two-tier client/server by extending the two tiers to three. A three-tier architecture adds to the two-tier model a new layer that isolates data processing in a central location and maximizes object reuse. Figure 7-3 shows how this new third layer might fit into an application architecture.

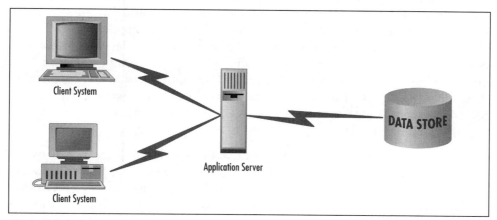

Figure 7-3. A three-tier architecture

Isolated database connectivity. I've already mentioned that JDBC frees you from concerns related to portability among proprietary database APIs. Unfortunately, it does not—it could not—provide us with a means to liberate your applications from your data model. If your application uses JDBC in a two-tier environment, it is still talking directly to the database. Any change in the database ends up costing you a change in the presentation layer.

To avoid this extra cost, you should isolate your database connection so that your presentation does not care anything about the way you store your data. You can take advantage of Java's object-oriented nature and create a system in which your clients talk only to objects on the server. Database connectivity becomes an issue hidden within each server object. Suddenly, the presentation layer stops caring about where the database is, or if you are even using a database at all. The client sees only middle-tier objects.

Centralized business processing. The middle tier of a three-tier architecture— the application server—handles the data-processing issues you have found out of place in either of the other tiers. The application server is populated by problem-specific objects commonly called *business objects.* Returning to the banking application, your business objects are such things as accounts, customers, and transactions that exist independently of how a user might see them. An account, for example, is concerned with processing new banking transactions. It does not care whether an ATM is viewing it, a teller is viewing it at his or her console, or the bank is planning to allow users to access it from the Web. An application server layer will generally consist of a data store interface and a public API.

The data store interface is hidden from external objects. Internally, a business object has methods to save it to and restore it from a database. Information about how this happens is not available outside the object, and thus does not affect other objects. On the other hand, the business object does provide a limited, public interface to allow external objects access to it. In a two-tier application, your GUI would have displayed account information directly from the database. In a three-tier system, however, the GUI learns everything about an account from an account business object instead of from the database. If the GUI wants to know something it should not be allowed to know, the business object can prevent it. Similarly, if the GUI wants to make a change to that object, it submits that change to the object instead of the database.

These centralized rules for processing data inside business objects are called *business rules.* No matter what your problem domain is, the rules for how data should be processed rarely change. For example, no matter what application talks to your account objects, that application should not (unfortunately) allow you to write checks for money you do not have. It is a rule that governs the way the bank does business. A three-tier architecture allows you to use the same business rules across all applications that operate on your business objects.

Business object presentation. User interfaces are very ephemeral things. They change constantly in the development process as users experiment with them; their final appearance depends heavily on the hardware being used, the application's user base, and the purpose of the application in question. The presentation layer of a three-tier application should therefore contain only user interface code that can be modified easily on a whim.

Your banking application could use any of these different presentation layers:

- The teller window's console at the bank
- The ATM machine
- The web applet

Figure 7-4 shows how you intend to present an account from a teller PC.

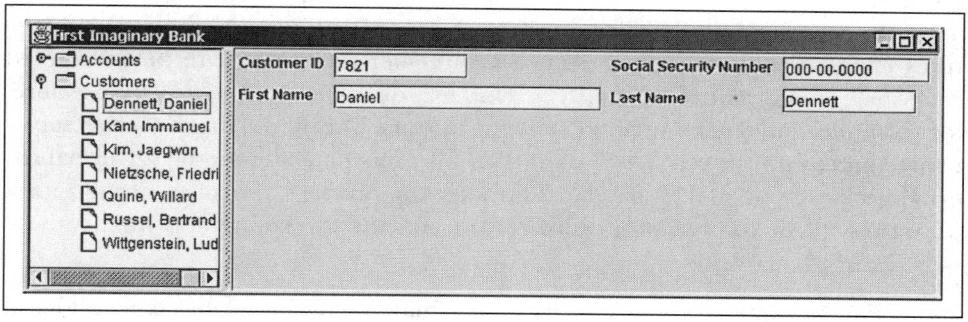

Figure 7-4. An account as viewed from the teller console

Database vendors know that data presentation is a central requirement, and they have developed some fancy solutions for creating GUIs. The good ones are easy to use and produce nice-looking results, but since they are based on a two-tiered vision, they allow rules and decision making to leak into the presentation layer. For instance, take PowerBuilder, which has been on the leading edge of designing a rapid application development environment for building database frontends. It uses GUI objects called DataWindows to map relational data to a graphical user interface display. With a DataWindow, you can use simple drag-and-drop to associate a database column with a particular GUI widget.

Because a DataWindow maps the user interface directly to the database, it does not work well in a three-tier system where you map the user interface to intermediary business objects. You will, however, create a user interface library in Chapter 10, *The User Interface*, that captures the DataWindow level of abstraction in a way that better suits a three-tier distributed architecture. Instead of mapping rows from a database to a display area on a user interface, you will create a one-to-one mapping of business objects to specific GUI views of them.

Drawbacks to the three-tier architecture

While the three-tier architecture provides some important advantages, it is not without its downside. Chief among its drawbacks is the level of complexity it adds to a system. You have more distinct components in your system, and therefore more to manage. It is also harder to find software engineers who are competent in three-tier programming skills such as transaction management and security. While tools like the EJB component model aim to minimize this complexity, they cannot elimintate it.

The Network Application Architecture

The term Network Application Architecture (NAA) is one I coined to describe a specific kind of three-tier architecture I found works best for enterprise Java systems. Variations on it are certain to work, but its essential characteristic is that it is a distributed three-tier application architecture. Distributed three-tier architectures enable the three logical tiers of a three-tier architecture to be distributed across many different process spaces. Under a distributed three-tier architecture, for example, my database could be split into an Oracle database on the server named **athens** for my business data and an Informix database on the server named **carthage** for my digital assets. Furthermore, my product and inventory business objects could be located on a third server, and the marketing and finance business objects on a fourth.

Figure 7-5 illustrates the NAA. It treats the mid-tier business objects as a logical mid-tier that can be split into many different partitions. This split is entirely transparent to the other tiers in the architecture. The result is that you can move objects around at runtime to enhance system performance without worrying that a client is looking for a particular object on a particular machine.

This principal also applies to the database layer. The business objects do not know or care whether the underlying database is a single or a distributed database.

The NAA makes a joke of the concept "web-enabled." Because the NAA is not specific to any kind of presentation layer, it can support ultra-thin web clients or just moderately thin Java clients. If access to your business systems via interactive television is the next great wave, your system is already enabled to support it.

The NAA addresses issues other than simple application partitioning. It is also based on the principles of enterprise systems I enumerated in Chapter 1, *Java in the Enterprise*. The NAA is not only a distributed three-tier architecture, it is a distributed three-tier architecture based on the EJB component model and RMI/IIOP for distributed computing support. It mandates full support for internationalization and localization and assumes a hostile security environment by requiring encrypted communications.

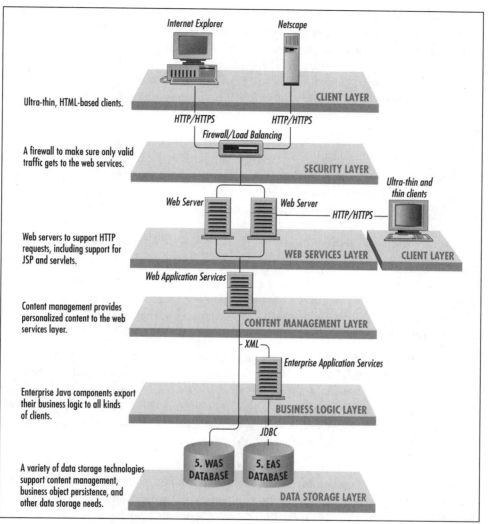

Figure 7-5. The Network Application Architecture

Design Patterns

Design patterns have been popularized by the book *Design Patterns* by Erich Gamma, Richard Helm, Ralph Johnson, John Vlissides, and Grady Booch (Addison-Wesley). They are recurring forms in software development that you can capture at a low level and reuse across dissimilar applications. Within any application scope are problems you have encountered; patterns are the result of your recognizing those common problems and creating a common solution.

The first step to identifying the design patterns is identifying problems in generic terms. You already know that you need to relate GUI widgets on the client to business objects in the application server; you should create GUI widgets that observe changes in centralized business objects. You also know that you need to make those business objects persistent by saving them to a database. You should therefore look at a few common patterns that will help accomplish these goals.

Client Patterns

The user interface provides a view of the business specific to the role of the user in question. In the Network Application Architecture, it provides this view by displaying the business components housed on a shared server. Good client design patterns will help keep the user interface decoupled from the server.

The model-view-controller pattern

Java Swing is based entirely on a very important user-interface pattern, the *model-view-controller pattern* (MVC). In fact, this key design pattern is part of what makes Java so perfect for distributed enterprise development. The MVC pattern separates a GUI component's visual display (the view) from the thing it is a view of (the model) and the way the user interacts with the component (the controller).

Imagine, for example, a simple two-tier application that displays the rows from a database table in a GUI table display. The columns of the GUI table match the columns of the database table, and the rows in the GUI table match those in the database table. The model is the database. The view is the GUI table. The controller is a less obvious object that handles the user mouse clicks and keypresses and determines what the model or view should do in response to those user actions.

Swing actually uses a variant of this pattern called the *model-delegate pattern*. The model-delegate pattern combines the view and the controller into a single object that delegates to its model. Applied to the Network Application Architecture, a single model can model the business objects on the server to provide a common look for multiple GUI components. As a result, you could have a user interface with a tree and table showing two different views of the same objects for which deleting an object in the table is immediately reflected in the tree on the left without any programming effort.

The listener pattern

Perhaps saying that the tree knows about the change "without any programming effort" is a bit of an overstatement. The tree and the table may be sharing the same model, but the tree will not know to repaint itself unless it somehow knows that the model has been changed. Swing uses another key design pattern to make sure the tree knows about the change: the *listener pattern*.

The listener pattern enables one object to listen to specific events that occur to another object. A common listener in the JavaBeans component architecture is something called a `PropertyChangeListener`. One object can declare itself a `PropertyChangeListener` by implementing the `PropertyChangeListener` interface. It then tells other objects that it is interested in property changes by calling the `addPropertyChangeListener()` method in any objects it cares about. The import part of this pattern is that the object being listened to needs to know nothing about its listeners except that those objects want to know when a property has changed. As a result, you can design objects that live well beyond the uses originally intended for them.

The distributed listener pattern

A variation of the listener pattern is the *distributed listener pattern*. It captures situations in which one object is interested in changes that occur in an object on another machine. Returning to the banking application, my spouse at the ATM can withdraw money from a checking account that I am looking at on the Web. If the GUI widgets in my applet are not actively observing those accounts, they will not know that my account has less money than it did a minute ago. If the application uses the distributed listener pattern, however, anytime a change occurs in the checking account, both the ATM and the web browser get notified.

Distributed computing adds unique challenges to the distributed listener pattern. First of all, Java RMI's JRMP protocol cannot support the server calling a method in a user interface object for which that user interface is hidden behind a firewall. You can get around this problem by creating a special smart proxy object that acts like an RMI stub but is in fact a local user interface object. This stub polls the actual RMI stub for changes in the remote object. If it detects a change, it fires an event that local user interface objects can listen for. Figure 7-6 shows a class diagram detailing the object relationships. Figure 7-7 provides a sequence diagram to show what happens when a change occurs.

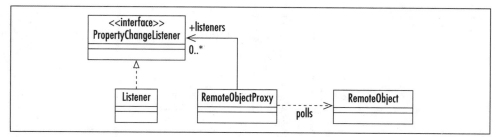

Figure 7-6. A UML class diagram of the distributed listener pattern

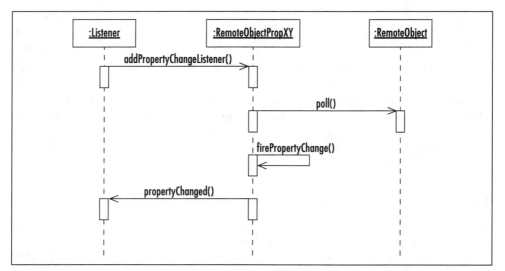

Figure 7-7. A sequence diagram describing sequences of events in the distributed listener pattern

Business Patterns

As a general rule, the mid-tier business logic is likely to use just about every design pattern in the *Design Pattern* book. The two most common general patterns I have encountered are the *composite* and *factory* patterns. I will provide a brief description of those two patterns here, but I strongly recommend the purchase of *Design Patterns* for greater insight into these and a wealth of other useful general patterns.

The composite pattern

The composite pattern appears everywhere in the real world. It represents a hierarchy in which some type of object may be both contained by similar objects and contain similar objects. Figure 7-8 shows a UML diagram describing the composite pattern.

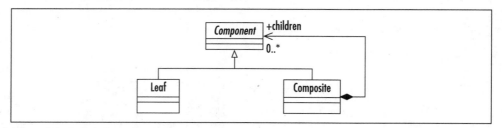

Figure 7-8. A class diagram of the composite pattern

To put a more concrete face on the composite pattern, think of a virtual reality game that attempts to model your movements through a maze. In your game, you might have a Room class that can contain Tangible objects, some of which can contain other Tangible objects (e.g., a bag). Your room is a container, and bags are containers. Things like stones and money, however, are unable to contain anything. The room, on the other hand, cannot be contained by anything greater than it. The result is the class diagram contained in Figure 7-9.

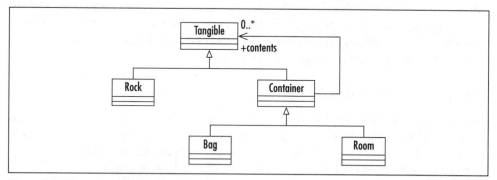

Figure 7-9. The composite pattern in practice

The factory pattern

Another common pattern found in the core Java libraries is the factory pattern. The AppServerImpl class from the previous chapter is an example of this pattern in use. The pattern encapsulates the creation of objects inside a single interface. The Java 1.1 internationalization support is peppered with factory classes. The java.util.ResourceBundle class, for example, contains logic that allows you to find a bundle of resources for a specific locale without having to know which subclass of ResourceBundle is the right one to instantiate. A ResourceBundle is an object that might contain translations of error messages, menu item labels, and text labels for your application. By using a ResourceBundle, you can create an application that will appear in French to French users, German to German users, and English to English users.

Because of the factory pattern, using a ResourceBundle is quite easy. To create a save button, for example, you might have the following code:

```
ResourceBundle bundle =
    ResourceBundle.getBundle("labels",Locale.getDefault());
Button button = new Button(bundle.getString("SAVE"));
```

This code actually uses two factory methods: Locale.getDefault() and ResourceBundle.getBundle(). Locale.getDefault() constructs a Locale instance representing the locale in which your application is being run. For a

French user, this `Locale` instance would represent France and the French language. For a German, it would represent Germany and the German language. The `ResourceBundle.getBundle()` method in turn finds a `ResourceBundle` instance that supports the language and customs for that locale. The French `ResourceBundle` will thus return "Enregistrer" for the `getString()` call and the English one would return "Save."

The goal of the factory pattern is to capture the creation logic of certain objects in one method. The benefit of providing a single location for the creation of certain objects is that you can handle any rules regarding the creation of those objects once. If you use new everywhere, however, a change in business rules will require a change and retest of every single new in your code.

Data Access Patterns

One key to smooth three-tier development is providing a clear division between data storage code and business logic code. At some point, a business object needs to save itself to a data store. You will use some key data access patterns to make sure that the business object knows nothing about how it stores itself to a database. It only knows that it is saving itself.

The persistence delegate pattern

To some degree, most applications are concerned about some sort of *persistence*. Persistence is simply the ability to have information from an application instance exist for later instances of the application (or even other applications) to use. An object-oriented database application uses a database to enable its business objects to exist beyond the traditional object lifecycle. You want your customer object to exist at least as long as the customer. You want the accounts to exist at least as long as they are open. The persistence pattern solves this problem by creating a single interface for any potential method of extending an object's life.

The simplest implementation of object persistence is the creation of flat files. Each time an object changes, it saves itself to a file. When your application recreates the object later on, it goes back to that file and restores itself. While this sort of persistence is useful for small systems, it is extremely inefficient and does not scale at all for big systems.

Another backend tool for object persistence is the relational database. Here you have arrived at your goal. Instead of saving to a file with each change in an object, your objects update the database. Although saving to a database is a lot different from saving to a file, the same basic concepts of saving, restoring, committing, and aborting apply to both. What differs is the system-dependent specifics; for instance, you execute a simple file write for a file save, but a SQL UPDATE for a database save. You can therefore write a generic persistence interface that provides a single set of methods for persistence, regardless of whether you use a database or flat files. Your business objects never care how they are being saved, so the business logic just calls a `store()` method and allows a persistence-specific class to handle how that saving is implemented.

The persistence pattern defines an interface that prescribes these four behaviors:

`create()`
> Creates a primary key for the object and inserts it into the data store

`load()`
> Tells the object to load its data from the data store

`remove()`
> Removes the object from the database

`store()`
> Attempts to save any changes made to the object to the data store

The memento pattern

In the persistence delegate pattern, how does the persistence delegate know about the state of the object it is persisting? You could pass the object to the persistence methods, but that action requires your delegate to know a lot more about the objects it supports than you would likely want. Another design pattern from the *Design Patterns* book comes to the rescue here, the *memento pattern*.

A memento is a tool for capturing an object's state and safely passing it around. The advantage of the memento pattern is that it enables you to modify the beans and the persistence handlers independent of one another. A change to the bean does not affect any code in the persistence handler. The memento knows how to capture that change. The persistence handler knows how to get data from the memento. Similarly, any change in the way data is retrieved or saved to the data store is irrelevant to the bean. It always just passes its state to the delegate and lets the delegate worry about all persistence issues. I provide a concrete implementation of the memento pattern later in the book when I discuss address persistence.

The Banking Application

It is time to put everything together into a concrete banking application. This application is naturally not something your local bank would want to implement to support its business, but it does illustrate all of the key concepts I have covered in this book. The application is specifically a simple user interface that enables you to view your accounts and transfer money between any of them. It is a three-tier application that takes advantage of the Network Application Architecture, but it is not EJB-based. You will therefore have to construct tools along the way that you get for free with EJB. As a result, you will get a very practical feel for all the issues involved in distributed software development that you can apply to both EJB and nonEJB development.

The Business Objects

With a distributed enterprise application, your starting point is the middle tier. The business classes that make up the middle tier are the key to a successful design. It is therefore the starting point for your development efforts.* Figure 7-10 is a UML class diagram describing the mid-tier business objects for the banking application. You will build these objects in Chapter 8, *Distributed Component Models.*

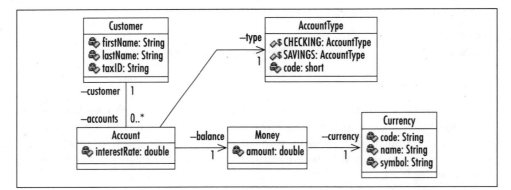

Figure 7-10. The middle tier of the banking application

Persistence

Persistence is a huge topic. A distributed application that persists its objects against a relational database has so many complex issues, such as security, locking, transaction management, object/database consistency, and performance to deal with. Enterprise JavaBeans worries about a lot of these issues for you. A book on database programming with JDBC and Java, however, would certainly be negligent if it did not address these problems. For the banking application, you will put together a library of objects that take care of these issues for you and apply it to the business objects in the banking application. Chapter 9, *Persistence,* covers the details of persistence in a distributed application.

---

* This fact is often in opposition to political considerations, namely that people want to see something. This urge is similar to asking a home builder to put up the siding on a house before building the frame, but it is a reality in software development today. My suggestion is to build time into your budget for a separate prototyping effort that involves a completely separate development team. That team can use rapid prototyping techniques both to provide some "feel good" enthusiasm and gather useful user interface (UI) design feedback for later stages of the system's design.

The User Interface

A good book on Swing, such as *Java Swing* by Robert Eckstein, Marc Loy, and Dave Wood, will tell you 99 percent of what you need to know about user interface programming in Java in a distributed environment. In Chapter 10 I focus on that extra one percent and the issues you need to deal with in Swing programming using the Network Application Architecture. The result will be the window in Figure 7-4 that enables users to view their accounts and make transfers.

8

Distributed Component Models

Beings are, so to speak, interrogated with regard to their being. But if they are to exhibit the characteristics of their being without falsification, they must for their part have become accessible in advance as they are in themselves. The question of being demands that the right access to being be gained and secured in advance with regard to what it interrogates.

—Martin Heidegger
Being and Time

As a phenomenologist, Heidegger believed that there was no purpose in seeking an underlying truth to a being beyond that truth it exposed to the world outside—in other words, one is what one does. The phenonomological approach actually applies very well to software engineering, in which one of your central tasks, especially in a business system, is to identify key concepts in the business, capture them in software, and expose them to the outside world. When I introduced Enterprise JavaBeans as the centerpiece of the Java 2 Enterprise Edition in Chapter 6, *Other Enterprise APIs*, I noted that EJB was a distributed component model. A component model specifies how objects should be written in order to make themselves accessible to the outside world. A good component model is backed by an open standard so that a system can be built from components developed by many independent sources.

EJB takes care of almost everything covered in this book for you. In other words, if you deploy a container-managed EJB application, you can be successful without knowing JDBC or component model issues. Java development, however, has not reached the point at which everyone is using Enterprise JavaBeans. Furthermore, EJB does not address all distributed-computing concerns perfectly. There are three common situations in which you will want to know more of the details of enterprise database application development than EJB requires:

- Container-managed persistence does not work for most EJB deployment environments. For example, systems that save some of their data to specialized data stores, such as a digital asset management repository, require bean-managed persistence.

- Not all applications require the power of an EJB solution.

- Even when the features supported by EJB are required, there may be other issues—for example, cost—that make the choice of EJB impractical.

You have already covered what you need to know for the first scenario, the JDBC API. Because EJB worries about the details of managing your JDBC-based transaction, a bean-managed EJB developer does not really need to understand all of the issues covered in this chapter. Anyone faced with the other two scenarios, however, will need to tackle some or all of the issues that distributed component models generally handle for you. This chapter shows you how to address those issues. It also introduces concepts, such as façades, that can help support EJB environments.

As I mentioned in Chapter 6, some of the issues EJB handles for you include security, searching, transactions, and persistence. In this chapter, you will look at three of those issues independent of EJB: security, searching, and transactions. Because the focus of this book is database programming, an entire chapter—Chapter 9, *Persistence*—is dedicated to persistence. The last part of the equation is building a client to use your component model. Chapter 10, *The User Interface*, addresses user interface issues.

Kinds of Distributed Components

Distributed components can be broken into two categories: *persistent components* and *process-oriented components*. Persistent components represent the fundamental, unchanging business concepts that make up your model. Process-oriented components, however, manage the business proceses that tie your persistent components together. EJB refers to process-oriented components as session beans; it refers to persistent components as entity beans.

If you think about the problem of a banking application, an Account is a persistent component, whereas a BankTransaction—not to be confused with a database transaction—is process-oriented. The Account is persistent because it is something the bank wants to track across an extended period of time. The BankTransaction, however, does not really represent a thing that needs to be tracked on its own across time. It simply exists during a client session to support the withdrawal of money from a checking account or the deposit of money into a savings account.

If you write your own distributed application without the assistance of EJB, nothing demands you make this distinction. For the sake of being able to best leverage the tools in this book for a migration to EJB, however, you will continue with this distinction. You need persistent business objects that represent our key concepts and non-persistent process objects that represent operations on those persistent business objects.

Process-Oriented Components

Process-oriented components manage your business transactions. Perhaps you have noticed by this point that the term *transaction* is heavily overloaded. On the one hand, I have used it for business transactions such as deposits, withdrawals, account creation, etc. On the other hand, I have used it in terms of database and component transactions. Process-oriented components support the former: business transactions.

In the banking application, the class `BankTransaction` represents common business processes that support account management. This "session" component has a one-to-one relationship with the client it serves. If you and I both use the application on our respective computers, we will each have our own `BankTransaction` instance. These session components do not require a lot of infrastructure to support them. They will use the architecture's underlying transaction support to manage your component transactions—to begin them and either to commit them or roll them back—and you will need to be able to get references to them from clients, but they have no issues unique to themselves that you need to support.

Persistent Components

Persistent components are more complex than session components; EJB did not even require support for persistent components until Version 1.1. Today, support for persistent components comes in the form of entity beans. These components represent something in your system that needs to last beyond the current session. One key feature of an entity component is that it has a clear identity. By identity, I refer to the same thing we mean when we talk about the identity of things in the real world. What is it about the persistent component that makes you consider it to be the same component across time?

My bank account, for example, is not interchangeable with your bank account. Furthermore, if you and I both need to see my account information, something needs to guarantee that we are both looking at the same thing. In the database, this is generally accomplished via primary keys. Anything about an object can change over time and we know it is still the same object because it shares the same primary key with its past state.

Depending on the nature of your application, what constitutes a unique identifier can be highly dependent on the kind of component you support. An ideal unique identifer has no meaning built into it; it is just a number or a string that uniquely identifies the component. Unfortunately, not all systems have been built with good unique identifiers. If you are tasked with building business components that persist against a legacy database, you may find that some use social security numbers, email addresses, or other meaningful values as their primary keys.

In a well-designed distributed system, you will generate unique identifiers to support the identification of your business objects. In the banking application, you use a Java `long` field, `objectID`, in each persistent component. No two components in the system will share the same `objectID`. You therefore need a mechanism for generating unique `long` values.

You could rely on the ID generation mechanism supported by your database of choice. Unfortunately, there is no standard for ID generation. Even if there were a standard supported by JDBC, you would leave out the ability to support such non-JDBC data stores as object databases and digital media repositories. You are therefore going to develop a custom, data-store-independent ID generation tool.

From a performance perspective, you do not want to have to go to your data store each time you need a new unique ID. Such a scheme could end up doubling the time it takes to create new objects in your system. It could also be very costly if you engage in clustering.* A solution to the problem of ID generation is a *node identifier*.

A node identifier is a unique key that enables a server to generate numbers within a process that are guaranteed to be unique even if other processes also generate unique IDs. On start up, a node in a cluster finds a sequence generator somewhere on the network and requests a unique node identifier. The sequence generator will go to some sort of persistent store to grab the next available node ID, increment it, and save the incremented value back to the persistent store. That value will then be returned to the requesting node to use as a seed in `objectID` generation.

Consider a banking application with two server nodes enabling clients to create new accounts. The first server gets a node identifier 1 from the sequence generator and the second server gets a 2. Using that 1, the first server can begin generating unique IDs without consulting the sequence generator again. It generates its unique `objectID` values by multiplying the node identifier by one million and then adding an internally incremented number. Thus, the first `objectID` it generates will be 1000000, the second, 1000001, and so on. It will continue until the process ends or

---

* *Clustering* is having multiple processes serving up objects to clients. In such an environment, you would end up with a bottleneck at the central ID generation point if that point were responsible for generating each and every identifier.

it reaches 1999999—whichever comes first. When it reaches one of those points, it goes to the sequence generator for a new node identifier and generates new `objectID` values all over again. It might, for example, get 3 as the next node identifier and thus generate 3000000 as the next `objectID` after it generates 1999999.

You may have noted that you have simply traded one central bottleneck for another. This bottleneck, however, is negligible. After all, a node only grabs a new node identifier at every million new objects or at every start up. Excepting for system startup, the chances of two nodes asking for a node identifier at the same time are quite slim. As a result, the bottleneck is more of a potential than an actual bottleneck.

Another potential downside of the node-identifier approach is that it is capable of rapidly burning unique identifiers. You therefore should tailor the number of object IDs generated before a new node identifier is retrieved to be representative of the uptime of a server. If, for example, a node is likely to be up only five minutes at a time, you want to make sure it is only going to multiply the node identifier by a small number such as 1,000 or 10,000. If the node is up for weeks, months, or years at a time, you can push that number up to 1,000,000 or 10,000,000. With the multiplier set correctly and a 64-bit object ID, it should be virtually impossible to run out of object IDs for most business systems.

You can probably come up with any number of alternate algorithms that accomplish the same task. Example 8-1 provides the code for an abstract `SequenceGenerator` class that implements this algorithm without relying on any specific data store technology. It provides a factory method for accessing a sequence generator specific to whatever data store you might be using.

Example 8-1. A Generic API for Generating Unique Sequences Across Multiple Processes

```
package com.imaginary.lwp;

import com.imaginary.lwp.jdbc.JDBCGenerator;

public abstract class SequenceGenerator {
    static private long             currentNode = -1L;
    static private SequenceGenerator generator   = null;
    static private long             nextID      = -1L;

    /**
     * Generates the next unique value in the sequence
     * having the specified name. By creating a generic
     * sequence generation scheme, we can re-use this
     * scheme for other kinds of sequences.
     * @param seq the name of the desired sequence
     * @return the next value in the specified sequence
     * @throws com.imaginary.lwp.SequenceException
     * the desired sequence could not be generated
     */
```

Example 8-1. A Generic API for Generating Unique Sequences Across Multiple Processes (continued)

```
static public synchronized long generateSequence(String seq)
    throws SequenceException {
    if( generator == null ) {
      // the class name for a concrete sequence generator
      // for example, com.imaginary.lwp.jdbc.JDBCGenerator
        String cname = System.getProperty(LWPProperties.SEQ_GEN);

        if( cname == null ) {
            // use the JDBC generator if none specified
            generator = new JDBCGenerator();
        }
        else {
            try {
                // instantiates a concrete sequence generator
                generator =
                    (SequenceGenerator)Class.forName(cname).newInstance();
            }
            catch( Exception e ) {
                throw new SequenceException(e);
            }
        }
    }
    return generator.generate(seq);
}


/**
 * A convenience method that uses the unique
 * object ID generation algorithm to create unique
 * object IDs without having to go to the data store
 * for every single ID.
 * @return a unique objectID
 * @throws com.imaginary.lwp.SequenceException
 * the next ID could not be determined
 */
static public synchronized long nextObjectID() throws SequenceException {
    // if this is the first object ID after process start,
    // (currentNode == -1)
    // or if we have used up all of our ID's
    // (nextID >= 999999L)
    // we need to go to the data store and get a new one
    if( currentNode == -1L || nextID >= 999999L ) {
        currentNode = generateSequence("node");
        // if currentNode < 1, this is the first ever
        if( currentNode < 1 ) {
            // start at 1, keep all objectID > 0
            nextID = 1;
        }
```

Example 8-1. A Generic API for Generating Unique Sequences Across Multiple Processes (continued)

```
            else {
                nextID = 0;
            }
        }
        else {
            nextID++;
        }
        return ((currentNode*1000000L) + nextID);
    }

    public SequenceGenerator() {
        super();
    }

    /**
     * Generators for specific data storage technologies
     * will implement this method to generate
     * the next value in the sequence.
     * @param seq the sequence to be generated
     * @return the next value in the specified sequence
     * @throws com.imaginary.lwp.SequenceException
     * the sequence could not be generated
     */
    public abstract long generate(String seq) throws SequenceException;
}
```

This class supports any kind of sequence generation, not simply node or `objectID` generation. Anything wanting a unique identifier asks for the next number in the sequence by calling the `generateSequence()` method with the name of the sequence to be generated. This method relies on a concrete implementation of the class to support the actual generation of unique identifiers. It specifically looks to a system property for the name of a `SequenceGenerator` subclass. It instantiates an instance of that class and then calls the `generate()` method to generate the next value in the sequence. By taking this indirect approach, your system can hide any number of sequence generation algorithms behind the same API. Your application is not at all dependent on any particular algorithm.

The `SequenceGenerator` class uses the `generateSequence()` method within a custom method for generating unique `objectID` values, `nextObjectID()`. Whatever your mechanism for generating sequences, the `nextObjectID()` method will use a sequence named `node` to generate node identifiers and the `objectID` values that follow.

The abstract `generate()` method must be implemented by concrete subclasses that provide the actual algorithm for generating sequences. Example 8-2 is a JDBC implementation of the abstract sequence generator from Example 8-1.

Example 8-2. A JDBC Implementation of the SequenceGenerator Abstract Class

```java
package com.imaginary.lwp.jdbc;

import com.imaginary.lwp.SequenceException;
import com.imaginary.lwp.SequenceGenerator;
import java.sql.Connection;
import java.sql.PreparedStatement;
import java.sql.ResultSet;
import java.sql.SQLException;
import javax.naming.Context;
import javax.naming.InitialContext;
import javax.naming.NamingException;
import javax.sql.DataSource;

/**
 * A JDBC-based sequence generator that implements LWP's
 * <CODE>SequenceGenerator</CODE> interface. To use this sequence
 * generator, your database must have the following data model:
 * <PRE>
 * CREATE TABLE SEQGEN(
 *      NAME            VARCHAR(25)     NOT NULL PRIMARY KEY,
 *      NEXT_SEQ        BIGINT          NOT NULL DEFAULT 1,
 *      LASTUPDATETIME BIGINT           NOT NULL);
 *
 * CREATE UNIQUE INDEX SEQGEN_IDX ON SEQGEN(NAME, LASTUPDATETIME);
 * </PRE>
 * <BR>
 * Last modified $Date: 2000/08/08 17:17:20 $
 * @version $Revision: 1.12 $
 * @author George Reese (borg@imaginary.com)
 */
public class JDBCGenerator extends SequenceGenerator {
    /**
     * The SQL to insert a new sequence number in the table.
     */
    static public final String INSERT =
        "INSERT INTO SEQGEN(NAME, NEXT_SEQ, LASTUPDATETIME) " +
        "VALUES(?, ?, ?)";

    /**
     * Selects the next sequence number from the database.
     */
    static public final String SELECT =
        "SELECT NEXT_SEQ, LASTUPDATETIME " +
        "FROM SEQGEN " +
        "WHERE NAME = ?";
```

Example 8-2. A JDBC Implementation of the SequenceGenerator Abstract Class (continued)

```java
/**
 * The SQL to one-up the current sequence number.
 */
static public final String UPDATE =
    "UPDATE SEQGEN " +
    "SET NEXT_SEQ = ?, " +
    "LASTUPDATETIME = ? " +
    "WHERE NAME = ? " +
    "AND LASTUPDATETIME = ?";

/**
 * Creates a new sequence.
 * @param conn the JDBC connection to use
 * @param seq the sequence name
 * @throws java.sql.SQLException a database error occurred
 */
private void createSequence(Connection conn, String seq)
    throws SQLException {
    PreparedStatement stmt = conn.prepareStatement(INSERT);

    stmt.setString(1, seq);
    stmt.setLong(2, 1L);
    stmt.setLong(3, (new java.util.Date()).getTime());
    stmt.executeUpdate();
}

/**
 * Generates a sequence for the specified sequence in accordance with
 * the <CODE>SequenceGenerator</CODE> interface.
 * @param seq the name of the sequence to generate
 * @return the next value in the sequence
 * @throws com.imaginary.lwp.SequenceException an error occurred
 * generating the sequence
 */
public synchronized long generate(String seq) throws SequenceException {
    Connection conn = null;

    try {
        PreparedStatement stmt;
        ResultSet rs;
        String dsn = System.getProperty(LWPProperties.DSN);
        Context ctx = new InitialContext();
        DataSource ds = (DataSource)ctx.lookup(dsn);
        long nid, lut, tut;

        conn = ds.getConnection();
        conn.setAutoCommit(false);
        stmt = conn.prepareStatement(SELECT);
```

Example 8-2. A JDBC Implementation of the SequenceGenerator Abstract Class (continued)

```
stmt.setString(1, seq);
rs = stmt.executeQuery();
if( !rs.next() ) {
    try {
        // if the sequence does not exist, create it
        createSequence(conn, seq);
    }
    catch( SQLException e ) {
        String state = e.getSQLState();

        // if a duplicate was found, retry sequence generation
        // 23505 == duplicate unique index field
        if( state.equals("23505") ) {
            return generate(seq);
        }
        throw new SequenceException(e);
    }
    return 0L;
}
// the next identifier
nid = rs.getLong(1);
// a last update ID to verify concurrency
lut = rs.getLong(2);
tut = (new java.util.Date()).getTime();
if( tut == lut ) {
    tut++;
}
stmt = conn.prepareStatement(UPDATE);
stmt.setLong(1, nid+1);
stmt.setLong(2, tut);
stmt.setString(3, seq);
stmt.setLong(4, lut);
try {
    int rc = stmt.executeUpdate();

    if( rc != 1 ) {
        conn.rollback();
        return generate(seq);
    }
    else {
        conn.commit();
    }
}
catch( SQLException e ) {
    throw new SequenceException(e);
}
return nid;
}
```

Example 8-2. A JDBC Implementation of the SequenceGenerator Abstract Class (continued)

```
    catch( SQLException e ) {
        throw new SequenceException(e);
    }
    catch( NamingException e ) {
        throw new SequenceException(e);
    }
    finally {
        if( conn != null ) {
            try { conn.close(); }
            catch( SQLException e ) { }
        }
    }
  }
}
```

Security

Security for distributed systems falls into two problem domains: *business component security* and *network security*. Proper business component security prevents users from doing things they should not be able to do to the shared business objects. Proper network security, on the other hand, prevents snoopers from intercepting your network traffic and seeing things they should not.

Component Security

Component security involves authenticating the people accessing your system and validating their access requests against a set of established privileges. Distributed computing, especially in a web environment, introduces a few quirks that make component security especially troublesome. Fortunately for EJB users, security is handled for you by your EJB container at every level. You just specify security policies at deployment time.[*]

Authentication

Today applications tend to rely on a weak authentication method based on a user ID/password combination. This authentication method requires you to store a list of users and their passwords in the system. When a client presents a user ID and password, and the specified password matches the password you have in your database for that user ID, your system is considered to have authenticated that user. In other words, your system views the fact that the correct password was provided as proof that the user is who that user claims to be.

---

[*] If you are intent on building your own security system, you should probably use the Java security API as specified in the `java.security` package. A discussion of this package is well beyond the scope of this book.

Upon initial authentication of a user, your system needs a way to keep track of that user, i.e., to keep track of the user's identity across time. One of the greater challenges of security in an Internet environment is that you cannot rely on a constant network connection between the client and server. While a client Java application maintains a constant connection, a servlet-based application uses HTTP and therefore does not maintain a connection. The challenge of identity is thus the challenge of knowing that two HTTP requests are in fact from the same user.

Once you know that the users are who they say they are, you need to validate at each step of the way the type of access they are requesting. To avoid the hassle of reauthentication, you should, upon authentication, provide a client with some sort of token that identifies the user to the system. The client then takes that token and sends it to the server every time it wishes to perform an operation. By placing this burden on the client, you make it responsible for solving the identity problem. Figure 8-1 is an activity diagram that illustrates what needs to happen at a conceptual level.

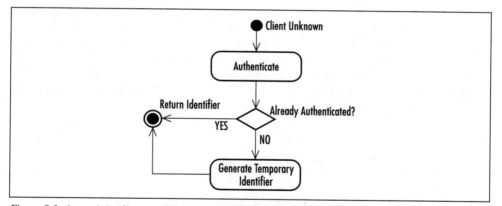

Figure 8-1. An activity diagram illustrating authentication

To avoid tying your infrastructure to a particular technology for storing users and passwords, you need to use a design similar to the one you used for sequence generation. Specifically, the banking application will rely on a generic Authenticator interface that can be implemented by any number of technology-specific classes, and these classes can be assigned to the application at deployment time. Example 8-3 shows the Authenticator interface.

Example 8-3. The Data Store Independent Authenticator Interface

```
package com.imaginary.lwp;

/**
 * Authenticates a user ID/password pair. Different applications may provide
```

Example 8-3. The Data Store Independent Authenticator Interface (continued)

```
 * their own authenticator and specify it in their LWP configuration
 * file using the &quot;imaginary.lwp.authenticator&quot; property.
 * <BR>
 * Last modified $Date: 2000/08/08 17:17:20 $
 * @version $Revision: 1.12 $
 * @author George Reese (borg@imaginary.com)
 */
public interface Authenticator {
    /**
     * Authenticates the specified user ID against the specified
     * password.
     * @param uid the user ID to authenticate
     * @param pw the password to use for authentication
     * @throws com.imaginary.lwp.AuthenticationException the
     * user ID failed to authenticate against the specified password
     */
    void authenticate(String uid, String pw) throws AuthenticationException;
}
```

Just as the `SequenceGenerator` class requires subclasses to implement a `generate()` method to perform the specific sequence generation tasks, the `Authenticator` interface requires subclasses to implement an `authenticate()` method to perform authentication specific to a given technology. The focus of this book is JDBC, so the banking application uses a JDBC implementation of the `Authenticator` interface in Example 8-4.

Example 8-4. A JDBC Implementation of the Authenticator Interface

```
package com.imaginary.lwp.JDBCAuthenticator;

import com.imaginary.lwp.Authenticator;
import com.imaginary.lwp.AuthenticationException;
import com.imaginary.lwp.AuthenticationRole;
import java.sql.Connection;
import java.sql.PreparedStatement;
import java.sql.ResultSet;
import java.sql.SQLException;
import javax.naming.Context;
import javax.naming.InitialContext;
import javax.naming.NamingException;
import javax.sql.DataSource;

/**
 * Implements the <CODE>Authenticator</CODE> interface to authenticate
 * a user ID/password against values stored in a database. This class
 * expects the following table structure:
 * <TABLE>
 * <TR>
```

Example 8-4. A JDBC Implementation of the Authenticator Interface (continued)

```
 * <TH><CODE>LWP_USER</CODE></TH>
 * </TR>
 * <TR>
 * <TD><CODE>USER_ID (VARCHAR(25))</CODE></TD>
 * </TR>
 * <TR>
 * <TD><CODE>PASSWORD (VARCHAR(25))</CODE></TD>
 * </TR>
 * </TABLE>
 * If you want a more complex authentication scheme, you should
 * write your own <CODE>Authenticator</CODE> implementation.
 * <BR>
 * Last modified $Date: 2000/08/08 17:17:20 $
 * @version $Revision: 1.12 $
 * @author George Reese (borg@imaginary.com)
 */
public class JDBCAuthenticator implements Authenticator {
    /**
     * The SQL SELECT statement.
     */
    static public final String SELECT =
        "SELECT USER_ID, PASSWORD FROM LWP_USER WHERE USER_ID = ?";

    /**
     * Authenticates the specified user ID against the specified
     * password.
     * @param uid the user ID to authenticate
     * @param pw the password to use for authentication
     * @throws com.imaginary.lwp.AuthenticationException the
     * user ID failed to authenticate against the specified password
     */
    public void authenticate(String uid, String pw)
        throws AuthenticationException {
        Connection conn = null;

        try {
            String dsn = System.getProperty(LWPProperties.DSN);
            Context ctx = new InitialContext();
            DataSource ds = (DataSource)ctx.lookup(dsn);
            PreparedStatement stmt;
            String actual;
            ResultSet rs;

            conn = ds.getConnection();
            stmt = conn.prepareStatement(SELECT);
            stmt.setString(1, uid);
            rs = stmt.executeQuery();
            if( !rs.next() ) {
```

Example 8-4. A JDBC Implementation of the Authenticator Interface (continued)

```
                throw new AuthenticationException("Invalid user ID or " +
                                              "password.");
            }
            actual = rs.getString(1);
            if( rs.wasNull() ) {
                throw new AuthenticationException("No password "+
                                                    "specified for " +
                                    uid);
            }
            if( !actual.equals(pw) ) {
                throw new AuthenticationException("Invalid user ID or " +
                                              "password.");
            }
        }
        catch( SQLException e ) {
            e.printStackTrace();
            throw new AuthenticationException(e);
        }
        catch( NamingException e ) {
            e.printStackTrace();
            throw new AuthenticationException(e);
        }
        finally {
            if( conn != null ) {
                try { conn.close(); }
                catch( SQLException e ) { }
            }
        }
    }
}
```

You should be concerned that this example relies on a data model with unencrypted passwords. Of course, it does not have to. Such databases as MySQL support the concept of password fields so that you do not have to store unencrypted passwords. Relying on such features, however, ties you to specific database engines. A better solution is to encrypt passwords before you store them in the database. The book *Java Cryptography* by Jonathan Knudsen (O'Reilly & Associates) provides an in-depth discussion of encrypting all kinds of data in Java.

Once a client is authenticated, it needs an identity token that it can use for future calls to the server. A primary goal of an identity token is to avoid continuous reauthentication of a client. If you are familiar with web development, an identity token is kind of like a cookie—without the privacy concerns. A good identity token has two requirements:

- It must live for only the lifetime of the client session.

- It must not be forgeable.

To support the banking application, you will use an identifier token class called `Identifier`. Once a person is successfully authenticated, the server generates and stores a unique `Identifier` instance. It also hands the client a copy of this instance. Whenever a client makes a call to the server, it passes its copy to the server. If the two copies match, the client is considered authenticated for that method call. After a certain amount of inactivity, the `Identifier` is invalidated, and the client must login again to generate a new `Identifier`.

The important security feature here is that the server associates a temporary unique number with a user ID. If an `Identifier` comes in when the unique number does not match the currently valid unique number, the operation is rejected. The only way for someone to forge access is to snoop, grab the entire serialized `Identifier`, and use it before the session is invalidated. Forgery is impossible using such encryption as SSL.

Because the `Identifier` instances expire, they should not live much longer than the expected lifetime of the client session they support. The hard part is making the identifier unforgable. In order to do that, the `Identifier` class has a key field that gets randomly generated upon login. To make it truly secure, you use Java's `java.security.SecureRandom` class. The actual code for this class is included in the examples on this book's web site at *http://www.oreilly.com/catalog/jdbc2*.

Validation

The picture you should have now is of a client that logs in to a server, gets an `Identifier` instance, and then passes it to every method it calls on the server. Under this component model, RMI remote interfaces must be written with every method accepting an `Identifier` as one of its arguments. As you will see when you get to the actual banking classes, I make the `Identifier` the first argument to every method. In a shared environment like the banking application, you probably need to move beyond authentication to validation. In other words, you need to not only make sure that the client represents who it claims to represent, but also that that person can actually perform the operation in bquestion.

The `Identifier` class provides static methods that enable a business object to check if a particular `Identifier` supports a specific operation. These methods come in the form of `validateXXX()` for which XXX is the name of an operation. These `validateXXX()` methods can then be coded to perform some sort of lookup in an access control list. The implementation class for the account entity, for example, might have a method `getBalance()` that will look like this:

```
public double getBalance(Identifier id) {
    if( !Identifier.validateRead(id, this) ) {
        throw new IllegalReadException();
    }
    return balance;
}
```

To simplify things, however, you will support a `prepareRead()` method in a
`BaseEntity` that performs the check for any read operation:

```
protected void prepareRead(Identifier id) {
    if( !Identifier.validateRead(id, this) ) {
        throw new IllegalReadException();
    }
}
```

As a result, `getBalance()` can be simplified:

```
public double getBalance(Identifier id) {
    // this will throw a runtime exception if access
    // is disallowed
    prepareRead(id);
    return balance;
}
```

While this simplification may appear trivial, it gains importance when the
`prepareXXX()` methods become larger vehicles for managing transactions.
Throughout the rest of this book, I will use a class called `BaseEntity` that provides convenience methods to be called from higher level methods.

Network Security

The default network communication in RMI is provided by the standard `java.
net.Socket` class. This is the same class you might use for non-RMI TCP/IP net-
work communication. It will send data across the network unchanged from its
original form. As long as you are not concerned with what prying eyes might see,
this state of affairs will work just fine for you.

Encrypting your network communications actually involves very few changes to the
way you write application code. It is largely a matter of installing a custom socket
factory. I will briefly outline the steps here required to install a custom socket
factory for RMI. A more detailed discussion of these issues can be found in *Java
Network Programming* by Elliotte Rusty Harold (O'Reilly & Associates).

Your first task is to decide what sort of socket will handle your network communications. In fact, this discussion is not limited to helping you encrypt your RMI
communications. It will also help you perform such things as compression of large
amounts of binary data. JDK 1.2 lets you support different sockets for different
objects, so the choice of which socket to use depends very much on the type of
data coming in and out of an object.

For encryption, you will likely want to use a secure socket layer (SSL) socket.
Unfortunately, Java does not ship with any SSL socket implementations. You have
to buy these from third-party vendors.

Next, you need to write an implementation of java.rmi.server.
RMIClientSocketFactory* to hand out the client sockets you wish to use. This
pattern is an excellent example of the factory design pattern mentioned in the
previous chapter. By relying on a class that constructs sockets rather than relying
on direct instantiation of the sockets themselves, you'll find that the sky is the limit
for the type of sockets you can use for your RMI communications. Example 8-5
shows a custom socket factory for creating a fictional SSLClientSocket.

Example 8-5. A Custom Client Socket Factory for RMI

```
import java.io.IOException;
import java.io.Serializable;
import java.net.Socket;
import java.rmi.server.RMIClientSocketFactory;

public class SSLClientSocketFactory
implements RMIClientSocketFactory, Serializable {
    public Socket createSocket(String h, int p)
    throws IOException  {
        return new SSLSocket(h, p);
    }
}
```

Naturally, you also have to write a server socket factory that implements java.
rmi.server.RMIServerSocketFactory. Example 8-6 is an example of an RMI
server socket factory.

Example 8-6. A Factory for Generating Server SSL Sockets

```
import java.io.IOException;
import java.io.Serializable;
import java.net.Socket;
import java.rmi.server.RMIServerSocketFactory;

public class SSLServerSocketFactory
implements RMIServerSocketFactory, Serializable {
    public ServerSocket createServerSocket(int p)
        throws IOException  {
        return new SSLServerSocket(p);
    }
}
```

---

* If you are lucky, the custom socket package you use will ship with RMI client and server socket factories,
so that you do not need to write them yourself.

After all this work, you still have not touched any application code. The final step is when you integrate your custom sockets into your application. Back in Chapter 6, you saw how RMI classes can export themselves either by extending `UnicastRemoteObject` or calling `UnicastRemoteObject.exportObject()`. The constructor for `UnicastRemoteObject` and the static method `exportObject()` both have alternate signatures that enable you to provide a custom socket factory for a specific object.

In Chapter 6, there was a `BallImpl` object that extended `UnicastRemoteObject`. If you wanted to install your SSL socket factories from this chapter, you would simply change the constructor to look like this:

```
public Ball() throws RemoteException {
    super(0,
        new SSLClientSocketFactory(),
        new SSLServerSocketFactory());
}
```

When RMI needs to create a sockets to handle its network communications for the ball component, it will now use these factory classes to generate those sockets instead of the normal socket factories.

Database Security

In a multitier environment, you generally put together multiple technologies with their own authentication and validation mechanisms. You might, for example, have EJB component authentication and validation in the middle tier, but also have database authentication and validation in the data storage tier. A servlet environment might even compound that with web server security.

Multitier applications generally grant a single user ID/password to the middle tier application server. The database trusts that the application server properly manages security. Other tools accessing that same database use different user ID and password combinations to distinguish them and their access rights. Individual users, in turn, are managed either at the web server or application server layer.

A web-based application, for example, could use the web server to manage which users can see which web pages. Those web pages present only the screens containing data a specific user is allowed to see or edit. The web server, in turn, will use a single user ID and password to authenticate itself with the application server. It does not matter who the actual end user is. Similarly, the application server will support access by a handful of different client applications authenticated by user ID/password combinations on a per-client application basis. Finally, the application server will use a single user ID/password pair for all database access.

Transactions

One of the most important features of EJB is transaction management. Whether you have a simple two-tier application or a complex three-tier application, if you have a database in the mix, you have to worry about transactions. Transactions were discussed in the context of JDBC in both Chapter 3, *Introduction to JDBC*, and Chapter 4, *Advanced JDBC*. Transactions in a three-tier environment are much more complex, but they face many of the same issues. For example, if you perform a transfer from a savings account object to a checking account object, you want to make sure that a failure at any point in that transaction results in a return to the original state of affairs. For example, if the savings account successfully debits itself but the crediting of the checking account fails, the savings account needs to get back the amount debited.

Transaction management at the distributed component level means worrying about a lot of details in the code for every single transaction; a mistake in any one of those details can place the system permanently in an inconsistent state. At the very least, a transaction in a distributed component environment needs to do the following:*

- Recognize when a transaction begins.

- Track changes that occur during a transaction.

- Lock down the modified objects against modification by other transactions for the duration of the transaction.

- Recognize when the transaction ends.

- Notify the persistence library that changes need to be saved and save them within a single data store transaction.

- Commit or roll back the data store transaction.

- Commit or roll back changes to the business objects.

- Unlock the locked objects so that they may be accessed again for subsequent transactions.

On top of this, components need to recognize when the transaction management has failed. In other words, once a change has been made to an object, it needs to expect a commit or rollback. If it does not receive one in a reasonable amount of time, it needs to roll itself back.

The best solution to the problem of transaction management is to use an infrastructure that manages it all for you, such as Enterprise JavaBeans.† If EJB is not an option, then you should attempt to write a shared library that captures as many of

---

* Even more is required to support transactions across multiple data sources, also called *two-phase commits*.

† I want to emphasize that I am not recommending writing your own transaction management system. I am covering these issues because they are important to understanding distributed database application programming. EJB is much simpler and more robust than what I present here in this book.

the details of transaction management as is possible. The solution is a
`Transaction` object that monitors a given transaction. You will leave the burden
of determining when a transaction begins and ends to the application developer,
but some tools in the `Transaction` class will be provided to make that task easier.
The `Transaction` class should handle everything else.*

Transaction Boundaries

The first attack on transaction-boundary recognition might be to have code that
looks like this:

```
public void debit(Identifier id, double amt) {
    // get a transaction
    Transaction trans = Transaction.getCurrent(id);

    trans.begin();
    // perform the application logic
    amount -= amt;
    trans.end();
}
```

One problem is that the `debit()` method cannot be reused in the context of
another transaction. You cannot, for example, call the `debit()` method from a
`transfer()` method because the `debit()` method attempts to end the transaction. The transaction will no longer be valid when you attempt to call `credit()` in
the other account!

A more flexible approach to transaction management would enable the developer
to write the same code in every single transactional method without worrying
about the context the method is being called in. Consider this modified version of
the `debit()` method:

```
public void debit(Identifier id, double amt)
throws TransactionException {
    Transaction trans = Transaction.getCurrent(id);
    boolean ip = trans.isInProcess();

    if( !ip ) {
        trans.begin();
    }
    amount -= amt;
    if( !ip ) {
        trans.end();
    }
}
```

---

* EJB does not require you to worry about transaction boundaries. It recognizes transaction boundaries
through a very complex transaction management mechanism. For a detailed discussion of EJB transaction management, look at *Enterprise JavaBeans* by Richard Monson-Haefel (O'Reilly & Associates).

If the application developer follows this paradigm for all method calls, it will not matter whether the method were called as part of a greater transaction or as its own transaction. The application developer has one more problem to worry about: exceptions. The debit method can only encounter Error conditions, so it may not seem like much of a concern. Consider the transfer() method, however:

```
public void transfer(Identifier id, Account a, Account b, double amt)
throws TransactionException {
    Transaction trans = Transaction.getCurrent(id);
    boolean ip = trans.isInProcess();
    boolean success = false;

    if( !ip ) {
        trans.begin();
    }
    try {
        a.debit(id, amt);
        b.credit(id, amt);
        success = true;
    }
    finally {
        // some exception may have occurred, rollback if it did
        if( success ) {
            if( !ip ) {
                trans.end();
            }
        }
        else if( !ip ) {
            try { trans.rollback(); }
            catch( Exception e ) { }
        }
    }
}
```

The success flag is made true only when the entire set of business logic has completed. Because the business logic is captured in a try block, any exception is certain to trigger a rollback if the business logic does not complete for any reason whatsoever, *and* this method is where the transaction began. The code could include a catch() block if you wanted special handling to occur for specific exceptions, but in this case there is no reason to catch particular exceptions.

Tracking Changes

The code for the debit() and transfer() methods is missing some of the security discussed earlier in the chapter; namely, it does not check with the Identifier class to see if the update is valid. I intentionally left this part out since you have another issue needs addressing: tracking changes.

For the `Transaction` class to intelligently manage transactional operations, it needs to know which objects are being created, modified, or deleted. You can take advantage of the `prepareXXX()` methods mentioned earlier to mark an object as modified in a particular way for a given transaction.

The security code alone might look something like this:

```
if( !Identifier.validateUpdate(id, this) ) {
    throw new ValidationException("Illegal access!");
}
```

By combining the change tracking code in a single method in the `BaseEntity` class, you would end up with code like this:

```
protected synchronized void prepareUpdate(Identifier id)
throws TransactionException {
    Transaction trans = Transaction.getCurrent(id);

    if( !Identifier.validateUpdate(id, this) ) {
        throw new ValidationException("Illegal access!");
    }
    // associate this change with the current
    // transaction
    trans.prepareUpdate(this);
}
```

The first part of this method performs the security check. The second part notifies the current transaction that the object has been modified by calling the `prepareUpdate()` method. The `debit()` method can now look like this:

```
public void debit(Identifier id, double amt)
throws TransactionException {
    Transaction trans = Transaction.getCurrent(id);
    boolean ip = trans.isInProcess();
    boolean success = false;

    if( !ip ) {
        trans.begin();
    }
    try {
        // security check and change notification
        prepareUpdate(id);
        amount -= amt;
        success = true;
    }
    finally {
        if( success ) {
            if( !ip ) {
                trans.end();
            }
        }
    }
```

```
        else {
            try { trans.rollback(); }
            catch( Exception e ) { }
        }
    }
}
```

Certainly there is a lot more code in that method than the core business logic of
amount -= amt, but it is code that can exist in each transactional method without the coder having to make a lot of transaction-based coding decisions. Because
the prepareUpdate() tells the transaction that the account has been modified,
the transaction can add it to a list of modified objects associated with the transaction. When you end the transaction, the Transaction class then goes through all
of the modified objects and makes sure that their new state is saved to the persistent data store. Among the complexities the Transaction class needs to handle
here is the complexity of a transaction that makes a change to an object and
deletes it. The Transaction class can make sure that only the delete operation is
sent to the persistent data store.

Other Transaction Management Issues

Once a transaction has been told it is over, it needs to save the current state of the
objects that took part in the transaction to the persistent data store. You will cover
the actual saving of the state to a relational database in Chapter 9. What you need
to think about at this point is that the transaction object be able to track which
objects have changed and what sort of changes occurred. Once the transaction
ends, it needs to tell the persistence mechanism to insert, update, or delete the
object in the data store. The prepareUpdate() method in the BaseEntity class
took care of that for us.

The only unaddressed piece other than persistence is making sure that two transactions do not interfere with each other. An example of such a situation might be a
transaction for which I am in the bank withdrawing cash and my wife is at the ATM
doing a transfer. We have $100 in our checking account, and we are both attempt-
ing to withdraw $75. Obviously, we should not both be able to succeed. The transac-
tion management infrastructure should make sure that does not happen.

We can make sure only one transaction is touching an object at a time by adding
the following code to the prepareUpdate() method just after the security check:

```
if( transaction != null ) {
    if( !trans.equals(transaction) ) {
        throw new TransactionException("Illegal " +
                "concurrent transactions!");
    }
}
```

```
else {
    transaction = trans;
}
```

By throwing an exception, this prevents the system from ending up in a situation called a *deadlock*, in which one transaction waits on a lock held by another, while that other transaction waits on a lock held by the first. Of course the `BaseEntity` also needs to set the transaction to null in its `commit()` and `rollback()` implementations.

Lookups and Searches

Before a client can make any changes to an object, it needs to find that object. There are three scenarios for getting a reference to a distributed component:

- Looking it up by its unique identifier
- Searching for it based on a set of criteria
- Asking another related component for a reference to it

The last scenario is the simplest and begs the question of the other two. Specifically, given a reference to a `Customer` component, you should be able to get all of that `Customer`'s `Account` objects. How did you get a reference to that `Customer` in the first place?

EJB uses a kind of meta-component called a *home* to manage operations on a component as a class, including lookups, searches, and creates. Whether you call it a home or something else, a distributed database application needs some way to get access to the business objects stored on the server. You will take advantage of the home metaphor, but you'll put a new spin on it.

Getting a reference to an object using its unique identifier is fairly simple. A `find()` method in the home accepts an `Identifier` and an `objectID` as parameters and returns a reference to the component identified by that `objectID`:

```
public abstract Account find(Identifier id,
                             long oid)
    throws FindException;
```

Using the persistence library that will be discussed in Chapter 9, you can then search the persistence store for an object that has the specified `objectID`.

Performing searches on criteria other than a unique identifier gets more complex. First, because the criteria may not identify an object instance uniquely, you need to handle a collection of those objects. Second, the number of search criteria combinations can become overwhelming. Whereas one client screen may want to search on balance and customer last names, other client screens may wish to search on social security numbers, gender, or marital status. A solid business component needs to be able to support all these permutations.

EJB actually encounters serious problems with these issues. Under the EJB component model, any bean has a home interface responsible for the creation of new instances of that component, destroying instances of it, and performing searches. When a client performs a search that returns a collection, most EJB implementations return a Java `Enumeration` or `Collection` that contains the full set of beans matching the specified criteria. Unfortunately, searches that return thousands or millions of records cause serious performance problems for EJB. In addition, EJB requires you to specify a distinct `find()` method for each combination of search criteria you wish to offer. To address these issues, you will use a generic search mechanism in the banking application that returns a specialized collection.*

The core of your searching library is a class called `SearchCriteria`. It can represent any arbitrary set of search criteria—independent of persistence technology—so the home can pass those search criteria to a persistence engine for interpretation. The `AccountHome` class thus has a single method for searches on arbitrary criteria:

```
public abstract Collection find(Identifier id,
                                SearchCriteria sc)
throws FindException;
```

The task of the `SearchCriteria` class is to associate attributes with values via some sort of operator. For example, if you want to search for all accounts with a balance of less than $100, the `SearchCriteria` class would have "balance" as the attribute, "<" as the operator, and 100.00 as the value. Such a triplet is encapsulated in a class called `SearchBinding`. The `SearchCriteria` ties multiple bindings together with an `AND` or `OR`. You can thus perform complex queries joining many bindings. Finally, a `SearchCriteria` is itself a `SearchBinding`. Using this feature, a person can perform a search that groups bindings together. Figure 8-2 shows how the following SQL search matches with a `SearchCriteria` instance:

```
"SELECT objectID FROM Account WHERE balance > 100 OR (openDate > '23-MAR-2000' AND
openDate < '31-MAR-2000')"
```

In Chapter 9, I will show how the persistence library actually implements searching by taking a `SearchCriteria` instance and turning it into a SQL query.

I am still begging the question as to how you get a reference to a home object in the first place. JNDI enters the picture here. When an application is deployed, the system administrator enters home objects into a JNDI-supported directory so that clients can perform a JNDI lookup for the home.

---

* The next release of the EJB specification will introduce a specialized query language, which should address some failings in its searching API.

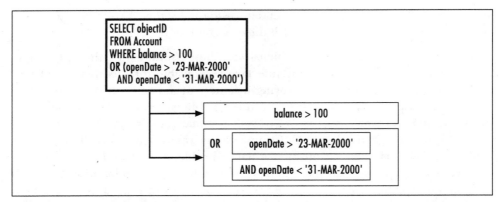

Figure 8-2. A graphic illustration of how bindings form a search criteria instance

Entity Relationships

Relationships among entities is one of the most complex problems to handle in the object-oriented world. Imagine a huge film server such as the Internet Movie Database (IMDB). A film can have many directors and actors. Each director and actor can, in turn, be related to many films. If your application restored a film from its data store with all of its relationships intact, the act of loading a single film would cause a huge amount of data—most of which you are definitely not interested in—to load into memory. An enterprise system therefore needs to be much smarter about managing entity relationships than the use of simple entity attributes.

Enterprise JavaBeans does not directly address the problem of entity relationships. The problems you face for the banking application are therefore the same problems you would face if you were using EJB. As a result, the solutions discussed in this section are directly applicable to an Enterprise JavaBean system.

A crude solution to the problem is to store the unique identifiers for related entities instead of the entities themselves; after all, this is what you do in the database. In other words, a bank account would have a `customerID` instead of a `Customer` attribute. The `Account` component would load the `Customer` into memory using the `customerID` only when it needed the reference.

Unfortunately, this solution is both cumbersome and not very object-oriented. It is cumbersome because the `Account` coder is forced to deal with the `Customer` relationship at two levels: as a unique identifier and as a entity component. This treatment of the same concept using two different representations opens the code up to error. The more serious architectural problem, however, is the move away from the object metaphor. The relationship being modeled in the code is no longer the relationship between a `Customer` and an `Account`, but between a `Customer` and a number.

A better solution is an object placeholder that looks to clients like the actual object it represents but does not contain all data associated with the actual object it represents. I call this approach a *façade*.* When a façade first comes into being, it knows only the unique identifier of the component it serves. It loads that component only if a method call is made on the façade. An entity can thus store its relationships with other entities as façades and treat them as if they were the real components.

Façades

A good façade can do much more than save you the effort of loading components. It can help performance by caching component attributes. The first benefit of caching attributes is the minimization of network calls to the component. If, for example, a client had a `JTable` with a list of `Account` components, it would make a network call to each account for each value stored in the table any time a redraw is requested. This chatty behavior results in a very slow GUI. By using façades and caching data in the façades, calls to get data from an account beyond the initial calls become local.

A façade can also poll its associated entity component to make sure nothing has changed. It can then integrate with the Swing event model on a client by supporting `PropertyChangeEvent` occurrences. When something does change, the façade can throw a `PropertyChangeEvent`. If you are not familiar with property change events, remember that they are a key part of the JavaBeans model. The idea is that objects can register themselves as being interested in changes that occur to the bound properties of other objects, a.k.a. beans. When a change occurs in a target object, it fires a `PropertyChangeEvent` that notifies all listening objects of the change. I will cover the Swing event model and how façades support it in detail in Chapter 10.

Example 8-7 shows the base class for a façade from which component-specific façades can be built. At its heart is the method `reconnect()`. This method performs a lookup for the entity behind this façade when circumstances demand it.

Example 8-7. A Generic Façade for Entity Components

```
package com.imaginary.lwp;

import java.beans.PropertyChangeEvent;
import java.beans.PropertyChangeListener;
import java.io.Serializable;
```

---

* Façades are actually an implementation of the classic "proxy" pattern, not the classic "façade" pattern. More specifically, they help implement the distributed listener pattern from earlier in the book. I call them façades because they are much more than simple proxies and are, in fact, façades in the more colloquial dictionary sense.

Example 8-7. A Generic Façade for Entity Components (continued)

```java
import java.net.MalformedURLException;
import java.rmi.Naming;
import java.rmi.NotBoundException;
import java.rmi.RemoteException;
import java.util.ArrayList;
import java.util.HashMap;
import java.util.Iterator;

/**
 * The base class for all façade objects. This class
 * captures all functionality common to façades. Subclasses
 * should be written for each entity class.
 */
public abstract class BaseFacade implements Serializable {
    private           HashMap            cache          = new HashMap();
    private           Entity             entity         = null;
    private           Home               home           = null;
    private transient ArrayList listeners    =
                                              new ArrayList();
    private           String             lastUpdateID   = null;
    private           long               lastUpdateTime = -1L;
    private           long               objectID       = -1L;

    public BaseFacade() {
        super();
    }

    /**
     * Constructs a new façade that represents the entity
     * identified by the specified object identifier.
     * @param oid the unique identifier of the associated entity
     */
    public BaseFacade(long oid) {
        super();
        objectID = oid;
    }

    /**
     * Constructs a new façade that represents the specified
     * entity object.
     * @param ent the entity being represented
     * @throws java.rmi.RemoteException the entity is inaccessible
     */
    public BaseFacade(Entity ent) throws RemoteException {
        super();
        entity = ent;
```

Example 8-7. A Generic Façade for Entity Components (continued)

```java
        objectID = entity.getObjectID();
    }

    /**
     * Supports the JavaBeans event model by allowing other
     * objects to know when a change has occurred in this object.
     * @param l the object listening to this façade
     */
    public void addPropertyChangeListener(PropertyChangeListener l) {
        if( listeners == null ) {
            listeners = new ArrayList();
        }
        listeners.add(l);
    }

    /**
     * Enables an object to listen for changes in a particular
     * property in this façade. This implementation does
     * not currently care what property the listeners are listening for.
     * @param p the property, this is ignored
     * @param l the object listening to this façade
     */
    public void addPropertyChangeListener(String p, PropertyChangeListener l) {
        if( listeners == null ) {
            listeners = new ArrayList();
        }
        listeners.add(l);
    }

    /**
     * Assigns this façade to support the entity identified
     * by the specific object identifier.
     * @param oid the unique object identifier
     */
    public void assign(long oid) {
        if( objectID != -1L ) {
            throw new ReferenceReuseException("Reference already assigned.");
        }
        else {
            objectID = oid;
        }
    }

    public void assign(long oid, Entity ent) {
        assign(oid);
        entity = ent;
    }
```

Example 8-7. A Generic Façade for Entity Components (continued)

```java
public void assign(long oid, HashMap vals) {
    assign(oid);
}


/**
 * Determines whether or not the specified attribute has
 * been cached.
 * @param attr the name of the attribute to test
 * @return true if the attribute has been cached
 */
protected boolean contains(String attr) {
    return cache.containsKey(attr);
}


// two are equal if they have the same objectID
public boolean equals(Object ob) {
    if( ob instanceof BaseReference ) {
        BaseReference ref = (BaseReference)ob;

        return (ref.getObjectID() == getObjectID());
    }
    else {
        return false;
    }
}


// fires a property change event
protected void firePropertyChange() {
    firePropertyChange(new PropertyChangeEvent(this, null, null, null));
}


protected void firePropertyChange(PropertyChangeEvent evt) {
    Iterator it;

    if( listeners == null ) {
        return;
    }
    it = listeners.iterator();
    while( it.hasNext() ) {
        PropertyChangeListener l = (PropertyChangeListener)it.next();

        l.propertyChange(evt);
    }
}


/**
 * Provides the cached value for the specified attribute.
 * This method will return null if the value has not been
```

Example 8-7. A Generic Façade for Entity Components (continued)

```java
     * cached, so a check to contains() should be made first.
     * @param attr the name of the attribute to get
     * @return the value of the cached attribute
     */
    protected Object get(String attr) {
        return cache.get(attr);
    }


    // Provides the entity behind this reference.
    public Entity getEntity() throws RemoteException {
        if( entity == null ) {
            reconnect();
        }
        return entity;
    }


    // Provides the last update ID.
    public String getLastUpdateID() throws RemoteException {
        if( lastUpdateID == null ) {
            try {
                lastUpdateID = getEntity().getLastUpdateID();
            }
            catch( RemoteException e ) {
                reconnect();
                lastUpdateID = getEntity().getLastUpdateID();
            }
        }
        return lastUpdateID;
    }


    // Provides the timestamp from the last update.
    public long getLastUpdateTime() throws RemoteException {
        if( lastUpdateTime == -1L ) {
            try {
                lastUpdateTime = getEntity().getLastUpdateTime();
            }
            catch( RemoteException e ) {
                reconnect();
                lastUpdateTime = getEntity().getLastUpdateTime();
            }
        }
        return lastUpdateTime;
    }


    // Provides the unique object identifier.
    public long getObjectID() {
        return objectID;
    }
```

Example 8-7. A Generic Façade for Entity Components (continued)

```java
public int hashCode() {
    Long l = new Long(getObjectID());

    return l.hashCode();
}

public boolean hasListeners(String prop) {
    if( listeners == null ) {
        return false;
    }
    if( listeners.size() > 0 ) {
        return true;
    }
    else {
        return false;
    }
}

/**
 * Inserts the specified attribute and value into the
 * object cache.
 * @param attr the name of the attribute
 * @param val the value to be associated with the attribute
 */
protected void put(String attr, Object val) {
    cache.put(attr, val);
}

/**
 * This method provides a level of failover support and
 * initializes entity polling. This method is called
 * only when the façade has determined it has to load
 * the associated entity.
 * @throws java.rmi.RemoteException the server is inaccessible
 */
protected void reconnect() throws RemoteException {
    final BaseFacade ref = this;
    Thread t;

    // the home object is used to find entities; load it if null
    if( home == null ) {
        String url = System.getProperty(LWPProperties.RMI_URL);
        ObjectServer svr;

        try {
            // the ObjectServer is an RMI object that provides homes
            svr = (ObjectServer)Naming.lookup(url);
        }
```

Example 8-7. A Generic Façade for Entity Components (continued)

```
            catch( MalformedURLException e ) {
                throw new RemoteException(e.getMessage());
            }
            catch( NotBoundException e ) {
                throw new RemoteException(e.getMessage());
            }
            try {
                // use the client identifier for doing a lookup
                Identifier id = Identifier.currentIdentifier();

                // if null, this is happening on the server
                // in that case, use a special server ID
                if( id == null ) {
                    id = Identifier.getServerID();
                }
              // ask the server for the home for this class
                home = (Home)svr.lookup(id, getClass().getName());
            }
            catch( LWPException e ) {
                throw new RemoteException(e.getMessage());
            }
        }
        try {
            Identifier id = Identifier.currentIdentifier();

            // look up the entity
            entity = home.findByObjectID(id, objectID);
            lastUpdateID = entity.getLastUpdateID();
            lastUpdateTime = entity.getLastUpdateTime();
        }
        catch( PersistenceException e ) {
            throw new RemoteException(e.getMessage());
        }
        catch( FindException e ) {
            throw new RemoteException(e.getMessage());
        }
        catch( RemoteException e ) {
            // give it a second chance
            e.printStackTrace();
            String url = System.getProperty(LWPProperties.RMI_URL);
            ObjectServer svr;

            try {
                svr = (ObjectServer)Naming.lookup(url);
            }
            catch( MalformedURLException salt ) {
                throw new RemoteException(salt.getMessage());
            }
```

Example 8-7. A Generic Façade for Entity Components (continued)

```
    catch( NotBoundException salt ) {
        throw new RemoteException(salt.getMessage());
    }
    try {
        Identifier id = Identifier.currentIdentifier();

        if( id == null ) {
            id = Identifier.getServerID();
        }
        home = (Home)svr.lookup(id, getClass().getName());
        entity = home.findByObjectID(id, objectID);
        lastUpdateID = entity.getLastUpdateID();
        lastUpdateTime = entity.getLastUpdateTime();
    }
    catch( LookupException salt ) {
        throw new RemoteException(salt.getMessage());
    }
    catch( PersistenceException salt ) {
        throw new RemoteException(salt.getMessage());
    }
    catch( FindException salt ) {
        throw new RemoteException(salt.getMessage());
    }
}
// With the entity loaded, begin polling for changes.
t = new Thread() {
    public void run() {
        while( true ) {
            synchronized( ref ) {
                if( entity == null ) {
                    return;
                }
                try {
                    if( lastUpdateTime == -1L ) {
                        lastUpdateTime = entity.getLastUpdateTime();
                    }
                    if( entity.isChanged(lastUpdateTime) ) {
                        lastUpdateTime = entity.getLastUpdateTime();
                        lastUpdateID = entity.getLastUpdateID();
                        firePropertyChange();
                    }
                }
                catch( RemoteException e ) {
                    // this will force a reload
                    entity = null;
                    return;
                }
            }
```

Example 8-7. A Generic Façade for Entity Components (continued)

```
                        try { Thread.sleep(30000); }
                        catch( InterruptedException e ) { }
                    }
                }
            };
            t.setPriority(Thread.MIN_PRIORITY);
            t.start();
        }

        public void removePropertyChangeListener(PropertyChangeListener l) {
            if( listeners == null ) {
                return;
            }
            listeners.remove(l);
        }

        public void removePropertyChangeListener(String p,
                                        PropertyChangeListener l) {
            if( listeners == null ) {
                return;
            }
            listeners.remove(l);
        }

        public synchronized void reset() {
            cache.clear();
            lastUpdateTime = -1L;
            lastUpdateID = null;
        }
    }
}
```

Collections

One-to-one relationships are clearly simplified with the use of façades. One-to-many and many-to-many relationships complicate things. How do you handle the modeling of a machine with one million parts?

You almost never want to send all one million parts across the network. When you do, users on the other end would certainly prefer not to wait for all one million parts to traverse the network before they work with the first part or even see any progress on the method call. This problem is more common when performing finds using home objects, since it is rare that an entity will have a one-to-one million relationship. It is all too common that people issue queries that will return one million rows. The standard Java Collections API does not address this problem.

The answer is a custom collection that hands the client elements in the collection just before the client goes to work with that row. It could grab the first 100 hits before it returns and then send the client back elements in groups of 100 as the client is approaching the point when it needs them. If the client uses only the first 100 results, at most 200 elements will get sent across the network. The other 999800 elements will sit on the server. The code supporting this book (*ftp://ftp.oreilly.com/pub/examples/java/jdbc*) comes with just such a collection.

9

Persistence

Objects contain the possibility of all situations.
—Ludwig Wittgenstein
Tractatus Logico Philisophicus

If RAM were unlimited and computers never shut down, you would now have all of the tools you need to finish the server side of the banking application. You cannnot, however, afford to have all your data in memory all of the time; computers shut down far too often, sometimes by design, sometimes by error. You need to grant your business objects a certain level of immortality, to make them persist beyond the lifecycle of the process in which they are created.

Persistence is the act of making the state of an application stretch through the end of this process instance of the application to the next. In order to make an application persist, its state needs to be recorded in a data store that can survive computer shutdowns and crashes. The most common persistence tool is by far the relational database—and for Java, that means JDBC.

Database Transactions

Transactions appear throughout this book. In the first half of this book, you saw how JDBC manages transaction isolation levels, commits, and rollbacks. Chapter 8, *Distributed Component Models*, spoke of component-level transactions. You now need to tie the two together at the persistence layer.

The component transaction choreographs a persistence operation. When that transaction is notified that it is complete, it creates a persistence transaction—in your case, a JDBC transaction—and tells each object modified in the business transaction to insert, update, or delete itself in the persistent store. The persistence transaction makes sure all data store accesses take place within a single data store transaction. In the case of JDBC, the persistence subsystem is responsible for making sure all of the objects are saved using the same `Connection` object and committed at the end.

The component model needs to remain impartial about the kind of persistence you use. To preserve this agnosticism, it uses a generic `Transaction` object to represent a component-level transaction. Besides sounding really cool, this agnosticism is actually intuitive once you step back and think about what it is to be an account or a customer. There is nothing about the concept of a bank account that says, "I save to a relational database." Instead, within the context of your application, you know that a bank account is something you wish to persist across time. How it persists is a technological detail that should not be melded into the essence of a bank account.

The core of a solid persistence library contains no code specific to any data storage type. This means, of course, that it does not use any of the JDBC API you learned in the first section of the book. Figure 9-1 shows how you can structure this library so that you can write plug-in modules that support different data-storage technologies without committing your applications to any particular technology.

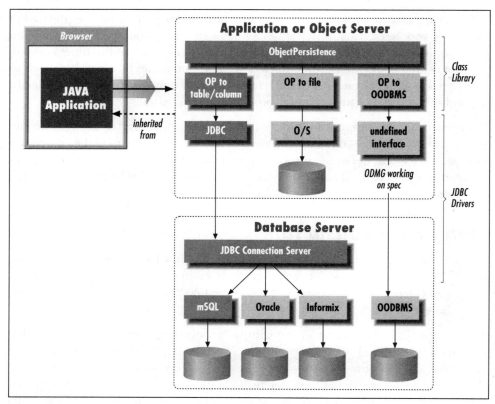

Figure 9-1. The persistence library architecture

A few key behaviors define bank accounts, customers, and any other kind of object as persistent. Specifically, they save to and restore from some kind of data store. Saving is much more complex than it sounds: each save could be creating a new account, updating an existing one, or deleting a closed one. Session components wanting to save an account or groups of accounts, however, should not be responsible for handling the logic that determines what kind of save a specific account requires. They should just begin transactions and end them; separate persistence tools figure out what the begins and ends really mean.

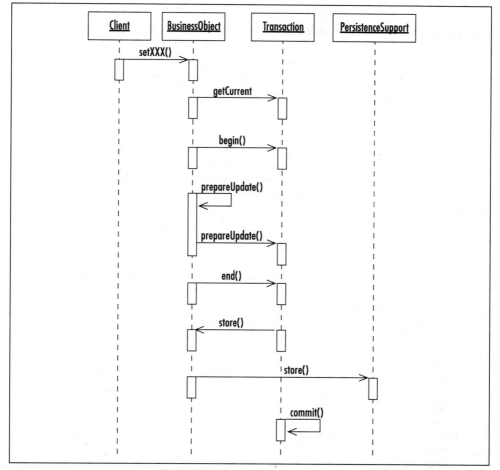

Figure 9-2. A sequence diagram showing a component transaction and its persistence transaction

To support this level of intelligence, persistent objects note when changes occur to them. You saw this change tracking in Chapter 8 inside the `prepareUpdate()` method in `BaseEntity`. When a transaction is ended and the transaction tells the component to save itself, the component knows what sort of save to perform based on what kind of change was made to it. Figure 9-2 provides a UML sequence diagram that illustrates this complex behavior.

Persistence operations may of course fail. Earlier in the book, you saw how JDBC defaults all Connection objects to auto-committing database transactions. In order to support component transactions, you turn this feature off and enable a JDBC-specific implementation of the Transaction class to manage the commit logic. Example 9-1 captures the generic transaction logic provided by the Transaction abstract class.

Example 9-1. The Abstract Transaction Class

```java
package com.imaginary.lwp;

import java.util.Date;
import java.util.HashMap;
import java.util.HashSet;
import java.util.Iterator;

/**
 * An abstract representation of a data storage transaction. This class
 * manages the lifecycle of a data storage transaction. Applications can
 * get a transaction instance by calling <CODE>getCurrent</CODE>. The
 * transaction does not begin, however, until the <CODE>begin</CODE> method
 * is called by an application.
 * <BR>
 * Last modified $Date: 2000/08/07 18:35:03 $
 * @version $Revision: 1.13 $
 * @author George Reese (borg@imaginary.com)
 */
public abstract class Transaction {
    static private HashMap transactions = new HashMap();

    /**
     * Provides access to the transaction currently in
     * process for the specified user identifier.
     * This method will create a new transaction if none
     * currently exists for the identifier in question.
     * @param id the user identifier
     * @return the current transaction
     * @throws com.imaginary.lwp.PersistenceTransaction
     * could not create the transaction
     */
    static public Transaction getCurrent(Identifier id)
        throws PersistenceException {
        Transaction trans;
        String cname;
```

Example 9-1. The Abstract Transaction Class (continued)

```
        if( id == null ) {
            // id was null, so create a new transaction
            // LWPProperties.XACTION is a property that
            // identifies the Transaction implementation class
            cname = System.getProperty(LWPProperties.XACTION);
            try {
                trans = (Transaction)Class.forName(cname).newInstance();
                trans.userID = id;
            }
            catch( Exception e ) {
                e.printStackTrace();
                throw new PersistenceException(e);
            }
        }
        synchronized( transactions ) {
            // if a transaction is in place, return it
            if( transactions.containsKey(id) ) {
                trans = (Transaction)transactions.get(id);
                return trans;
            }
            cname = System.getProperty(LWPProperties.XACTION);
            try {
                trans = (Transaction)Class.forName(cname).newInstance();
                trans.userID = id;
            }
            catch( Exception e ) {
                e.printStackTrace();
                throw new PersistenceException(e);
            }
            transactions.put(id, trans);
        }
        return trans;
    }

    private long       timestamp = -1L;
    private HashSet     toCreate  = new HashSet();
    private HashSet     toRemove  = new HashSet();
    private HashSet     toStore   = new HashSet();
    private Identifier userID     = null;

    public Transaction() {
        super();
    }

    /**
     * Starts a new transaction.
     * This method establishes the transaction timestamp.
     */
```

Example 9-1. The Abstract Transaction Class (continued)

```java
public synchronized final void begin() throws PersistenceException {
    if( timestamp == -1L ) {
        timestamp = (new Date()).getTime();
    }
    else {
        throw new PersistenceException("Duplicate begin() call.");
    }
}


/**
 * Each data store implements this method
 * to perform the actual commit.
 */
public abstract void commit() throws PersistenceException;

/**
 * Ends the transaction at the component level and
 * executes the persistence transaction. This method
 * moves through each of the modified components and
 * tells it to save to the data store. If all saves are
 * successful, it sends a commit to the persistence layer.
 * Otherwise, it sends an abort.
 */
public synchronized final void end() throws PersistenceException {
    try {
        Iterator obs;

        // perform the different operations
        // the order here is unimportant (remove vs. create vs. store)
        // as long as there are no database constraints
        // in place
        obs = toRemove.iterator();
        while( obs.hasNext() ) {
            BaseEntity p = (BaseEntity)obs.next();

            p.remove(this);
        }
        obs = toCreate.iterator();
        while( obs.hasNext() ) {
            BaseEntity p = (BaseEntity)obs.next();

            p.create(this);
        }                obs = toStore.iterator();
        while( obs.hasNext() ) {
            BaseEntity p = (BaseEntity)obs.next();

            p.store(this);
        }
```

Example 9-1. The Abstract Transaction Class (continued)

```
                // commit the changes
                commit();
                // let the objects know about the commit
                obs = toRemove.iterator();
                while( obs.hasNext() ) {
                    BaseEntity p = (BaseEntity)obs.next();

                    p.commit(this);
                }
                obs = toCreate.iterator();
                while( obs.hasNext() ) {
                    BaseEntity p = (BaseEntity)obs.next();

                    p.commit(this);
                }
                obs = toStore.iterator();
                while( obs.hasNext() ) {
                    BaseEntity p = (BaseEntity)obs.next();

                    p.commit(this);
                }
                toCreate.clear();
                // invalidate all removed objects
                obs = toRemove.iterator();
                while( obs.hasNext() ) {
                    BaseEntity p = (BaseEntity)obs.next();

                    p.invalidate();
                }
                toRemove.clear();
                toStore.clear();
                // remove the transaction from the list of transactions
                Transaction.transactions.remove(userID);
            }
            catch( Throwable t ) {
                Transaction trans;
                Iterator obs;

                // an exception occurred, rollback
                rollback();
                Transaction.transactions.remove(userID);
                // use a different transaction to reload everyone
                trans = Transaction.getCurrent(userID);
                // force everyone to reload
                obs = toRemove.iterator();
                while( obs.hasNext() ) {
                    BaseEntity ob = (BaseEntity)obs.next();
```

Example 9-1. The Abstract Transaction Class (continued)

```
                try {
                    ob.reload(trans);
                }
                catch( Exception disaster ) {
                    ob.invalidate();
                }
            }
            obs = toStore.iterator();
            while( obs.hasNext() ) {
                BaseEntity ob = (BaseEntity)obs.next();

                try {
                    ob.reload(trans);
                }
                catch( Exception disaster ) {
                    ob.invalidate();
                }
            }
            if( t instanceof PersistenceException ) {
                throw (PersistenceException)t;
            }
            else {
                throw new PersistenceException(t);
            }
        }
        finally {
            timestamp = -1L;
        }
    }


    // the identifier of the user behind this transaction
    public synchronized final Identifier getIdentifier() {
        return userID;
    }


    // the timestamp of this transaction
    public synchronized final long getTimestamp() {
        return timestamp;
    }


    /**
     * Called by prepareCreate() in the BaseEntity class.
     * This method adds the specified object to the list
     * of objects to be created in this transaction.
     * @param ob the entity to be added to the transaction
     */
    synchronized final void prepareCreate(BaseEntity ob) {
```

Example 9-1. The Abstract Transaction Class (continued)

```
        if( toCreate.contains(ob) ) {
            return;
        }
        toCreate.add(ob);
    }


    // identifies whether the transaction has been begun
    public synchronized final boolean isInProcess() {
        return (timestamp != -1L);
    }


    /**
     * Adds the specified entity to the list of entities
     * to delete from the data store. If this entity is
     * already marked for modification, it is removed from
     * that list. If it is marked for creation, it is removed
     * from that list and <EM>not</EM> added to the list of
     * entities to be removed.
     * @param ob the entity to be removed
     */
    synchronized final void prepareRemove(BaseEntity ob) {
        // It is already in the list, so do nothing.
        if( toRemove.contains(ob) ) {
            return;
        }
        // It is supposed to be created, which means
        // there is now nothing to delete.
        // Remove it from the list of things to create.
        if( toCreate.contains(ob) ) {
            toCreate.remove(ob);
            return;
        }
        // It was modified before the remove() was called
        // so remove it from the list of things to save.
        if( toStore.contains(ob) ) {
            toStore.remove(ob);
        }
        toRemove.add(ob);
    }


    /**
     * Adds the specified entity to the list of entities
     * modified in this transaction. If the entity is already
     * marked as created or removed, it is not added.
     * @param ob the entity that was modified
     */
    synchronized final void prepareStore(BaseEntity ob) {
        // if it already is part of this transaction in
```

Example 9-1. The Abstract Transaction Class (continued)

```
        // any capacity, leave it be
        if( toStore.contains(ob) || toCreate.contains(ob) ) {
            return;
        }
        if( toRemove.contains(ob) ) {
            return;
        }
        toStore.add(ob);
    }


    /**
     * Each data store implements this method to
     * perform the actual rollbacks here.
     */
    public abstract void rollback() throws PersistenceException;
}
```

The abstract `Transaction` class manages all component transaction issues. The `end()` method goes through and tells each object to perform the appropriate persistence operation. It assumes an implementation of the `Persistent` interface in Example 9-2 that is implemented by `BaseEntity`.

Example 9-2. The Persistent Interface

```
package com.imaginary.lwp;

public interface Persistent {
    String getLastUpdateID();

    long getLastUpdateTime();

    long getObjectID();

    void create(Transaction trans) throws PersistenceException;

    void load(Transaction trans, long oid) throws PersistenceException;

    void reload(Transaction trans) throws PersistenceException;

    void remove(Transaction trans) throws PersistenceException;

    void store(Transaction trans) throws PersistenceException;
}
```

The `Transaction` base class that makes these calls leaves the `commit()` and `rollback()` methods to the persistence subsystem. For a JDBC transaction, the `commit()` should look like this:

```
    public void commit() throws PersistenceException {
        if( connection == null ) {
            return;
        }
        if( connection.isClosed() ) {
            throw new PersistenceException("Connection closed.");
        }
        try {
            connection.commit();
            connection.close();
            connection = null;
        }
        catch( SQLException e ) {
            throw new PersistenceException(e);
        }
    }
```

Similarly, the rollback() should look like this:

```
    public void rollback() throws PersistenceException {
        try {
            if( connection == null ) {
                return;
            }
            if( connection.isClosed() ) {
                throw new PersistenceException("Invalid transactional "+
                                "state.");
            }
            connection.rollback();
            connection.close();
            connection = null;
        }
        catch( SQLException e ) {
            throw new PersistenceException(e);
        }
    }
```

Mementos and Delegates

One of the key features of a solid persistence architecture is a separation of business logic from persistence logic. This separation is critical for these reasons:

- The skill set required for writing business components is very different from that required for database programming. By separating different kinds of behavior in various components, different people can easily "own" the development and maintenance of those components.

- If a business component is independent of the persistence logic, it requires no changes should the persistence logic change; even if that change involves a migration to a new database engine or even a new persistence mechanism.

You will use two key design patterns to support the separation of business logic from persistence logic: the memento pattern and delegation. `BaseEntity` specifically delegates its implementation of the `Persistent` interface in Example 9-2 to a specialized persistence component. This sample code shows how that delegation works:

```
public final void store(Transaction trans)
    throws StoreException {
    Memento mem = new Memento(this);

    if( !isValid ) {
        throw new StoreException("This object is no longer valid.");
    }
    handler.store(trans, mem);
}
```

The `BaseEntity` class references an attribute called `handler` that is an instance of a class implementing the `PersistenceSupport` interface. This object is called the *delegate*. It supports the persistence operations for an entity. Each method delegated to it requires a `Transaction` object to identify what transaction governs the persistence operation and a memento that captures the entity's current state.

I briefly introduced the classic memento design pattern in Chapter 7, *Distributed Application Architecture*. The memento pattern enables an object's state to be decoupled from its implementation. In order to perform a persistence operation, the delegate depends only on the `Memento` class.* It gets all of the entity's state information from that memento. As a result, an entity can go through major code changes without any impact on its persistence delegate. Using these two tools, you now have a system for which a business component has no dependencies on the underlying data model, and a persistence delegate has no depencies on the business component it persists. Example 9-3 shows the generic `PersistenceSupport` interface.

Example 9-3. The PersistenceSupport Interface for Delegating Persistence Operations

```
package com.imaginary.lwp;

import java.util.Collection;

public interface PersistenceSupport {
    public abstract void create(Transaction trans, Memento mem)
        throws CreateException;

    public abstract Collection find(Transaction trans, SearchCriteria sc)
        throws FindException;
```

---

* The full source code for the Memento class comes with the code supporting this book (*ftp://ftp.ora.com/ pub/examples/java/jdbc*).

Example 9-3. The PersistenceSupport Interface for Delegating Persistence Operations (continued)

```
    public abstract void load(Transaction trans, Memento mem)
        throws LoadException;

    public abstract void remove(Transaction trans, Memento mem)
        throws RemoveException;

    public abstract void store(Transaction trans, Memento mem)
        throws StoreException;
}
```

This interface contains no mention of JDBC or of the entity it is saving. It knows only about its transaction context and the memento.

JDBC Persistence

Now that you have a general foundation for object persistence, you can use these classes to create a JDBC-based persistence package. The generic library has set aside implementations of the `PersistenceSupport` and `Transaction` interfaces as the places where data store-specific persistence operations should occur. To create a database persistence library, you thus need to create database-specific extensions of these two classes.

Here you get the chance to put your JDBC skills to use. I already showed how a `JDBCTransaction` class might implement `commit()` and `rollback()` methods. JDBC support requires still more work. You need to create JDBC `Connection` instances used to talk to the database. You also need to write the actual methods that talk to the database. A `getConnection()` method in the `JDBCTransaction` class takes care of the first problem:

```
    public Connection getConnection() throws SQLException {
        if( connection == null ) {
            Context ctx = new InitialContext();
            DataSource ds = (DataSource)ctx.lookup("jdbc/ora");

            connection = ds.getConnection("borg", "pw");
            connection.setAutoCommit(false);
        }
        return connection;
    }
```

In this code, I use the JDBC 2.0 Optional Package method for connecting to a database. You may not have the JDBC 2.0 Optional Package available to you, in which case you may want to use the old-fashioned `DriverManager` approach to making a `Connection`. Either way, you definitely want a pooled connection. Without access to the JDBC 2.0 Optional Package, you have to roll your own connection pooling.

The heart of JDBC persistence rests in the persistence delegate. As you saw before in the `PersistenceSupport` interface, an implementation is responsible for the SQL that inserts, updates, or deletes the object in question from the database. Each implementation is dependent on the particular entity it is persisting. Example 9-4 provides the `store()` method in the `AccountSupport` class to save an `Account` entity to the database.

Example 9-4. The store( ) Method for an Account Persistence Delegate

```
static private String UPDATE =
    "UPDATE Account " +
    "SET balance = ?, " +
    "lastUpdateID = ?, " +
    "lastUpdateTime = ? " +
    "WHERE objectID = ? " +
    "AND lastUpdateID = ? " +
    "AND lastUpdateTime = ?";

public void store(Transaction trans, Memento mem)
throws StoreException {
    long oid = mem.getObjectID();
    long lut = mem.getLastUpdateTime();
    String luid = mem.getLastUpdateID();
    Connection conn = null;

    try {
        PreparedStatement stmt;
        Double d;

        conn = ((JDBCTransaction)trans).getConnection();
        stmt = conn.prepareStatement(UPDATE);
        d = (Double)mem.get(Account.class,
                            Account.BALANCE);
        if( d == null ) {
            stmt.setNull(1, Types.REAL);
        }
        else {
            stmt.setDouble(1, d.doubleValue());
        }
        stmt.setString(2, trans.getIdentifier().getUserID());
        stmt.setLong(3, trans.getTimestamp());
        stmt.setLong(4, oid);
        stmt.setString(5, luid);
        stmt.setLong(6, lut);
        if( stmt.executeUpdate() != 1 ) {
            throw new StoreException("No row modified.");
        }
        stmt.close();
    }
```

Example 9-4. The store( ) Method for an Account Persistence Delegate (continued)

```
catch( SQLException e ) {
    throw new CreateException(e);
}
}
```

You may have noticed the `getLastUpdateID()` and `getLastUpdateTime()` methods in the `Persistent` interface earlier in the chapter and wondered what their purpose was. They specifically enable you to work with a database in optimistic concurrency mode. Pessimistic concurrency means that the database will lock data on read and not release that lock without a commit. In other words, if you do a `SELECT` to find an account, the row—or perhaps more—will be locked until you issue a commit. No one else can read or write to that row.

As you can imagine, pessimistic concurrency is very bad for performance. With optimistic concurrency, however, you risk dirty writes. A dirty write is a situation in which two clients have read the same data simultaneously and then attempt to make different writes. For example, consider when a teller reads customer information to change the customer address, and the bank manager reads information about the same customer to add a comment to the customer file. If they both read the data at the same time, the person to save last risks erasing the changes made by the first person to save. By using the user ID of the last person to make a change, along with a timestamp noting when the change was made, you can get the performance benefit of optimistic concurrency with the protection against dirty writes of pessimistic concurrency.

Under this model, when you query the database, you get the user ID of the last user to make a change and the time the change was made. When you update the database with that data, you use that user ID and timestamp in the `WHERE` clause. If someone else changed the data before you, your `WHERE` clause will not match any rows in the database and will thus throw an exception.

Searches

Not only does the persistence delegate support the basic database inserts, updates, and deletes, but it also supports the component model's searches. Writing logic to support arbitrary searches, however, can be very complex. You really do not want to have to repeat the complexity of search logic for every single component in your system if you can avoid it. Fortunately, you can avoid it by capturing search logic in a single place, the persistence delegate.

The final example in this chapter, Example 9-5, is the full source code to the `JDBCSupport` class, an implementation of the `PersistenceSupport` class. It does not, on its own, provide implementations of the persistence operations you discussed so far in the chapter. Business components require subclasses of JDBCSupport that specifically map a specific business component to a data model.* The base class does have, however, a generalized search engine that accepts the SearchCriteria object, translates it into SQL, and finally returns the results.

Example 9-5. The Abstract JDBCSupport Class with a Generic SQL Search Algorithm

```
package com.imaginary.lwp.jdbc;

import com.imaginary.lwp.BaseFacade;
import com.imaginary.lwp.FindException;
import com.imaginary.lwp.PersistenceSupport;
import com.imaginary.lwp.SearchBinding;
import com.imaginary.lwp.SearchCriteria;
import com.imaginary.lwp.Transaction;
import com.imaginary.util.DistributedList;
import java.sql.Connection;
import java.sql.PreparedStatement;
import java.sql.ResultSet;
import java.sql.ResultSetMetaData;
import java.sql.SQLException;
import java.util.ArrayList;
import java.util.Collection;
import java.util.HashMap;
import java.util.Iterator;


/**
 * Persistence support for JDBC-based persistence.
 * <BR>
 * Last modified $Date: 2000/08/07 18:35:03 $
 * @version $Revision: 1.13 $
 * @author George Reese (borg@imaginary.com)
 */
public abstract class JDBCSupport implements PersistenceSupport {
    /**
     * Provides a generalized mechanism for binding a set
     * of values to any possible prepared statement. A calling
     * method specifies a statement and the index from which
     * binding should begin, as well as the actual bindings.
     * This index is the index that gets passed to a
     * prepared statement's setXXX() method for binding
     * the values in the bindinds list
     * @param stmt the statement being set up
     * @param ind the index to start binding at
     * @param bindings the bindings to bind
```

---

* A mostly automated mapping of any generic component to a data model would be possible, but it is very complex and much beyond the scope of the book. The biggest obstacle to automated mapping is the lack of parameterized types in Java.

Example 9-5. The Abstract JDBCSupport Class with a Generic SQL Search Algorithm (continued)

```
 * @throws com.imaginary.lwp.FindException
 * @throws java.sql.SQLException an error occurred binding the bindings
 * to the statement
 */
private void bind(PreparedStatement stmt, int ind, Iterator bindings)
    throws FindException, SQLException  {
    while( bindings.hasNext() ) {
        SearchBinding bdg = (SearchBinding)bindings.next();
        Object val = bdg.getValue();

        if( val instanceof SearchCriteria ) {
            SearchCriteria sc = (SearchCriteria)val;

            bind(stmt, ind, sc.bindings());
        }
        else if( val instanceof BaseFacade ) {
            BaseFacade ref = (BaseFacade)val;

            stmt.setLong(ind++, ref.getObjectID());
        }
        else {
            stmt.setObject(ind++, val);
        }
    }
}

/**
 * Executes a search for objects meeting the specified criteria
 * using the specified transaction.
 * @param tr the transaction to use for the find operation
 * @param sc the search criteria to base the find on
 * @return an iterator of matching objects
 * @throws com.imaginary.lwp.FindException an error occurred
 * searching for objects meeting the search criteria
 */
public Collection find(Transaction tr, SearchCriteria sc)
    throws FindException {
    Iterator bindings = sc.bindings();
    DistributedList list = new DistributedList();
    String sql = getFindSQL(sc);

    try {
        JDBCTransaction trans;
        Connection conn;

        trans = (JDBCTransaction)tr;
        try {
            conn = trans.getConnection();
        }
```

Example 9-5. The Abstract JDBCSupport Class with a Generic SQL Search Algorithm (continued)

```
            catch( Exception e ) {
                e.printStackTrace();
                return null;
            }
            PreparedStatement stmt = conn.prepareStatement(sql);
            ResultSetMetaData meta;
            ResultSet rs;
            int cc;

            bind(stmt, 1, bindings);
            rs = stmt.executeQuery();
            meta = rs.getMetaData();
            cc = meta.getColumnCount();
            // This loop places result set values into
            // a hash map with the column name as the key
            // and the column value as the value. This
            // map then gets passed to a new facade for
            // pre-caching values.
            while( rs.next() ) {
                HashMap map = new HashMap();
                long oid = rs.getLong(1);
                String cls = rs.getString(2);

                for(int i=3; i<=cc; i++) {
                    String tbl = meta.getTableName(i).toUpperCase();
                    String name = meta.getColumnLabel(i).toUpperCase();
                    Object val = rs.getObject(i);

                    if( tbl.equals("") ) {
                        tbl = getPrimaryTable().toUpperCase();
                    }
                    name = tbl + "." + name;
                    if( rs.wasNull() ) {
                        val = null;
                    }
                    map.put(name, val);
                }
                list.add(getFacade(oid, cls, map));
            }
            return list;
        }
        catch( SQLException e ) {
            throw new FindException(e);
        }
    }
```

Example 9-5. The Abstract JDBCSupport Class with a Generic SQL Search Algorithm (continued)

```java
/**
 * Provides the facade object for entities supported by this
 * persistence support delegate.
 * @param oid the object ID of the desired object
 * @param cls the reference class name
 * @param vals the initial cache values
 * @return an instance of the reference class pointing to the specified
 * object
 * @throws com.imaginary.lwp.FindException the specified class could not
 * be loaded
 */
public final BaseFacade getFacade(long oid, String cls, HashMap vals)
    throws FindException {
    try {
        BaseFacade ref;

        ref = (BaseFacade)Class.forName(cls).newInstance();
        ref.assign(oid, vals);
        return ref;
    }
    catch( Exception e ) {
        e.printStackTrace();
        throw new FindException(e);
    }
}

/**
 * Special method for building a <CODE>SELECT</CODE> statement that
 * will perform a search using the named search critieria.
 * @param sc the search criteria to build SQL from
 * @return the SQL that performs the select
 * @throws com.imaginary.lwp.FindException the SQL could not be built
 */
protected String getFindSQL(SearchCriteria sc) throws FindException {
    StringBuffer sql = new StringBuffer("SELECT ");
    ArrayList tables = new ArrayList();
    String where, order;
    Iterator it;

    sql.append(getPrimaryTable() + ".OBJECTID");
    sql.append(", " + getPrimaryTable() + ".CRT_CLASS");
    tables.add(getPrimaryTable());
    it = sc.preloads();
    while( it.hasNext() ) {
        String fld = mapField((String)it.next());
        int i = fld.indexOf(".");
        String tbl;
```

Example 9-5. The Abstract JDBCSupport Class with a Generic SQL Search Algorithm (continued)

```
            if( i != -1 ) {
                tbl = fld.substring(0, i);
                if( !tables.contains(tbl) ) {
                    tables.add(tbl);
                }
            }
            sql.append(", ");
            sql.append(fld);
        }
        where = getWhere(sc.bindings(), tables);
        order = getOrder(sc.sorts(), tables);
        it = tables.iterator();
        sql.append(" FROM ");
        while( it.hasNext() ) {
            sql.append((String)it.next());
            if( it.hasNext() ) {
                sql.append(", ");
            }
        }
        if( where.length() > 0 ) {
            sql.append(" WHERE ");
            sql.append("(" + where + ")");
        }
        else if( tables.size() > 1 ) {
            sql.append(" WHERE ");
        }
        it = tables.iterator();
        while( it.hasNext() ) {
            String tbl = (String)it.next();
            JDBCJoin join;

            if( tbl.equals(getPrimaryTable()) ) {
                continue;
            }
            join = getJoin(tbl);
            sql.append(" AND " + join.toString() + " ");
        }
        if( order.length() > 0 ) {
            sql.append(" ORDER BY " + order);
        }
        return sql.toString();
    }

    /**
     * Given a table, this method needs to provide a portion of a
     * <CODE>WHERE</CODE> clause that supports joining to the specified
     * table.
     * @param tbl the table to join to
```

Example 9-5. The Abstract JDBCSupport Class with a Generic SQL Search Algorithm (continued)

```
     * @return the join object that represents a join for the primary
     * table to the specified table
     * @throws com.imaginary.lwp.FindException a join could not be constructed
     */
    protected abstract JDBCJoin getJoin(String tbl) throws FindException;

    /**
     * Provides the <CODE>ORDER BY</CODE> clause to support ordering of
     * the results.
     * @param sorts the sort criteria from the search criteria object
     * @param a pass by reference thing where any new tables that need
     * to be joined to are added to this list
     * @return a string with the <CODE>ORDER BY</CODE> clause
     * @throws com.imaginary.lwp.FindException the clause could not be
     * built
     */
    private String getOrder(Iterator sorts, ArrayList tables)
        throws FindException {
        StringBuffer order = null;

        if( !sorts.hasNext() ) {
            return "";
        }
        do {
            String col = (String)sorts.next();
            int i;

            if( order == null ) {
                order = new StringBuffer();
            }
            else {
                order.append(", ");
            }
            col = mapField(col);
            order.append(col);
            i = col.indexOf(".");
            if( i != -1 ) {
                String tbl = col.substring(0, i);

                if( !tables.contains(tbl) ) {
                    tables.add(tbl);
                }
            }
        } while( sorts.hasNext() );
        return order.toString();
    }
```

Example 9-5. The Abstract JDBCSupport Class with a Generic SQL Search Algorithm (continued)

```
/**
 * Implemented by subclasses to provide the name of the primary
 * table for storing objects supported by this class.
 * @return the name of the primary table
 */
protected abstract String getPrimaryTable();

/**
 * Provides the <CODE>WHERE</CODE> clause to support a find.
 * @param bindings the search bindings from the search criteria object
 * @param a pass by reference thing where any new tables that need
 * to be joined to are added to this list
 * @return a string with the <CODE>WHERE</CODE> clause
 * @throws com.imaginary.lwp.FindException the clause could not be
 * built
 */
private String getWhere(Iterator bindings, ArrayList tables)
    throws FindException {
    StringBuffer where = null;

    if( !bindings.hasNext() ) {
        return "";
    }
    do {
        SearchBinding bdg = (SearchBinding)bindings.next();
        Object val = bdg.getValue();
        String fld = bdg.getField();

        if( where == null ) {
            where = new StringBuffer();
        }
        else {
            where.append(" " + bdg.getBoolean().toString() + " ");
        }
        if( val instanceof SearchCriteria ) {
            SearchCriteria sc = (SearchCriteria)val;

            where.append("(");
            where.append(getWhere(sc.bindings(), tables));
            where.append(")");
        }
        else {
            int i;

            fld = mapField(fld);
            where.append(fld);
            i = fld.indexOf(".");
            if( i != -1 ) {
```

Example 9-5. The Abstract JDBCSupport Class with a Generic SQL Search Algorithm (continued)

```
                    String tbl = fld.substring(0, i);

                    if( !tables.contains(tbl) ) {
                        tables.add(tbl);
                    }
                }
                where.append(" " + bdg.getOperator().toString() + " ?");
            }
        } while( bindings.hasNext() );
        if( where == null ) {
            return "";
        }
        else {
            return where.toString();
        }
    }


    /**
     * Maps a field from the supported object's attributes to a database
     * field.
     * @param fld the Java object.attribute for the field to map
     * @return the database table to map the field to
     * @throws com.imaginary.lwp.FindException the field could not be mapped
     */
    protected abstract String mapField(String fld) throws FindException;
}
```

The bulk of work done in this class is done by the `getFindSQL()` method. It takes a `SearchCriteria` instance and builds SQL to support the desired criteria. The `SearchCriteria` represents a set of criteria on which to perform a search independent of the underlying data store semantics. You can arbitrarily associate attributes with values and the nature of that relationship. For example, you can use the `SearchCriteria` to specify that an attribute must equal some value and a second attribute be greater than another value. Your client might construct a search in the following way:

```
String[] precache = { "lastName", "firstName" };
SearchCriteria sc = new SearchCriteria(precache);

// ssn is the social security number being sought
sc.addBinding("taxID", ssn);
sc.addBinding(SearchBoolean.OR, "birthDate",
            SearchOperator.EQUALS, bd);
```

The result is a collection of façades containing customers who either have the specified social security number or the specified birth date. Each façade will be precached with the customer's first and last name.

All other methods in the class basically support the SQL building: the getWhere()
providing the WHERE clause and the getOrder() supporting any potential ORDER
BY clause. Once the SQL is built, the find() method uses that SQL and help from
ResultSetMetaData to execute the SQL and process the results. For each matching row, a Façade is instantiated and placed into a Collection specially opti-
mized for distributed searches.

10

The User Interface

*We say that error is appearance. This is false. On the
contrary, appearance is always true if we confine
ourselves to it. Appearance is being.*
—Jean-Paul Sartre
Truth and Existence

Appearance is truth. Whatever data you have stored in your database, it is what your users see that ultimately matters. As you explored in previous chapters, a two-tier application creates copies of database data on the client. The database can change and leave the client with a different set of data from that sitting in the database. The users, however, continue to interface with the client under the belief that what they see is reality.

You want to create a user interface that is not a copy of the data in the business objects, but a mirror of the business objects themselves. You want to know that whatever the users see on the screen reflects the state of the business object on the server. You have been through the hardest part of this application: the abstraction of application functionality into reusable components. These appearance tasks become easier and less tangled.

In Chapter 7, *Distributed Application Architecture*, I presented a design for client interaction that treats the client as a system of business component listeners (see Figure 7-4). While this GUI is not the most usable interface from a user perspective, it does demonstrate many of the issues surrounding Swing development in a distributed database application. We will now dive into the details of that design and see how it plays out in the Java environment.

Swing at a Glance

Swing is Java's user interface API. A full discussion of Swing is of course well beyond the scope of this book. In order to fully apply the information in this chapter, you should have some background in Swing programming. *Java Swing* by Robert Eckstein, Marc Loy, and Dave Wood (O'Reilly & Associates) provides excellent coverage of the Swing API. Before diving into the issues of Swing development in a distributed computing environment, however, I do want to take a moment to review some of the Swing concepts I rely on in this chapter.

Model-View-Controller

Swing is much more than a bunch of GUI components that you paste into a window. It is an entire architecture for building user interfaces in Java. At the heart of this architecture is is the model-view-controller (MVC) paradigm. The MVC GUI architecture breaks user interface components into three elements: the *model*, the *view*, and the *controller*:

Model

> The model captures the state of one or more components independent of its appearance. Each user interface component is driven by some underlying model object. The model for a JTree, for example, captures the data and the heirarchy that are displayed in the tree. The model does not care at all about how the component is displayed on the screen. In fact, the same model can be used to support multiple components.

View

> The view is how a component appears on the screen. It is the actual GUI widget. The view is responsible for determining how to display the data in the model object. Two different views can have different takes on the same data.

Controller

> A controller reacts to actions such as key presses and mouse clicks. When some event occurs, the controller is responsible for determining how the GUI component should behave.

Under this architecture, you perform an action—for example, a mouse click—and a controller interprets that action. The controller may respond by modifying the model. Whenever the model is modified, it notifes the view via an event model. Upon learning of the change, the view changes the way it displays itself on screen.

Swing uses a variation of the MVC architecture called the *model-delegate architecture*. The model-delegate architecture combines the roles of view and controller into a single object, the UI delegate. As a result, a GUI component, such as a tree, is represented in Swing by a UI delegate (the JTree class) and a model (the TreeModel interface).

Threads in Swing

One of the core features of the Java language is the fact that it has multithreading built into its basic nature. Multithreading in Swing applications, however, is not trivial. While you can avoid its complexities in desktop applications, you absolutely cannot avoid multithreading in a distributed application.

Because Swing works independently of the underlying operating system, it cannot rely on OS events to paint components on the user's screen. Swing therefore uses a special thread called the event queue to paint the user interface. Because a change to a model in a thread other than the event queue can result in a faulty drawing of a widget on the screen, Swing has to assume that no changes can occur to GUI model objects outside of the event queue. As a Swing programmer, you must therefore never make changes to the model except in the event queue.

This limitation is generally not a problem since all event dispatches occur in the event queue. In other words, your code that responds to a key press, component focus gain, or mouse click will occur in the event queue. Unfortunately, another rule of thumb for Swing programming is that long-lived events—events lasting a second or longer—should occur in a separate thread.* As luck would have it, events requiring network access often fall into this category. When a Swing developer handles a user event requiring network access, the event handler must start a new thread that will perform the actual network access. If the network access needs to make a change to a model object, it must notify the event queue that it has a modification to make. In the next cycle of the event queue, the event queue thread will then make that modification.

The keys to successful multithreaded updates of model objects are the invokeAndWait() and invokeLater() methods in the SwingUtilities class. These methods accept a Runnable instance as an argument and then invoke that Runnable's run() method from inside the event queue. The invokeAndWait() method makes the calling thread wait until the event queue has called run() before continuing. On the other hand, invokeLater() simply pushes the Runnable onto a queue to be executed in the event queue, and moves on. The effective difference is that you are guaranteed that your run() method has been called after invokeAndWait() returns, but you have no such guarantee with invokeLater(). The following code shows invokeLater() in action:

```
public void actionPerformed(ActionEvent evt) {
    Thread t = new Thread() {
```

---

* This rule of thumb cannot be emphasized enough. Much of Java's bad reputation on the client is actually a result of bad programmers failing to multithread long-lived events or failing to properly modify models inside the event queue.

```
            public void run() {
                longMethod();
            }
        };

        // start this thread that performs the long-lived event
        t.start();
    }

    // the long-lived event
    private void longMethod() {
        Runnable r = new Runnable() {
            public void run() {
                changeModel();
            }
        };

        // do some extensive processing here
        // do the model change in the event queue
        SwingUtilities.invokeLater(r);
    }
```

In this code, you first start a thread for handling the long-lived event. The action triggered from the event queue returns immediately. While the long-lived event is processing in a background thread, the UI is responsive to user actions—even if the user interaction does nothing more than display an hourglass and properly redraw the screen as the user moves the window around. When that background thread finishes, it creates an anonymous Runnable object that makes changes to the UI in its run() method. The event queue is then told to invoke that method during the next run through the event queue via invokeLater().

Models for Database Applications

The model contains the state information that drives the UI display. It is therefore the starting point for understanding how to build a Swing application. The banking application needs to provide a model that organizes the banking business objects for the appropriate UI component models. Before we dive into the complexities of three-tier UI component modeling, however, I want to step back and look at a simpler two-tier example. This two-tier example presents the basic concepts we will see later in a more flexible three-tier model without the need to worry about distributed computing issues.

A Two-Tier Model

The simplest example of a two-tier database application is one that queries a database and stores the results in a table. In Swing, the JTable UI delegate and

`TableModel` model represent the table component. The table model captures a database result set and tells the table view what the column and value names are for each row. The table view then provides a nice tabular display of the data.

Swing makes it possible for you to ignore all of the display issues. Your concern is handling events and providing accurate state information in the model. It is surprising just how easy it is to construct such a model for database access. You need only to extend the `AbstractTableModel` class provided in the Swing API and delegate to the `RowSet` class covered in Chapter 5, *The JDBC Optional Package*. The result is the class in Example 10-1.

Example 10-1. A RowSet Model for Constructing a Table from a RowSet

```
package com.imaginary.swing;

import javax.swing.table.AbstractTableModel;
import java.sql.ResultSetMetaData;
import java.sql.SQLException;
import java.sql.Types;
import javax.sql.RowSet;
import javax.sql.RowSetEvent;
import javax.sql.RowSetListener;

public class RowSetModel extends AbstractTableModel implements RowSetListener {
    private RowSet rowSet    = null;

    public RowSetModel(RowSet set) {
        super();
        rowSet = set;
        rowSet.addRowSetListener(this);
    }

    public void cursorMoved(RowSetEvent event) {
    }

    /**
     * The JTable uses the column class to figure out how to
     * format cells. This method finds out the SQL type of
     * the column and returns its Java type.
     * @param column the table column number sought
     * @return the Java Class for the column
     */
    public Class getColumnClass(int column) {
        String cname;
        int type;

        try {
            ResultSetMetaData meta = rowSet.getMetaData();
```

Example 10-1. A RowSet Model for Constructing a Table from a RowSet (continued)

```
                if( meta == null ) {
                    return null;
                }
                // remember, JTable columns start at 0, JDBC at 1!
                type = meta.getColumnType(column+1);
            }
        catch( SQLException e ) {
            e.printStackTrace();
            return super.getColumnClass(column);
        }
        switch( type ) {
        case Types.BIT:
            {
                cname = "java.lang.Boolean";
                break;
            }
        case Types.TINYINT:
            {
                cname = "java.lang.Byte";
                break;
            }
        case Types.SMALLINT:
            {
                cname = "java.lang.Short";
                break;
            }
        case Types.INTEGER:
            {
                cname = "java.lang.Integer";
                break;
            }
// CASE STATEMENTS FOR THE FULL SET OF SQL TYPES OMITTED
// FOR THE SAKE OF BREVITY
// FULL EXAMPLE AT http://www.oreilly.com/catalog/jdbc2
        default:
            {
                return super.getColumnClass(column);
            }
        }
        try {
            return Class.forName(cname);
        }
        catch( Exception e ) {
            e.printStackTrace();
            return super.getColumnClass(column);
        }
    }
```

Example 10-1. A RowSet Model for Constructing a Table from a RowSet (continued)

```java
    // the number of columns in the result set
    public int getColumnCount() {
        try {
            ResultSetMetaData meta = rowSet.getMetaData();

            if( meta == null ) {
                return 0;
            }
            return meta.getColumnCount();
        }
        catch( SQLException e ) {
            return 0;
        }
    }


    // a label for the column
    public String getColumnName(int col) {
        try {
            ResultSetMetaData meta = rowSet.getMetaData();

            if( meta == null ) {
                return null;
            }
            return meta.getColumnName(col+1);
        }
        catch( SQLException e ) {
            return "Error";
        }
    }


    public int getRowCount() {
        try {
            if( rowSet.last() ) {
                return (rowSet.getRow());
            }
            else {
                return 0;
            }
        }
        catch( SQLException e ) {
            return 0;
        }
    }


    // the actual value for the column at the specified row
    public Object getValueAt(int row, int col) {
        try {
```

Example 10-1. A RowSet Model for Constructing a Table from a RowSet (continued)

```java
            if( !rowSet.absolute(row+1) ) {
                return null;
            }
            return rowSet.getObject(col+1);
        }
        catch( SQLException e ) {
            return null;
        }
    }

    // this is called when the row set is modified
    public void rowChanged(RowSetEvent event) {
        try {
            int row = rowSet.getRow();

            if( rowSet.rowDeleted() ) {
                fireTableRowsDeleted(row, row);
            }
            else if( rowSet.rowInserted() ) {
                fireTableRowsInserted(row, row);
            }
            else if( rowSet.rowUpdated() ) {
                fireTableRowsUpdated(row, row);
            }
        }
        catch( SQLException e ) {
        }
    }

    // this is called when the SQL has changed
    public void rowSetChanged(RowSetEvent event) {
        fireTableStructureChanged();
    }

    // called if the user changes a cell value in the table
    public void setValueAt(Object value, int row, int column) {
        try {
            if( !rowSet.absolute(row+1) ) {
                return;
            }
            rowSet.updateObject(column+1, value);
        }
        catch( SQLException e ) {
        }
    }
}
```

One key of the model is to make sure to fire an event associated with the model whenever it changes in some way. Because the view is always listening to its model, firing these events will cause the view to requery the model and change its appearance based on the new state of the model.

You now have basically everything you need for an application that displays database results in a table. The methods implemented in this class are all from the `TableModel` interface. The class implements them by making calls to a `RowSet`.

A Three-Tier Model

While the two-tier model provides a good look at how the model piece of the model-delegate picture works, it does not address everything you need to support the banking application. The single most evident point in the banking application is that your primary navigational tool is a tree, not a table. A tree is, of course, more complicated to model. The second point is that you have two panels in this user interface: the tree and the detail view on the right.

The tree has a "Customers" node and an "Accounts" node at the root of the tree. Under the "Customers" node are all the bank's customers with their accounts located under them. The "Accounts" node, on the other hand, provides an account-oriented view with an account's customers underneath each account.

Swing's support for tree components comes with a handy default model, the `javax.swing.tree.DefaultTreeModel` class. This model handles all basic functionality required in a tree model—just add `TreeNode` implementations to provide the data. To support the tree in this environment, you need to build three `TreeNode` implementations: one to represent the root node of the tree,* one to represent customer objects, and another to represent accounts.

The simplest node is the root node. It has two children representing the customers and accounts hierarchies, respectively. Because it is not concerned with any distributed computing issues, it is a great place to start learning how basic `TreeNode` implementations work. Example 10-2 shows the `RootNode` class.

Example 10-2. The Root Node for the Tree View

```
package com.imaginary.bank;

import java.util.ArrayList;
import java.util.Enumeration;
import java.util.Iterator;
import javax.swing.tree.TreeNode;
```

---

* While it appears that your tree has two roots, a `JTree` must actually always have a single root. You can, however, make that root invisible via the `setRootVisible()` method. The root node's children ultimately appear as multiple root nodes.

Example 10-2. The Root Node for the Tree View (continued)

```java
public class RootNode implements TreeNode {
    private ArrayList nodes = new ArrayList();

    public class IteratorEnumeration implements Enumeration {
        private Iterator iterator;

        public IteratorEnumeration(Iterator it) {
            super();
            iterator = it;
        }

        public boolean hasMoreElements() {
            return iterator.hasNext();
        }

        public Object nextElement() {
            return iterator.next();
        }
    }

    public RootNode(CustomerNode cn, AccountNode an) {
        super();
        nodes.add(cn);
        nodes.add(an);
    }

    public Enumeration children() {
        return new IteratorEnumeration(nodes.iterator());
    }

    public boolean getAllowsChildren() {
        return true;
    }

    public TreeNode getChildAt(int ind) {
        return (TreeNode)nodes.get(ind);
    }

    public int getChildCount() {
        return nodes.size();
    }

    public int getIndex(TreeNode chld) {
        return nodes.indexOf(chld);
    }
```

Example 10-2. The Root Node for the Tree View (continued)

```
    public TreeNode getParent() {
        return null;
    }

    public boolean isLeaf() {
        return false;
    }

    public String toString() {
        return "Root";
    }
}
```

This class comes with an inner class called `IteratorEnumeration` that helps convert a JDK 1.2 `Iterator` into its JDK 1.1 counterpart, an `Enumeration`. This conversion is necessary since I use an `ArrayList` to store the nodes, but the `TreeNode` interface requires an `Enumeration` for the `children()` method.

The methods in the `RootNode` implementation all exist to tell the `DefaultTreeModel` about the root node and its children. The rest of the nodes supporting this model follow this paradigm. Of course, those `TreeNode` implementations have the added complexity of network communication.

When your application has a widget such as a `JTree`, there is a real danger of loading too much data at once. The `JTree` is structured so that it will ask its model only for the information it needs to properly display the current screen data. From the programmer implementing this model, however, it is very easy to make the mistake of loading a node, all its children, and all its children's children at once. In your application, such a mistake would result in all customers and accounts being sent across the network and loaded into memory on the client. Example 10-3 shows how the `AccountNode` class addresses these issues.

Example 10-3. An AccountNode That Loads Its Children Only When Necessary

```
package com.imaginary.bank;

import com.imaginary.bank.AccountFacade;
import java.util.ArrayList;
import java.util.Collection;
import java.util.Enumeration;
import java.util.Iterator;
import javax.swing.tree.TreeNode;

public class AccountNode implements TreeNode {
    private AccountFacade account  = null;
    private ArrayList     children = null;
    private TreeNode      parent   = null;
```

Example 10-3. An AccountNode That Loads Its Children Only When Necessary (continued)

```java
public AccountNode(TreeNode prnt, AccountFacade acct) {
    super();
    parent = prnt;
    account = acct;
}

public Enumeration children() {
    return new RootNode.EnumerationIterator(children.iterator());
}

public boolean getAllowsChildren() {
    return !isLeaf();
}

public TreeNode getChildAt(int ind) {
    return getChildren().get(ind);
}

public int getChildCount() {
    return getChildren().size();
}

private synchronized ArrayList getChildren() {
    if( children == null ) {
        load();
    }
    return children;
}

public int getIndex(TreeNode chld) {
    return getChildren().indexOf(chld);
}

public TreeNode getParent() {
    return parent;
}

public boolean isLeaf() {
    if( parent instanceof CustomerNode ) {
        return true;
    }
    else {
        return false;
    }
}

private void load() {
```

Example 10-3. An AccountNode That Loads Its Children Only When Necessary (continued)

```
        if( account == null ) {
            children = new ArrayList();
        }
        else {
            Iterator it = account.getCustomers();

            children = new ArrayList();
            while( it.hasNext() ) {
                children.add(it.next());
            }
        }
    }

    public String toString() {
        if( account == null ) {
            return "Accounts";
        }
        else {
            return ("" + account.getNumber());
        }
    }
}
```

In Example 10-3, you should pay particular attention to the fact that the node never asks its façade for the account's customers until something causes the UI to ask for them. The downside to this approach is that you cause a long-lived transaction to take place in the Swing event queue. This tradeoff is necessary as the costs for loading an entire tree are certain to outweigh the costs of a single, long-lived event queue transaction.

Distributed Listeners

Swing uses an event model that enables UI delegates to monitor their models for changes. Under this model, a UI delegate registers itself with its model as a listener. It listens for specific events, including property changes, that may require it to redraw itself. This event model, however, is sufficiently abstract to allow any object to listen for changes in a model. In fact, any object that has interesting things happen to it—a change in a value, a change in its internal structure, etc.— can allow other objects to listen for when those things occur. When one of those things occur, the object of interest notifies its listeners of the occurrence.

The example most people are familiar with is a button component. When you place a button on a screen, your application probably wants to know when someone clicks on the button so that an appropriate action can be performed. A button supports `ActionListener` listeners. An `ActionEvent` is an event that occurs when a user requests a GUI component to do its thing. The user request usually comes in the form of hitting the Enter key or clicking on the component. Using the following code, an application can register what should happen when the button is clicked:

```
JButton button = new JButton("Save");

button.addActionListener(new ActionListener() {
    public void actionPerformed(ActionEvent evt) {
        save();
    }
});
```

This code creates an anonymous class that listens to the button for `ActionEvent` occurrences. This example is mercifully simple because you are only executing a save. It could contain more complex logic. As a result, when an `ActionEvent` occurs, the button notifies its listeners by calling `actionPerformed()` in each listener. This particular listener calls the `save()` method to perform a save.

As I mentioned previously, the UI delegate is generally interested in property or structural changes that occur in its model. The JavaBeans event that represents property changes is called the `PropertyChangeEvent`. In the three-tier world, the model wants to be notified in turn when properties change in the server components it models. Unfortunately, the Swing event model does not translate across virtual machine boundaries for two reasons: First, the `PropertyChangeListener` and all other listener interfaces do not extend `java.rmi.Remote`. As a result, `PropertyChangeListener` instances cannot be called remotely. Second, a distributed application should not rely on method calls from the server to the client since you can never rely on being able to get through a client's network firewall.

The solution to these two problems is the distributed listener design pattern. Under this design pattern, the component's façade is implemented as a JavaBean that can throw `PropertyChangeEvent` occurrences. A model can thus implement `PropertyChangeListener` and listen to the façade. Internally, the façade polls its entity component for any changes. When it detects a change, it fires a `PropertyChangeEvent`. Using this design pattern, a client developer works only under a single paradigm, the Swing event model. The façade objects hide all complexities of distributed computing.

One of the worst mistakes you can make in distributed computing is assuming unlimited bandwidth. A danger of the distributed listener pattern is that it can be abused to eat up network resources by overpolling components. If, for example, each component instance on the server had 100 clients, each polling it twice a second, your system could begin to hog bandwidth quickly. You should therefore make sure to poll only often enough to be sure clients will notice changes in a reasonable time frame.

You saw this design pattern put into play in Example 8-7 from Chapter 8. Specifically, the reconnect() method that makes the actual connection between a façade and an entity starts a polling thread once the entity has been contacted. That thread then periodically checks the last modification time on the entity with the last modification time on the façade. If the two differ, the façade throws a PropertyChangeEvent. The challenge for the listener is to handle the event inside the Swing event queue. We address these multithreading issues in the next section.

Worker Threads

The book has discussed two constraints that make Swing programming difficult in a multithreaded environment:

- Changes to models are supposed to occur only in the Swing event queue.

- Processing in the Swing event queue should be nearly instantaneous.

The reality of the distributed computing world is that things happen asynchronously all over the network, and the network requests made by a client application are rarely instantaneous. You saw an instance of the first problem in your distributed listener pattern. Specifically, you have an alternate thread polling for changes to server objects. Those changes are noted inside your polling thread, but Swing demands that they not be effective until the event-queue thread touches them.

A common technique to dealing with these problems in Swing is called *worker threads.* A worker thread acts much like the Swing event queue, except that it executes long-lived operations and then notifies the event queue when it should take note of something. You can have any number of worker threads. The more you have, however, the more complex your transaction processing needs to be on the server. For example, the server would need the ability to deal with multiple concurrent connections from the same client. The library shown so far is fairly simplistic, so you will use a single worker thread.

In your application, a WorkerThread object helps support this paradigm. Example 10-4 is a simple class that addresses both of the previous issues.

Example 10-4. A WorkerThread Class to Support the Worker Thread Pattern

```
package com.imaginary.lwp;

import com.imaginary.util.FifoStack;
import javax.swing.SwingUtilities;

public abstract class WorkerThread {
    static private FifoStack queue  = new FifoStack();
    static private Thread    worker = null;
```

Example 10-4. A WorkerThread Class to Support the Worker Thread Pattern (continued)

```java
/**
 * Places a worker thread object onto the worker queue for
 * execution in the worker thread. When the time is right, the
 * <CODE>run()</CODE> method in the specified <CODE>WorkerThread</CODE>
 * object will run inside the worker thread. Upon completion,
 * the <CODE>complete()</CODE> method will then be executed inside
 * the event queue.
 * @param wt the worker to be executed inside the worker thread
 */
static public void invokeWorker(WorkerThread wt) {
    synchronized( queue ) {
        queue.push(wt);
        if( worker == null ) {
            worker = new Thread() {
                    public void run() {
                        runThread();
                    }
                };
            worker.setDaemon(true);
            worker.setPriority(Thread.NORM_PRIORITY);
            worker.setName("Worker Queue");
            worker.start();
        }
    }
}

static private void runThread() {
    while( true ) {
        WorkerThread wt;

        synchronized( queue ) {
            if( queue.isEmpty() ) {
                worker = null;
                return;
            }
            wt = queue.pop();
        }
        try {
            Runnable r;

            wt.run();
            r = new Runnable() {
                public void run() {
                    wt.complete();
                }
            };
            // place the call to complete() in the event queue
            SwingUtilities.invokeLater(r);
        }
```

Example 10-4. A WorkerThread Class to Support the Worker Thread Pattern (continued)

```
            catch( Exception e ) {
                e.printStackTrace();
            }
        }
    }


    /**
     * This method is called inside the Swing event queue. An implementation
     * of this class does not need to implement this method unless it
     * wants processing to occur specifically in the event queue.
     */
    public void complete() {
    }


    /**
     * Implementors must implement this method to specify the processing
     * that should occur in the worker thread.
     */
    public abstract void run();
}
```

The key method in this class is the invokeWorker() method. It accepts implementations of this class and adds them to a FIFO queue. If there is no worker thread running, it will start one up. The worker thread pulls WorkerThread implementations off the worker queue and executes their run() methods sequentially.

The task of calling long-lived operations across the network is now much simpler. Consider the following code that calls the transfer() method in the AccountTransactionSession class:

```
WorkerThread wt = new WorkerThread() {
    public void run() {
        try {
            session.transfer(Identifier.currentIdentifier(),
                            checking, savings, 100.0);
        }
        catch( Exception e ) {
            e.printStackTrace();
        }
    }
};

WorkerThread.invokeWorker(wt);
```

If you had any processing that needed to occur in the Swing event queue, you could have written that code in a complete() method. In a more complex application, you might want to add more complex processing, such as changing the cursor to an hourglass and possibly disabling the user from performing certain actions while the client is accessing the server.

III

REFERENCE

This final section of the book presents, in a style like *Java in a Nutshell,* the classes of the JDBC Core API and the JDBC Optional Package.

11

JDBC Reference

The `java.sql` package listed in Figure 11-1 contains the entire JDBC API. It first became part of the core Java libraries with the 1.1 release. Classes new as of JDK 1. 2 are indicated by the "Availability" header. Deprecated methods are preceded by a diamond (◆) mark. New JDK 1.2 methods in old JDK 1.1 classes are shown in **bold**. Table 11-1 shows the mapping of JDK version support to JDBC versions.

Table 11-1. JDK to JDBC Version Mapping

JDK Version	JDBC Version
1.0	1.1
1.1	1.2
1.2	2.0

Array

Synopsis

Interface Name:	`java.sql.Array`
Superclass:	None
Immediate Subclasses:	None
Interfaces Implemented:	None
Availability:	New as of JDK 1.2

Description

`Array` represents a SQL3 array object. The default duration of a reference to a SQL array is for the life of the transaction in which it was created.

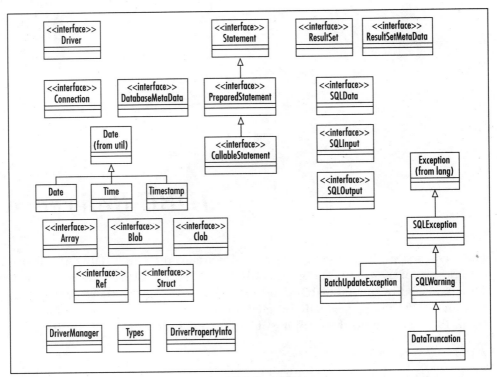

Figure 11-1. All classes and interfaces of the JDBC Core API

Class Summary

```
public interface Array {
    Object getArray() throws SQLException;
    Object getArray(Map map) throws SQLException;
    Object getArray(long index, int count)
        throws SQLException;
    Object getArray(long index, int count, Map map)
        throws SQLException;
    int getBaseType() throws SQLException;
    String getBaseTypeName() throws SQLException;
    ResultSet getResultSet() throws SQLException;
    ResultSet getResultSet(Map map) throws SQLException;
    ResultSet getResultSet(long index, int count)
        throws SQLException;
    ResultSet getResultSet(long index, int count,
                    Map map) throws SQLException
}
```

Object Methods

getArray()

```
public Object getArray() throws SQLException
public Object getArray(Map map) throws SQLException
public Object getArray(long index, int count)
    throws SQLException
public Object getArray(long index, int count, Map map)
    throws SQLException
```

Description

This method retrieves the contents of this SQL array into a Java language array or, instead, into the Java type specified by a provided Map. If a map is specified but no match is found in it, then the default mapping to a Java array is used. The two versions that accept an array index and element count enable you to retrieve a subset of the elements in the array.

getBaseType()

```
public int getBaseType() throws SQLException
```

Description

This method provides the JDBC type of the elements of this array.

getBaseTypeName()

```
public String getBaseTypeName() throws SQLException
```

Description

This method provides the SQL type name for the elements of this array.

getResultSet()

```
public ResultSet getResultSet() throws SQLException
public ResultSet getResultSet(Map map)
    throws SQLException
public ResultSet getResultSet(long index, int count)
    throws SQLException
public ResultSet getResultSet(long index, int count,
                                        Map map)
    throws SQLException
```

Description

This method provides a result set that contains the array's elements as rows. If appropriate, the elements are mapped using the type map for the connection or the specified type map if you pass one. Each row contains two columns: the first column is the index number (starting with 1), and the second column is the actual value.

Blob

Synopsis

Interface Name: `java.sql.Blob`
Superclass: None
Immediate Subclasses: None
Interfaces Implemented: None
Availability: New as of JDK 1.2

Description

This object represents a SQL BLOB. BLOB stands for "binary large object" and is a relational database representation of a large piece of binary data. The value of using a BLOB is that you can manipulate the BLOB as a Java object without retrieving all of the data behind the BLOB from the database. A BLOB object is only valid for the duration of the transaction in which it was created.

Class Summary

```
public interface Blob {
    InputStream getBinaryStream() throws SQLException;
    byte[] getBytes(long pos, int count)
        throws SQLException;
    long length() throws SQLException;
    long position(byte[] pattern, long start)
        throws SQLException;
    long position(Blob pattern, long start)
        throws SQLException;
}
```

Object Methods

getBinaryStream()

```
public InputStream getBinaryStream() throws SQLException
```

Description

This method retrieves the data that makes up the binary object as a stream from the database.

getBytes()

```
public byte[] getBytes(long pos, int count)
    throws SQLException
```

Description

This method returns the data that makes up the underlying binary object in part or in whole as an array of bytes. You can get a subset of the binary data by specifying a nonzero starting index or a number of bytes less than the object's length.

length()

```
public long length() throws SQLException
```

Description

This method provides the number of bytes that make up the BLOB.

position()

```
public long position(byte[] pattern, long start)
    throws SQLException
public long position(Blob pattern, long start)
    throws SQLException
```

Description

This method searches this Blob for the specified pattern and returns the byte at which the specified pattern occurs within this Blob. If the pattern does not occur, then this method will return −1.

CallableStatement

Synopsis

Interface Name:	java.sql.CallableStatement
Superclass:	java.sql.PreparedStatement
Immediate Subclasses:	None
Interfaces Implemented:	None
Availability:	JDK 1.1

Description

This extension of the PreparedStatement interface provides support for SQL stored procedures. It specifies methods that handle the binding of output parameters. JDBC prescribes a standard form in which stored procedures should appear independent of the DBMS being used. The format is:

```
{? = call ...}
{call ...}
```

Each question mark is a place holder for an input or output parameter. The first syntax provides a single result parameter. The second syntax has no result parameters. The parameters are referred to sequentially with the first question mark holding the place for parameter 1.

Before executing a stored procedure, all output parameters should be registered using the registerOutParameter() method. You then bind the input parameters using the various set methods and execute the stored procedure.

Class Summary

```
public interface CallableStatement extends PreparedStatement {
    Array getArray(int index) throws SQLException;
    BigDecimal getBigDecimal(int index)
        throws SQLException;
    #BigDecimal getBigDecimal(int index, int scale)
        throws SQLException;
    Blob getBlob(int index) throws SQLException;
    boolean getBoolean(int index) throws SQLException;
    byte getByte(int index) throws SQLException;
    byte[] getBytes(int index) throws SQLException;
    Clob getClob(int index) throws SQLException;
    java.sql.Date getDate(int index, Calendar cal)
        throws SQLException;
    java.sql.Date getDate(int index) throws SQLException;
    double getDouble(int index) throws SQLException;
    float getFloat(int index) throws SQLException;
    int getInt(int index) throws SQLException;
    long getLong(int index) throws SQLException;
    Object getObject(int index) throws SQLException;
    Object getObject(int index, Map map)
        throws SQLException;
    Ref getRef(int index) throws SQLException;
    short getShort(int index) throws SQLException;
    String getString(int index) throws SQLException;
    java.sql.Time getTime(int index) throws SQLException;
    java.sql.Time getTime(int index, Calendar cal)
        throws SQLException;
    java.sql.Timestamp getTimestamp(int index)
        throws SQLException;
    java.sql.Timestamp getTimestamp(int index,
                                    Calendar cal)
        throws SQLException;
    void registerOutParameter(int index, int type)
        throws SQLException;
    void registerOutParameter(int index, int type,
                              int scale)
        throws SQLException;
    void registerOutParameter(int index, int type,
                              String typename)
        throws SQLException;
    boolean wasNull() throws SQLException;
}
```

Object Methods

getBigDecimal()

```
public BigDecimal getBigDecimal(int index)
    throws SQLException
```

◆public BigDecimal getBigDecimal(int index, int scale)
        throws SQLException

Description

> This method returns the value of the parameter specified by the index
> parameter as a Java BigDecimal with a scale specified by the scale argu-
> ment. The scale is a nonnegative number representing the number of dig-
> its to the right of the decimal. Parameter indices start at 1; parameter 1 is
> thus index 1.

getArray(), getBlob(), getBoolean(), getByte(), getBytes(), get-Clob(), getDouble(), getFloat(), getInt(), getLong(), getRef(), getShort(), and getString()

```
public Array getArray(int index)
        throws SQLException
public Blob getBlob(int index) throws SQLException
public boolean getBoolean(int index) throws SQLException
public byte getByte(int index) throws SQLException
public byte[] getBytes(int index) throws SQLException
public Clob getClob(int index) throws SQLException
public double getDouble(int index) throws SQLException
public float getFloat(int index) throws SQLException
public int getInt(int index) throws SQLException
public long getLong(int index) throws SQLException
public Ref getRef(int index) throws SQLException
public short getShort(int index) throws SQLException
public String getString(int index) throws SQLException
```

Description

> These methods return the value of the parameter specified by the index
> argument as the Java datatype indicated by the method name.

getDate(), getTime(), and getTimestamp()

```
public Date getDate(int index) throws SQLException
public Date getDate(int index, Calendar cal)
        throws SQLException
public Time getTime(int index) throws SQLException
public Time getTime(int index, Calendar cal)
        throws SQLException
public Timestamp getTimestamp(int index)
        throws SQLException
public Timestamp getTimestamp(int index, Calendar cal)
        throws SQLException
```

Description

> These methods refine the basic java.util.Date object to be more suit-
> able for database programming. They provide ways to access return values
> from a CallableStatement as a Date, Time, or Timestamp object. The
> new JDK 1.2 variants allow you to specify a Calendar

getObject()

```
public Object getObject(int index) throws SQLException
public Object getObject(int index, Map map)
    throws SQLException
```

Description

This method returns the value of the specified output parameter as a Java object. The JDBC driver chooses the Java class that corresponds to the SQL type registered for this parameter using registerOutParameter(), or according to the specified type map.

registerOutParameter()

```
public void registerOutParameter(int index, int type)
    throws SQLException
public void registerOutParameter(int index, int type,
                                 int scale)
    throws SQLException
public void registerOutParameter(int index, int type,
                                 String typename)
    throws SQLException
```

Description

Before executing any stored procedure using a CallableStatement, you must register each of the output parameters. This method registers the java.sql.Type of an output parameter for a stored procedure. The first parameter specifies the output parameter being registered, and the second specifies the java.sql.Type to register. The three-argument version of this method is for BigDecimal types that require a scale. You later read the output parameters using the corresponding getXXX() method or getObject(). The third version of this method is new to JDK 1.2 and provides a way to map REF SQL types or custom SQL types.

wasNull()

```
public boolean wasNull() throws SQLException
```

Description

This method returns true if the last value you read using a getXXX() call was SQL null.

Clob

Synopsis

Interface Name:	java.sql.Clob
Superclass:	None
Immediate Subclasses:	None

Interfaces Implemented: None
Availability: New as of JDK 1.2

Description

A CLOB is an SQL3 type that stands for "character large object." Like a BLOB, a
CLOB represents a very large chunk of data in the database. Unlike a BLOB, it represents text stored using some sort of character encoding. The point of a CLOB type,
as opposed to a CHAR or VARCHAR type, is that CLOB data, like BLOB data, can be
retrieved as a stream instead of all at once.

Class Summary

```
public interface Clob {
    InputStream getAsciiStream() throws SQLException;
    Reader getCharacterStream() throws SQLException;
    String getSubString(long pos, int count)
        throws SQLException;
    long length() throws SQLException;
    long position(String pattern, long start)
        throws SQLException;
    long position(Clob pattern, long start)
        throws SQLException;
}
```

Object Methods

getAsciiStream()

```
public InputStream getAsciiStream() throws SQLException
```

Description

This method provides access to the data that makes up this Clob via an
ASCII stream.

getCharacterStream()

```
public Reader getCharacterStream() throws SQLException
```

Description

This method provides access to the data that makes up this Clob via a Unicode stream.

getSubString()

```
public String getSubString(long pos, int count)
    throws SQLException
```

Description

This method returns a substring of the Clob starting at the named position up to the number of characters specified by the count value.

length( )

```
public long length() throws SQLException
```

Description

This method provides the number of characters that make up the `Clob`.

position( )

```
public long position(String pattern, long start)
    throws SQLException;
public long position(Clob pattern, long start)
    throws SQLException;
```

Description

This method searches the `Clob` for the specified pattern starting at the specified start point. If the pattern is found within the `Clob`, the index at which the pattern first occurs is returned. If it does not exist within the `Clob`, then this method 'returns –1.

Connection

Synopsis

Interface Name: `java.sql.Connection`
Superclass: None
Immediate Subclasses: None
Interfaces Implemented: None
Availability: JDK 1.1

Description

`Connection` is the JDBC representation of a database session. It provides an application with `Statement` objects (and its subclasses) for that session. It also handles the transaction management for those statements. By default, each statement is committed immediately upon execution. You can use the `Connection` object to turn off this auto-commit feature for the session. In that event, you must expressly send commits, or any statements executed will be lost.

Class Summary

```
public interface Connection {
    static public final int TRANSACTION_NONE;
    static public final int TRANSACTION_READ_UNCOMMITTED;
    static public final int TRANSACTION_READ_COMMITTED;
    static public final int TRANSACTION_REPEATABLE_READ;
    static public final int TRANSACTION_SERIALIZABLE;
```

```
    void clearWarnings() throws SQLException;
    void close() throws SQLException;
    void commit() throws SQLException;
    Statement createStatement() throws SQLException;
    Statement createStatement(int type, int concur)
        throws SQLException;
    boolean getAutoCommit() throws SQLException;
    String getCatalog() throws SQLException;
    Map getTypeMap() throws SQLException;
    DatabaseMetaData getMetaData() throws SQLException;
    int getTransactionIsolation() throws SQLException;
    SQLWarning getWarnings() throws SQLException;
    boolean isClosed() throws SQLException;
    boolean isReadOnly() throws SQLException;
    String nativeSQL(String sql) throws SQLException;
    CallableStatement prepareCall(String sql)
        throws SQLException;
    CallableStatement prepareCall(String sql, int type,
                                  int concur)
        throws SQLException;
    PreparedStatement prepareStatement(String sql)
        throws SQLException;
    PreparedStatement prepareStatement(String sql,
                                       int type,
                                       int concur)
        throws SQLException;
    void rollback() throws SQLException;
    void setAutoCommit(boolean ac) throws SQLException;
    void setCatalog(String catalog) throws SQLException;
    void setReadOnly(boolean ro) throws SQLException;
    void setTransactionIsolation(int level)
        throws SQLException;
    void setTypeMap(Map map) throws SQLException;
}
```

Class Attributes

TRANSACTION_NONE

```
static public final int TRANSACTION_NONE
```

Description

Transactions are not supported.

TRANSACTION_READ_UNCOMMITTED

```
static public final int TRANSACTION_READ_UNCOMMITTED
```

Description

Uncommitted changes by one transaction are readable by other transactions.

TRANSACTION_READ_COMMITTED

    static public final int TRANSACTION_READ_COMMITTED

Description

> This attribute prevents dirty reads. In other words, changes by a TRANSACTION_READ_COMMITTED transaction are invisible to other transactions until the transaction making the change commits those changes.

TRANSACTION_REPEATABLE_READ

    static public final int TRANSACTION_REPEATABLE_READ

Description

> This attribute prevents dirty and nonrepeatable reads. A nonrepeatable read is one in which one transaction reads a row, a second transaction alters the row, and the first transaction rereads the row, getting different values the second time.

TRANSACTION_SERIALIZABLE

    static public final int TRANSACTION_SERIALIZABLE

Description

> This attribute prevents dirty, nonrepeatable, and phantom reads.

Object Methods

clearWarnings()

    public void clearWarnings() throws SQLException

Description

> This method clears out all the warnings associated with this Connection so that getWarnings() will return null until a new warning is reported.

close()

    public void close() throws SQLException

Description

> This method manually releases all resources (such as network connections and database locks) associated with a given JDBC Connection. This method is automatically called when garbage collection occurs; however, it is best to manually close a Connection once you are done with it, as it can leave resources open and result in an unresponsive database. This method implicitly closes any statements and result sets created by this connection.

commit()

    public void commit() throws SQLException

Description

> This method makes permanent the changes created by all statements associated with this Connection since the last commit or rollback was issued.

It should be used only when auto-commit is off. It does not commit changes made by statements associated with other Connection objects.

createStatement()

```
public Statement createStatement() throws SQLException
public Statement createStatement(int type, int concur)
    throws SQLException
```

Description

This method creates a Statement object associated with this Connection session. The no argument version of this method creates a Statement whose ResultSet instances are type-forward-only and read-only concurrency.

getAutoCommit() and setAutoCommit()

```
public boolean getAutoCommit() throws SQLException
public void setAutoCommit(boolean ac)
    throws SQLException
```

Description

By default, all Connection objects are in auto-commit mode. With auto-commit mode turned on, each statement is committed as it is executed. An application may instead choose to manually commit a series of statements together as a single transaction. In this case, you use the setAutoCommit() method to turn auto-commit off. You then follow your statements with a call to commit() or rollback(), depending on the success or failure of the transaction.

When in auto-commit mode, a statement is committed either when the statement is completed or when the next statement is executed, whichever is first. For statements returning a ResultSet, the statement is completed when the last row has been retrieved or the ResultSet has been closed. If a statement returns multiple result sets, the commit occurs when the last row of the last ResultSet object has been retrieved.

getCatalog() and setCatalog()

```
public String getCatalog() throws SQLException
public void setCatalog(String catalog) throws SQLException
```

Description

If a driver supports catalogs, use setCatalog() to select a subspace of the database with the specified catalog name. If the driver does not support catalogs, it will ignore this request.

getMetaData()

```
public DatabaseMetaData getMetaData() throws SQLException
```

Description

The DatabaseMetaData class provides methods that describe a database's tables, SQL support, stored procedures, and other information relating to the database and this Connection that are not directly related to executing statements and retrieving result sets. This method provides an instance of the DatabaseMetaData class for this Connection.

getTransactionIsolation() and setTransactionIsolation()

```
public int getTransactionIsolation() throws SQLException
public void setTransactionIsolation(int level)
    throws SQLException
```

Description

This method sets the Connection object's current transaction isolation level using one of the class attributes for the Connection interface. These levels are called TRANSACTION_NONE, TRANSACTION_READ_UNCOMMITTED, TRANSACTION_READ_COMMITTED, TRANSACTION_SERIALIZABLE, and TRANSACTION_REPEATABLE_READ.

getTypeMap() and setTypeMap()

```
public Map getTypeMap() throws SQLException
public void setTypeMap(Map map) throws SQLException
```

Description

You can use these methods to define or retrieve a custom mapping for SQL-structured and distinct types for all statements associated with this connection.

getWarnings()

```
public SQLWarning getWarnings() throws SQLException
```

Description

This method returns the first warning in the chain of warnings associated with this Connection object.

isClosed()

```
public boolean isClosed() throws SQLException
```

Description

This method returns true if the Connection has been closed.

isReadOnly() and setReadOnly()

```
public boolean isReadOnly() throws SQLException
public void setReadOnly(boolean ro) throws SQLException
```

Description

Some databases can optimize for read-only database access. The setReadOnly() method provides you with a way to put a Connection into read-only mode so that those optimizations occur. You cannot call setReadOnly() while in the middle of a transaction.

nativeSQL()

```
public String nativeSQL(String sql) throws SQLException
```

Description

Many databases may not actually support the same SQL required by JDBC. This method allows an application to see the native SQL for a given JDBC SQL string.

prepareCall()

```
public CallableStatement prepareCall(String sql)
    throws SQLException
public CallableStatement prepareCall(String sql,
                                    int type,
                                    int concur)
    throws SQLException
```

Description

Given a particular SQL string, this method creates a CallableStatement object associated with this Connection session. This is the preferred way of handling stored procedures. The default (no argument) version of this method provides a CallableStatement whose ResultSet instances are type-forward-only and read-only concurrency.

prepareStatement()

```
public PreparedStatement prepareStatement(String sql)
    throws SQLException
public PreparedStatement prepareStatement(String sql,
                                         int type,
                                         int concur)
    throws SQLException
```

Description

This method provides a PreparedStatement object to be associated with this Connection session. This is the preferred way of handling precompiled SQL statements. The default (no argument) version of this method provides a PreparedStatement whose ResultSet instances are type-forward-only and read-only concurrency.

rollback()

```
public void rollback() throws SQLException
```

Description

This method aborts all changes made by statements associated with this Connection since the last time a commit or rollback was issued. If you want to make those changes at a later time, your application will have to re-execute the statements that made those changes. This step should be used only when auto-commit is off.

DatabaseMetaData

Synopsis

Interface Name:	`java.sql.DatabaseMetaData`
Superclass:	None
Immediate Subclasses:	None
Interfaces Implemented:	None
Availability:	JDK 1.1

Description

This class provides a lot of information about the database to which a `Connection` object is connected. In many cases, it returns this information in the form of JDBC `ResultSet` objects. `DatabaseMetaData` will throw a SQLException for databases that do not support a particular kind of meta-data.

`DatabaseMetaData` methods take string patterns as arguments in which specific tokens within the `String` are interpreted to have a certain meaning. `%` matches any substring of 0 or more characters, and _ matches any one character. You can pass `null` to methods in place of string pattern arguments; this means that the argument's criteria should be dropped from the search.

Class Summary

```
public interface DatabaseMetaData {
    static public final int bestRowTemporary;
    static public final int bestRowTransaction;
    static public final int bestRowSession;
    static public final int bestRowUnknown;
    static public final int bestRowNotPseudo;
    static public final int bestRowPseudo;
    static public final int columnNoNulls;
    static public final int columnNullable;
    static public final int columnNullableUnknown;
    static public final int importedKeyCascade;
    static public final int importedKeyRestrict;
    static public final int importedKeySetNull;
    static public final int importedKeyNoAction;
    static public final int importedKeySetDefault;
    static public final int importedKeyInitiallyDeferred;
    static public final int importedKeyInitiallyImmediate;
    static public final int importedKeyNotDeferrable;
```

```
        static public final int procedureResultUnknown;
        static public final int procedureNoResult;
        static public final int procedureReturnsResult;
        static public final int procedureColumnUnknown;
        static public final int procedureColumnIn;
        static public final int procedureColumnOut;
        static public final int procedureColumnReturn;
        static public final int procedureColumnResult;
        static public final int procedureNoNulls;
        static public final int procedureNullable;
        static public final int procedureNullableUnknown;
        static public final short tableIndexStatistic;
        static public final short tableIndexClustered;
        static public final short tableIndexHashed;
        static public final short tableIndexOther;
        static public final int typeNoNulls;
        static public final int typeNullable;
        static public final int typeNullableUnknown;
        static public final int typePredNone;
        static public final int typePredChar;
        static public final int typePredBasic;
        static public final int typeSearchable;
        static public final int versionColumnUnknown;
        static public final int versionColumnNotPseudo;
        static public final int versionColumnPseudo;

    boolean allProceduresAreCallable()
        throws SQLException;
    boolean allTablesAreSelectable() throws SQLException;
    boolean dataDefinitionCausesTransactionCommit()
        throws SQLException;
    boolean dataDefinitionIgnoredInTransactions()
        throws SQLException;
    ResultSet getBestRowIdentifier(String catalog,
        String schema, String table, int scope,
        boolean nullable)
        throws SQLException;
    ResultSet getCatalogs() throws SQLException;
    String getCatalogSeparator() throws SQLException;
    String getCatalogTerm() throws SQLException;
    ResultSet getColumnPriveleges(String catalog,
            String spat, String table,
            String cpat) throws SQLException;
    ResultSet getColumns(String catalog,
            String spat, String tpat,
            String cpat) throws SQLException;
    ResultSet getCrossReference(String primaryCatalog,
            String primarySchema, String primaryTable,
            String foreignCatalog, String foreignSchema,
            String foreignTable) throws SQLException;
```

```
String getDatabaseProductName() throws SQLException;
String getDatabaseProductVersion()
     throws SQLException;
int getDefaultTransactionIsolation()
     throws SQLException;
int getDriverMajorVersion();
int getDriverMinorVersion();
String getDriverName() throws SQLException;
String getDriverVersion() throws SQLException;
ResultSet getExportedKeys(String catalog,
     String schema, String table)
     throws SQLException;
String getExtraNameCharacters() throws SQLException;
String getIdentifierQuoteString() throws SQLException;
ResultSet getImportedKeys(String catalog,
     String schema, String table) throws SQLException;
ResultSet getIndexInfo(String catalog,
     String schema, String table, boolean unique,
     boolean approximate) throws SQLException;
int getMaxBinaryLiteralLength() throws SQLException;
int getMaxCatalogNameLength() throws SQLException;
int getMaxCharLiteralLength() throws SQLException;
int getMaxcnameLength() throws SQLException;
int getMaxColumnsInGroupBy() throws SQLException;
int getMaxColumnsInIndex() throws SQLException;
int getMaxColumnsInOrderBy() throws SQLException;
int getMaxColumnsInSelect() throws SQLException;
int getMaxColumnsInTable() throws SQLException;
int getMaxConnections() throws SQLException;
int getMaxIndexLength() throws SQLException;
int getMaxProcedureNameLength()
     throws SQLException;
int getMaxRowSize() throws SQLException;
int getMaxRowSizeIncludeBlobs()
     throws SQLException;
int getMaxSchemaNameLength() throws SQLException;
int getMaxStatementLength() throws SQLException;
int getMaxStatements() throws SQLException;
int getMaxTableNameLength() throws SQLException;
int getMaxTablesInSelect() throws SQLException;
int getMaxUserNameLength() throws SQLException;
String getNumericFunctions() throws SQLException;
ResultSet getPrimaryKeys(String catalog,
     String schema, String table) throws SQLException;
ResultSet getProcedureColumns(String catalog,
     String schemePattern, String procedureNamePattern,
     String cnamePattern) throws SQLException;
String getProcedureTerm() throws SQLException;
ResultSet getProcedures(String catalog,
     String schemaPattern, String procedureNamePattern)
     throws SQLException;
```

```
public abstract ResultSet getSchemas() throws SQLException;
public abstract String getSchemaTerm() throws SQLException;
String getSearchStringEscape() throws SQLException;
String getSQLKeywords() throws SQLException;
String getStringFunctions() throws SQLException;
String getSystemFunctions() throws SQLException;
ResultSet getTablePriveleges(String catalog,
     String schemaPattern, String tableNamePattern)
     throws SQLException;
ResultSet getTableTypes() throws SQLException;
ResultSet getTables(String catalog,
     String schemaPattern, String tableNamePattern,
     String types[]) throws SQLException;
String getTimeDateFunctions() throws SQLException;
ResultSet getTypeInfo() throws SQLException;
String getURL() throws SQLException;
String getUserName() throws SQLException;
ResultSet getVersionColumns(String catalog,
     String schema, String table) throws SQLException;
boolean isCatalogAtStart() throws SQLException;
boolean isReadOnly() throws SQLException;
boolean nullPlusNonNullIsNull() throws SQLException;
boolean nullsAreSortedHigh() throws SQLException;
boolean nullsAreSortedLow() throws SQLException;
boolean nullsAreSortedAtStart() throws SQLException;
boolean nullsAreSortedAtEnd() throws SQLException;
boolean storesLowerCaseIdentifiers()
     throws SQLException;
boolean storesLowerCaseQuotedIdentifiers()
     throws SQLException;
boolean storesMixedCaseIdentifiers()
     throws SQLException;
boolean storesMixedCaseQuotedIdentifiers()
     throws SQLException;
boolean storesUpperCaseIdentifiers()
     throws SQLException;
boolean storesUpperCaseQuotedIdentifiers()
     throws SQLException;
boolean supportsAlterTableWithAddColumn()
     throws SQLException;
boolean supportsAlterTableWithDropColumn()
     throws SQLException;
boolean supportsANSI92FullSQL() throws SQLException;
boolean supportsANSI92IntermediateSQL()
     throws SQLException;
boolean supportsCatalogsInDataManipulation()
     throws SQLException;
boolean suppportsCatalogsInIndexDefinitions()
     throws SQLException;
boolean supportsCatalogsInPrivelegeDefinitions()
```

```
        throws SQLException;
boolean supportsCatalogsInProcedureCalls()
        throws SQLException;
boolean supportsCatalogsInTableDefinitions()
        throws SQLException;
boolean supportsColumnAliasing() throws SQLException;
boolean supportsConvert() throws SQLException;
boolean supportsConvert(int fromType, int toType)
        throws SQLException;
boolean supportsCoreSQLGrammar() throws SQLException;
boolean supportsCorrelatedSubqueries()
        throws SQLException;
boolean supportsDataDefinitionAndDataManipulationTransactions()
        throws SQLException;
boolean supportsDataManipulationTransactionsOnly()
        throws SQLException;
boolean supportsDifferentTableCorrelationNames()
        throws SQLException;
boolean supportsExpressionsInOrderBy()
        throws SQLException;
boolean supportsExtendedSQLGrammar()
        throws SQLException;
boolean supportsFullOuterJoins() throws SQLException;
boolean supportsGroupBy() throws SQLException;
boolean supportsGroupByBeyondSelect()
        throws SQLException;
boolean supportsGroupByUnrelated()
        throws SQLException;
boolean supportsIntegrityEnhancementFacility()
        throws SQLException;
boolean supportsLikeEscapeClause()
        throws SQLException;
boolean supportsLimitedOuterJoins()
        throws SQLException;
boolean supportsMinimumSQLGrammar()
        throws SQLException;
boolean supportsMixedCaseIdentifiers()
        throws SQLException;
boolean supportsMixedCaseQuotedIdenfitiers()
        throws SQLException;
boolean supportsMultipleResultSets()
        throws SQLException;
boolean supportsMultipleTransactions()
        throws SQLException;
boolean supportsNonNullableColumns()
        throws SQLException;
boolean supportsOpenCursorsAcrossCommit()
        throws SQLException;
```

```
boolean supportsOpenCursorsAcrossRollback()
    throws SQLException;
boolean supportsOpenStatementsAcrossCommit()
    throws SQLException;
boolean supportsOpenStatementsAcrossRollback()
    throws SQLException;
boolean supportsOrderByUnrelated()
    throws SQLException;
boolean supportsOuterJoins() throws SQLException;
boolean supportsPositionedDelete()
    throws SQLException;
boolean supportsPositionedUpdate()
    throws SQLException;
boolean supportsSchemasInDataManipulation()
    throws SQLException;
boolean supportsSchemasInIndexDefinitions()
    throws SQLException;
boolean supportsSchemasInPrivilegeDefinitions()
    throws SQLException;
boolean supportsSchemasInProcedureCalls()
    throws SQLException;
boolean supportsSchemasInTableDefinitions()
    throws SQLException;
boolean supportsSelectForUpdate()
    throws SQLException;
boolean supportsStoredProcedures()
    throws SQLException;
boolean supportsSubqueriesInComparisons()
    throws SQLException;
boolean supportsSubqueriesInExists()
    throws SQLException;
boolean supportsSubqueriesInIns()
    throws SQLException;
boolean supportsSubqueriesInQuantifieds()
    throws SQLException;
boolean supportsTableCorrelationNames()
    throws SQLException;
boolean supportsTransactionIsolationLevel(int level)
    throws SQLException;
boolean supportsTransactions() throws SQLException;
boolean supportsUnion() throws SQLException;
boolean supportsUnionAll() throws SQLException;
boolean usesLocalFilePerTable()
    throws SQLException;
boolean usesLocalFiles() throws SQLException;
}
```

Date

Synopsis

Class Name:	`java.sql.Date`
Superclass:	`java.util.Date`
Immediate Subclasses:	None
Interfaces Implemented:	None
Availability:	JDK 1.1

Description

This class deals with a subset of functionality found in the `java.util.Date` class. It specifically worries only about days and ignores hours, minutes, and seconds.

Class Summary

```
public class Date extends java.util.Date {
    static public Date valueOf(String s);
    #public Date(int year, int month, int day);
    public Date(long date);
    public void setTime(long date);
    public String toString();
}
```

Class Methods

valueOf()

```
static public Date valueOf(String s)
```

Description

> Given a `String` in the form of `yyyy-mm-dd`, this method will return a corresponding instance of the `Date` class representing that date.

Object Constructors

Date()

```
public Date(long date)
◆public Date(int year, int month, int day)
```

Description

> Date () constructs a new `Date` instance. Constructing a `Date` requires use of the new JDK 1.2 `Date(long)` constructor. The date argument specifies the number of milliseconds since January 1, 1970 00:00:00 GMT. A negative number represents the milliseconds before that date. The second, deprecated constructor naturally should never be used since it is ambiguous with respect to calendar and time zone.

Object Methods

setTime()

```
public void setTime(long date)
```

Description

> This method sets the time represented by this Date object to the specified number of milliseconds since January 1, 1970 00:00:00 GMT. A negative number represents the milliseconds before that date.

toString()

```
public String toString()
```

Description

> This method provides a String representing this Date in the form yyyy-mm-dd.

Driver

Synopsis

Interface Name:	java.sql.Driver
Superclass:	None
Immediate Subclasses:	None
Interfaces Implemented:	None
Availability:	JDK 1.1

Description

This class represents a specific JDBC implementation. When a Driver is loaded, it should create an instance of itself and register that instance with the DriverManager class. This action allows applications to create instances of it using the Class.forName() call to load a driver.

The Driver object then provides the ability for an application to connect to one or more databases. When a request for a specific database comes through, the DriverManager passes the data source request to each Driver registered as a URL. The first Driver to connect to the data source using that URL will be used.

Class Summary

```
public interface Driver {
    boolean acceptsURL(String url) throws SQLException;
    Connection connect(String url, Properties info)
        throws SQLException;
    int getMajorVersion();
```

```
    int getMinorVersion();
    DriverPropertyInfo[] getPropertyInfo(String url,
                                           Properties info)
        throws SQLException;
    boolean jdbcCompliant();
}
```

Object Methods

acceptsURL()

    public boolean acceptsURL(String url) throws SQLException

Description

This method returns true if the specified URL matches the URL subprotocol used by this driver.

connect()

    public Connection connect(String url, Properties info)
        throws SQLException

Description

This method attempts a connect using the specified URL and Property information (usually containing the username and password). If the URL is not right for this driver, connect() simply returns null. If it is the right URL but an error occurs during the connection process, a SQLException should be thrown.

getMajorVersion()

    public int getMajorVersion()

Description

This method returns the major version number for the driver.

getMinorVersion()

    public int getMinorVersion()

Description

Returns the minor version number for the driver.

getPropertyInfo()

    public DriverPropertyInfo[] getPropertyInfo(String url,
                                           Properties info)
        throws SQLException;

Description

This method allows GUI-based RAD environments to determine which properties the driver needs on connect so it can prompt a user to enter values for those properties.

jdbcCompliant()

```
public boolean jdbcCompliant()
```

Description

> A driver can return true here only if it passes the JDBC compliance tests. This means that the driver implementation supports the full JDBC API and full SQL 92 Entry Level.

DriverManager

Synopsis

Class Name:	`java.sql.DriverManager`
Superclass:	None
Immediate Subclasses:	None
Interfaces Implemented:	None
Availability:	JDK 1.1

Description

The `DriverManager` holds the master list of registered JDBC drivers for the system. Upon initialization, it loads all classes specified in the `jdbc.drivers` property. You can thus specify any runtime information about the database being used by an application on the command line.

During program execution, other drivers may register themselves with the `DriverManager` by calling the `registerDriver()` method. The `DriverManager` uses a JDBC URL to find an application's desired driver choice when requests are made through `getConnection()`.

The `DriverManager` class is likely to disappear one day as the new JDBC 2.0 Standard Extension provides a more application-friendly way of getting a database connection.

Class Summary

```
public class DriverManager {
    static void deregisterDriver(Driver driver)
        throws SQLException;
    static public synchronized Connection getConnection(String url,
        Properties info) throws SQLException;
    static public synchronized Connection getConnection(String url,
        String user, String password) throws SQLException;
    static public synchronized Connection getConnection(String url)
        throws SQLException;
```

```
    static public Driver getDriver(String url) throws SQLException;
    static public Enumeration getDrivers();
    static public int getLoginTimeout();
    #static public PrintStream getLogStream();
    static public PrintWriter getLogWriter();

    static public void println(String message);
    static public synchronized void registerDriver(Driver driver)
            throws SQLException;
    #static public void setLogStream(PrintStream out);
    static public void setLogWriter(PrintWriter out);
    static public void setLoginTimeout(int seconds);
}
```

Class Methods

deregisterDriver()

```
    static public void deregisterDriver(Driver driver) throws SQLException
```

Description

This method removes a Driver from the list of registered drivers.

getConnection()

```
    static public synchronized Connection getConnection(String url,
            Properties info) throws SQLException
    static public synchronized Connection getConnection(String url,
            String user, String password) throws SQLException
    static public synchronized Connection getConnection(String url)
            throws SQLException
```

Description

This method establishes a connection to the data store represented by the given URL. The DriverManager then looks through its list of registered Driver instances for one that will handle the specified URL. If none is found, it throws a SQLException. Otherwise it returns the Connection instance from the connect() method in the Driver class.

getDriver()

```
    static public Driver getDriver(String url) throws SQLException
```

Description

This method returns a driver than can handle the specified URL.

getDrivers()

```
    static public Enumeration getDrivers()
```

Description

This method returns a list of all registered drivers.

getLoginTimeout() and setLoginTimeout()

```
static public int getLoginTimeout()
static public int setLoginTimeout()
```

Description

The login timeout is the maximum time in seconds that a driver can wait while attempting to log in to a database.

getLogStream() and setLogStream()

```
◆static public PrintStream getLogStream()
◆static public void setLogStream(PrintStream out)
static public PrintWriter getLogWriter()
static public void setLogWriter(PrintWriter out)
```

Description

This method sets the stream used by the DriverManager and all drivers. The LogStream variant is the old JDK 1.1 version and should be avoided in favor of log writers

println()

```
static public void println(String message)
```

Description

This method prints a message to the current log stream.

registerDriver()

```
static public synchronized void registerDriver(Driver driver)
        throws SQLException
```

Description

This method allows a newly loaded Driver to register itself with the DriverManager class.

DriverPropertyInfo

Synopsis

Class Name: java.sql.DriverPropertyInfo
Superclass: None
Immediate Subclasses: None
Interfaces Implemented: None
Availability: JDK 1.1

Description

This class provides information required by a driver to connect to a database. Only development tools are likely to require this class. It has no methods, but simply a list of public attributes.

Class Summary

```
public class DriverPropertyInfo {
    public String[] choices;
    public String description;
    public String name;
    public boolean required;
    public String value;
    public DriverPropertyInfo(String name, String value);
}
```

Object Attributes

choices

`public String[] choices`

Description

> This attribute provides a list of choices from which a user may be prompted to specify a value for this property. This value can be null.

description

`public String description`

Description

> This attribute gives a brief description of the property or null.

name

`public String name`

Description

> This attribute gives the name of the property.

required

`public boolean required`

Description

> This attribute indicates whether or not this property must be set in order to make a connection.

value

`public String value`

Description

> This attribute gives the current value of the property or null, if no current value is set.

Object Constructors

DriverPropertyInfo()

> public DriverPropertyInfo(String name, String value)

> *Description*

> This constructor creates a new `DriverPropertyInfo` object with the name and value attributes set to the specified parameters. All other values are set to their default values.

PreparedStatement

Synopsis

Interface Name:	java.sql.PreparedStatement
Superclass:	java.sql.Statement
Immediate Subclasses:	java.sql.CallableStatement
Interfaces Implemented:	None
Availability:	JDK 1.1

Description

This class represents a precompiled SQL statement.

Class Summary

```
public interface PreparedStatement extends Statement {
    void addBatch() throws SQLException;
    void clearParameters() throws SQLException;
    boolean execute() throws SQLException;
    ResultSet executeQuery() throws SQLException;
    int executeUpdate() throws SQLException;
    ResultSetMetaData getMetaData() throws SQLException;
    void setArray(int index, Array arr)
        throws SQLException;
    void setAsciiStream(int index, InputStream is,
        int length) throws SQLException;
    void setBigDecimal(int index, BigDecimal d)
        throws SQLException;
    void setBinaryStream(int index, InputStream is,
        int length) throws SQLException;
    void setBlob(int index, Blob b) throws SQLException;
    void setBoolean(int index, boolean b)
        throws SQLException;
    void setByte(int index, byte b) throws SQLException;
    void setBytes(int index, byte[] bts)
```

```
            throws SQLException;
    void setCharacterStream(int index, Reader rdr,
        int length) throws SQLException;
    void setClob(int index, Clob c) throws SQLException;
    void setDate(int index, Date d) throws SQLException;
    void setDate(int index, Date d, Calendar cal)
        throws SQLException;
    void setDouble(int index, double x)
        throws SQLException;
    void setFloat(int index, float f) throws SQLException;
    void setInt(int index, int x) throws SQLException;
    void setLong(int index, long x) throws SQLException;
    void setNull(int index, int type) throws SQLException;
    void setNull(int index, int type, String tname)
        throws SQLException;
    void setObject(int index, Object ob)
        throws SQLException;
    void setObject(int index, Object ob, int type)
        throws SQLException;
    void setObject(int index, Object ob, int type,
        int scale) throws SQLException;
    void setRef(int index, Ref ref) throws SQLException;
    void setShort(int index, short s) throws SQLException;
    void setString(int index, String str)
        throws SQLException;
    void setTime(int index, Time t) throws SQLException;
    void setTime(int index, Time t, Calendar cal)
        throws SQLException;
    void setTimestamp(int index, Timestamp ts)
        throws SQLException;
    void setTimestamp(int index, Timestamp ts, Calendar cal)
        throws SQLException;
    #void setUnicodeStream(int index, InputStream is,
        int length) throws SQLException;
}
```

Object Methods

addBatch()

```
public void addBatch() throws SQLException
```

Description

This method adds a set of parameters to the batch for batch processing.

clearParameters()

```
public abstract void clearParameters() throws SQLException
```

Description

> Once set, a parameter value remains bound until either a new value is set for the parameter or until `clearParameters()` is called. This method clears all parameters associated with the `PreparedStatement`.

`execute()`, `executeQuery()`, and `executeUpdate()`

```
public abstract boolean execute() throws SQLException
public abstract ResultSet executeQuery() throws SQLException
public abstract int executeUpdate() throws SQLException
```

Description

> These methods execute the `PreparedStatement`. The first method, `execute()`, allows you to execute the `PreparedStatement` when you do not know if it is a query or an update. It returns `true` if the statement has result sets to process. The `executeQuery()` method is used for executing queries. It returns a result set for processing. The `executeUpdate()` statement is used for executing updates. It returns the number of rows affected by the update.

`getMetaData()`

```
public ResultSetMetaData getMetaData() throws SQLException;
```

Description

> This method retrieves the number, types, and properties of a `ResultSet`'s columns.

`setArray()`, `setAsciiStream()`, `setBigDecimal()`, `setBinaryStream()`, `setBlob()`, `setBoolean()`, `setByte()`, `setBytes()`, `setCharacterStream()`, `setClob()`, `setDate()`, `setDouble()`, `setFloat()`, `setInt()`, `setLong()`, `setNull()`, `setObject()`, `setRef()`, `setShort()`, `setString()`, `setTime()`, `setTimestamp()`, and `setUnicodeStream()`

```
public void setArray(int index, Array arr)
    throws SQLException
public void setAsciiStream(int index, InputStream is,
    int length) throws SQLException
public void setBigDecimal(int index, BigDecimal d)
    throws SQLException
public void setBinaryStream(int index, InputStream is,
    int length) throws SQLException
public void setBlob(int index, Blob b)
    throws SQLException
public void setBoolean(int index, boolean b)
    throws SQLException
public void setByte(int index, byte b)
    throws SQLException
public void setBytes(int index, byte[] bts)
    throws SQLException
public void setCharacterStream(int index, Reader rdr,
```

```
    int length) throws SQLException
public void setClob(int index, Clob c)
    throws SQLException
public void setDate(int index, Date d)
    throws SQLException
public void setDate(int index, Date d, Calendar cal)
    throws SQLException
public void setDouble(int index, double d)
    throws SQLException
public void setFloat(int index, float f)
    throws SQLException
public void setInt(int index, int x)
    throws SQLException
public void setLong(int index, long x)
    throws SQLException
public void setNull(int index, int type)
    throws SQLException
public void setNull(int index, int type, String tname)
    throws SQLException
public void setObject(int index, Object ob)
    throws SQLException
public void setObject(int index, Object ob, int type)
    throws SQLException
public void setObject(int index, Object ob, int type,
    int scale) throws SQLException
public void setRef(int index, Ref ref)
    throws SQLException
public void setShort(int index, short s)
    throws SQLException
public void setString(int index, String str)
    throws SQLException
public void setTime(int index, Time t)
    throws SQLException
public void setTime(int index, Time t, Calendar cal)
    throws SQLException
public void setTimestamp(int index, Timestamp ts)
    throws SQLException
public void setTimestamp(int index, Timestamp ts,
    Calendar cal) throws SQLException
◆public void setUnicodeStream(int index, InputStream is,
    int length) throws SQLException
```

Description

Binds a value to the specified parameter.

Ref

Synopsis

Interface Name:	java.sql.Ref
Superclass:	None
Immediate Subclasses:	None
Interfaces Implemented:	None
Availability:	New as of JDK 1.2

Description

A Ref is a reference to a value of a SQL structured type in the database. You can dereference a Ref by passing it as a parameter to a SQL statement and executing the statement.

Class Summary

```
public interface Ref {
    String getBaseTypeName() throws SQLException;
}
```

Object Methods

getBaseTypeName()

```
public String getBaseTypeName() throws SQLException
```

Description

This method provides the SQL structured type name for the referenced item.

ResultSet

Synopsis

Interface Name:	java.sql.ResultSet
Superclass:	None
Immediate Subclasses:	None
Interfaces Implemented:	None
Availability:	JDK 1.1

Description

This class represents a database result set. It provides an application with access to database queries one row at a time. During query processing, a ResultSet maintains a pointer to the current row being manipulated. The application then moves through the results sequentially until all results have been processed or the ResultSet is closed. A ResultSet is automatically closed when the Statement that generated it is closed, re-executed, or used to retrieve the next ResultSet in a multiple result set query.

Class Summary

```
public interface ResultSet {
    static public final int CONCUR_READ_ONLY;
    static public final int CONCUR_UPDATABLE;
    static public final int FETCH_FORWARD;
    static public final int FETCH_REVERSE;
    static public final int FETCH_UNKNOWN;
    static public final int TYPE_FORWARD_ONLY;
    static public final int TYPE_SCROLL_INSENSITIVE;
    static public final int TYPE_SCROLL_SENSITIVE;
    boolean absolute(int row) throws SQLException;
    void afterLast() throws SQLException;
    void beforeFirst() throws SQLException;
    void cancelRowUpdates() throws SQLException;
    void clearWarnings() throws SQLException;
    void close() throws SQLException;
    void deleteRow() throws SQLException;
    int findColumn(String cname) throws SQLException;
    boolean first() throws SQLException;
    Array getArray(int index) throws SQLException;
    Array getArray(String cname) throws SQLException;
    InputStream getAsciiStream(int index)
        throws SQLException;
    InputStream getAsciiStream(String cname)
        throws SQLException;
    InputStream getBinaryStream(int index)
        throws SQLException;
    InputStream getBinaryStream(String cname)
        throws SQLException;
    BigDecimal getBigDecimal(int index)
        throws SQLException;
    #BigDecimal getBigDecimal(int index, int scale)
        throws SQLException;
    BigDecimal getBigDecimal(String cname)
        throws SQLException;
    #BigDecimal getBigDecimal(String cname, int scale)
        throws SQLException;
    InputStream getBinaryStream(int index)
```

```
                    throws SQLException;
          InputStream getBinaryStream(String cname)
              throws SQLException;
        Blob getBlob(int index) throws SQLException;
        Blob getBlob(String cname) throws SQLException;
        boolean getBoolean(int index) throws SQLException;
        boolean getBoolean(String cname) throws SQLException;
        byte getByte(int index) throws SQLException;
        byte getByte(String cname) throws SQLException;
        byte[] getBytes(int index) throws SQLException;
        byte[] getBytes(String cname) throws SQLException;
        Reader getCharacterStream(int index)
              throws SQLException;
        Reader getCharacterStream(String cname)
              throws SQLException;
        Clob getClob(int index) throws SQLException;
        Clob getClob(String cname) throws SQLException;
        int getConcurrency() throws SQLException;
        String getCursorName() throws SQLException;
        Date getDate(int index) throws SQLException;
        Date getDate(int index, Calendar cal)
              throws SQLException;
        Date getDate(String cname) throws SQLException;
        Date getDate(String cname, Calendar cal)
              throws SQLException;
        double getDouble(int index) throws SQLException;
        double getDouble(String cname) throws SQLException;
        int getFetchDirection() throws SQLException;
        int getFetchSize() throws SQLException;
        float getFloat(int index) throws SQLException;
        float getFloat(String cname) throws SQLException;
        int getInt(int index) throws SQLException;
        int getInt(String cname) throws SQLException;
        long getLong(int index) throws SQLException;
        long getLong(String cname) throws SQLException;
        ResultSetMetaData getMetaData() throws SQLException;
        Object getObject(int index) throws SQLException;
        Object getObject(int index, Map map)
              throws SQLException;
        Object getObject(String cname) throws SQLException;
        Object getObject(String cname, Map map)
              throws SQLException;
        Ref getRef(int index) throws SQLException;
        Ref getRef(String cname) throws SQLException;
        int getRow() throws SQLException;
        short getShort(int index) throws SQLException;
        short getShort(String cname) throws SQLException;
        Statement getStatement() throws SQLException;
        String getString(int index) throws SQLException;
```

```
String getString(String cname) throws SQLException;
Time getTime(int index) throws SQLException;
Time getTime(int index, Calendar cal)
    throws SQLException;
Time getTime(String cname) throws SQLException;
Time getTime(String cname, Calendar cal)
    throws SQLException;
Timestamp getTimestamp(int index) throws SQLException;
Timestamp getTimestamp(int index, Calendar cal)
    throws SQLException;
Timestamp getTimestamp(String cname) throws SQLException;
Timestamp getTimestamp(String cname, Calendar cal)
    throws SQLException;
int getType() throws SQLException;
#InputStream getUnicodeStream(int index)
    throws SQLException;
#InputStream getUnicodeStream(String cname)
    throws SQLException;
SQLWarning getWarnings() throws SQLException;
void insertRow() throws SQLException;
boolean isAfterLast() throws SQLException;
boolean isBeforeFirst() throws SQLException;
boolean isFirst() throws SQLException;
boolean isLast() throws SQLException;
boolean last() throws SQLException;
void moveToCurrentRow() throws SQLException;
void moveToInsertRow() throws SQLException;
boolean next() throws SQLException;
boolean previous() throws SQLException;
void refreshRow() throws SQLException;
boolean relative(int rows) throws SQLException;
boolean rowDeleted() throws SQLException;
boolean rowInserted() throws SQLException;
boolean rowUpdated() throws SQLException;
void setFetchDirection(int dir) throws SQLException;
void setFetchSize(int rows) throws SQLException;
void updateAsciiStream(int index, InputStream is,
    int length) throws SQLException;
void updateAsciiStream(String cname, InputStream is,
    int length) throws SQLException;
void updateBigDecimal(int index, BigDecimal d)
    throws SQLException;
void updateBigDecimal(String cname, BigDecimal d)
    throws SQLException;
void updateBinaryStream(int index, InputStream is)
    throws SQLException;
void updateBinaryStream(String cname, InputStream is)
    throws SQLException;
void updateBoolean(int index, boolean b)
```

```
        throws SQLException;
void updateBoolean(String cname, boolean b)
        throws SQLException;
void updateByte(int index, byte b)
        throws SQLException;
void updateByte(String cname, byte b)
        throws SQLException;
void updateBytes(int index, byte[] bts)
        throws SQLException;
void updateBytes(String cname, byte[] bts)
        throws SQLException;
void updateCharacterStream(int index, Reader rdr,
        int length) throws SQLException;
void updateCharacterStream(String cname, Reader rdr,
        int length) throws SQLException;
void updateDate(int index, Date d)
        throws SQLException;
void updateDate(String cname, Date d)
        throws SQLException;
void updateDouble(int index, double d)
        throws SQLException;
void updateDouble(String cname, double d)
        throws SQLException;
void updateFloat(int index, float f)
        throws SQLException;
void updateFloat(String cname, float f)
        throws SQLException;
void updateInt(int index, int x) throws SQLException;
void updateInt(String cname, int x)
        throws SQLException;
void updateLong(int index, long x)
        throws SQLException;
void updateLong(String cname, long x)
        throws SQLException;
void updateNull(int index) throws SQLException;
void updateNull(String cname) throws SQLException;
void updateObject(int index, Object ob)
        throws SQLException;
void updateObject(int index, Object ob, int scale)
void updateObject(String cname, Object ob)
        throws SQLException;
void updateObject(String cname, Object ob, int scale)
        throws SQLException;
void updateRow() throws SQLException;
void updateShort(int index, short s)
        throws SQLException;
void updateShort(String cname, short s)
        throws SQLException;
void updateString(int index, String str)
```

```
        throws SQLException;
    void updateString(String cname, String str)
        throws SQLException;
    void updateTime(int index, Time t)
        throws SQLException;
    void updateTime(String cname, Time t)
        throws SQLException;
    void updateTimestamp(int index, Timestamp ts)
        throws SQLException;
    void updateTimestamp(String cname, Timestamp ts)
        throws SQLException;
    boolean wasNull() throws SQLException;
}
```

Class Attributes

CONCUR_READ_ONLY

    static public final int CONCUR_READ_ONLY

Description

This concurrency mode specifies that a result set may not be updated.

CONCUR_UPDATABLE

    static public final int CONCUR_UPDATABLE

Description

This concurrency mode specifies that a result set is updatable.

FETCH_FORWARD

    static public final int FETCH_FORWARD

Description

This value specifies that a result set's fetch direction is in the forward direction, from first to last.

FETCH_REVERSE

    static public final int FETCH_REVERSE

Description

This value specifies that a result set's fetch direction is in the reverse direction, from last to first.

FETCH_UNKNOWN

    static public final int FETCH_UNKNOWN

Description

This value specifies that the order of result-set processing is unknown.

TYPE_FORWARD_ONLY

    static public final int TYPE_FORWARD_ONLY

Description

> This result set type specifies that a result set can be only navigated in the forward direction.

TYPE_SCROLL_INSENSITIVE

`static public final int TYPE_SCROLL_INSENSITIVE`

Description

> This result set type specifies that a result set may be navigated in any direction, but it is not sensitive to changes made by others.

TYPE_SCROLL_SENSITIVE

`static public final int TYPE_SCROLL_SENSITIVE`

Description

> This result set type specifies that a result set may be navigated in any direction and that changes made by others will be seen in the result set.

Object Methods

absolute()

`public boolean absolute(int row) throws SQLException`

Description

> This method moves the cursor to the specified row number starting from the beginning for a positive number or the end for a negative number.

afterLast()

`public void afterLast() throws SQLException`

Description

> This method moves the cursor to the end of the result set, after the last row.

beforeFirst()

`public void beforeFirst() throws SQLException`

Description

> This method moves the cursor to the beginning of the result set, before the first row.

cancelRowUpdates()

`public void cancelRowUpdates() throws SQLException`

Description

> This method cancels any updates made to this row.

clearWarnings()

`public void clearWarnings() throws SQLException`

Description

> This method clears all warnings from the SQLWarning chain. Subsequent calls to getWarnings() then returns null until another warning occurs.

close()

```
public void close() throws SQLException
```

Description

> This method performs an immediate, manual close of the ResultSet. This is generally never required, as the closure of the Statement associated with the ResultSet will automatically close the ResultSet.

deleteRow()

```
public void deleteRow() throws SQLException
```

Description

> This method deletes the current row from this result set and from the database.

findColumn()

```
public int findColumn(String cname) throws SQLException
```

Description

> For the specified column name, this method will return the column number associated with it.

first()

```
public boolean first() throws SQLException
```

Description

> This method moves the cursor to the first row of a result set.

getAsciiStream(), getBinaryStream(), getCharacterStream(), and getUnicodeStream()

```
public InputStream getAsciiStream(int index)
    throws SQLException
public InputStream getAsciiStream(String cname)
    throws SQLException
public InputStream getBinaryStream(int index)
    throws SQLException
public InputStream getBinaryStream(String cname)
    throws SQLException
public Reader getCharacterStream(int index)
    throws SQLException
public Reader getCharacterStream(String cname)
    throws SQLException
◆public InputStream getUnicodeStream(int index)
    throws SQLException
◆public InputStream getUnicodeStream(String cname)
    throws SQLException
```

Description

In some cases, it may make sense to retrieve large pieces of data from the database as a Java InputStream. These methods allow an application to retrieve the specified column from the current row in this manner. You should notice that the getUnicodeStream() method has been deprecated in favor of the new getCharacterStream() method.

getArray(), getBlob(), getBoolean(), getByte(), getBytes(), getClob(), getDate(), getDouble(), getFloat(), getInt(), getLong(), getRef(), getShort(), getString(), getTime(), and getTimestamp()

```
public Array getArray(int index) throws SQLException
public Array getArray(String cname) throws SQLException
public Blob getBlob(int index) throws SQLException
public Blob getBlob(String cname) throws SQLException
public boolean getBoolean(int index) throws SQLException
public boolean getBoolean(String cname) throws SQLException
public byte getByte(int index) throws SQLException
public byte getByte(String cname) throws SQLException
public byte[] getBytes(int index) throws SQLException
public byte[] getBytes(String cname) throws SQLException
public Clob getClob(int index) throws SQLException
public Clob getClob(String cname) throws SQLException
public Date getDate(int index) throws SQLException
public Date getDate(String cname) throws SQLException
public double getDouble(int index) throws SQLException
public double getDouble(String cname) throws SQLException
public float getFloat(int index) throws SQLException
public float getFloat(String cname) throws SQLException
public int getInt(int index) throws SQLException
public int getInt(String cname) throws SQLException
public long getLong(int index) throws SQLException
public long getLong(String cname) throws SQLException
public Ref getRef(int index) throws SQLException
public Ref getRef(String cname) throws SQLException
public short getShort(int index) throws SQLException
public short getShort(String cname) throws SQLException
public String getString(int index) throws SQLException
public String getString(String cname) throws SQLException
public Time getTime(int index) throws SQLException
public Time getTime(String cname) throws SQLException
public Timestamp getTimestamp(int index)
    throws SQLException
public Timestamp getTimestamp(String cname)
    throws SQLException
```

Description

These methods return the specified column value for the current row as the Java data type that matches the method name.

getConcurrency(), and setConcurrency()

```
public int getConcurrency() throws SQLException
```

Description

These methods access the result set concurrency mode. It initially takes its value from the statement that generated this result set.

getCursorName()

```
public String getCursorName() throws SQLException
```

Description

Because some databases allow positioned updates, an application needs the cursor name associated with a ResultSet to perform those positioned updates. This method provides the cursor name.

getMetaData()

```
public ResultSetMetaData getMetaData() throws SQLException
```

Description

This method provides the meta-data object for this ResultSet.

getFetchDirection(), setFetchDirection(), getFetchSize(), and setFetchSize()

```
public int getFetchDirection() throws SQLException
public void setFetchDirection(int dir) throws SQLException
public int getFetchSize() throws SQLException
public void setFetchSize(int rows) throws SQLException
```

Description

These methods provide optimization hints for the driver. The driver is free to ignore these hints. The fetch size is the suggested number of rows the driver should prefetch each time it grabs data from the database. The direction is a hint to the driver about the direction in which you intend to work.

getObject()

```
public Object getObject(int index) throws SQLException
public Object getObject(int index, Map map)
    throws SQLException
public Object getObject(String cname) throws SQLException
public Object getObject(String cname, Map map)
    throws SQLException
```

Description

This method returns the specified column value for the current row as a Java object. The type returned will be the Java object that most closely matches the SQL type for the column. It is also useful for columns with database-specific datatypes.

getRow()

public int getRow() throws SQLException

Description

This method returns the current row number.

getStatement()

public Statement getStatement() throws SQLException

Description

This method returns the Statement instance generating this result set.

getType()

public int getType() throws SQLException

Description

This method returns the result set type for this result set.

getWarnings()

public SQLWarning getWarnings() throws SQLException

Description

This method returns the first SQLWarning object in the warning chain.

insertRow()

public void insertRow() throws SQLException

Description

This method inserts the contents of the insert row into the result set and the database.

isAfterLast()

public boolean isAfterLast() throws SQLException

Description

This method returns true if this result set is positioned after the last row in the result set.

isBeforeLast()

public boolean isBeforeFirst() throws SQLException

Description

This method returns true if this result set is positioned before the first row in the result set.

isFirst()

public boolean isFirst() throws SQLException

Description

This method returns true if the result set is positioned on the first row of the result set.

isLast()

public boolean isLast() throws SQLException

Description

This method returns true if result set is positioned after the last row in the result set.

last()

public boolean last() throws SQLException

Description

This method moves the cursor to the last row in the result set.

moveToCurrentRow()

public void moveToCurrentRow() throws SQLException

Description

This method moves the result set to the current row. It is used after you insert a row.

moveToInsertRow()

public void moveToInsertRow() throws SQLException

Description

This method moves the result to a new insert row. You need to call moveToCurrentRow() to get back.

next() and previous()

public boolean next() throws SQLException
public boolean previous() throws SQLException

Description

These methods navigate one row forward or one row backward in the ResultSet. Under a newly created result set, the result set is positioned before the first row. The first call to next() would thus move the result set to the first row. These methods return true as long as there is a row to move to. If there are no further rows to process, it returns false. If an InputStream from the previous row is still open, it is closed. The SQLWarning chain is also cleared.

refreshRow()

public void refreshRow() throws SQLException

Description

This method refreshes the current row with its most recent value from the database.

relative()

```
public boolean relative(int rows) throws SQLException
```

Description

This method moves the cursor the specified number of rows forward or backward. A positive number indicates that the cursor should be moved forward and a negative number indicates it should be moved backward.

rowDeleted(), rowInserted(), and rowUpdated()

```
public boolean rowDeleted() throws SQLException
public boolean rowInserted() throws SQLException
public boolean rowUpdated() throws SQLException
```

Description

These methods return true if the current row has been deleted, inserted, or updated.

updateAsciiStream(), updateBigDecimal(), updateBinaryStream(), updateBoolean(), updateByte(), updateBytes(), updateCharacterStream(), updateDate(), updateDouble(), updateFloat(), updateInt(), updateLong(), updateNull(), updateObject(), updateShort(), updateString(), updateTime(), and updateTimestamp()

```
public void updateAsciiStream(int index, InputStream is,
    int length) throws SQLException
public void updateAsciiStream(String cname, InputStream is,
    int length) throws SQLException
public void updateBigDecimal(int index, BigDecimal d)
    throws SQLException
public void updateBigDecimal(String cname, BigDecimal d)
    throws SQLException
public void updateBinaryStream(int index, InputStream is)
    throws SQLException
public void updateBinaryStream(String cname, InputStream is)
    throws SQLException
public void updateBoolean(int index, boolean b)
    throws SQLException
public void updateBoolean(String cname, boolean b)
    throws SQLException
public void updateByte(int index, byte b)
    throws SQLException
public void updateByte(String cname, byte b)
    throws SQLException
public void updateBytes(int index, byte[] bts)
    throws SQLException
public void updateBytes(String cname, byte[] bts)
    throws SQLException
public void updateCharacterStream(int index, Reader rdr,
    int length) throws SQLException
```

```
public void updateCharacterStream(String cname, Reader rdr,
    int length) throws SQLException
public void updateDate(int index, Date d)
    throws SQLException
public void updateDate(String cname, Date d)
    throws SQLException
public void updateDouble(int index, double d)
    throws SQLException
public void updateDouble(String cname, double d)
    throws SQLException
public void updateFloat(int index, float f)
    throws SQLException
public void updateFloat(String cname, float f)
    throws SQLException
public void updateInt(int index, int x)
    throws SQLException
public void updateInt(String cname, int x)
    throws SQLException
public void updateLong(int index, long x)
    throws SQLException
public void updateLong(String cname, long x)
    throws SQLException
public void updateNull(int index) throws SQLException
public void updateNull(String cname) throws SQLException
public void updateObject(int index, Object ob)
    throws SQLException
public void updateObject(int index, Object ob, int scale)
    throws SQLException
public void updateObject(String cname, Object ob)
    throws SQLException
public void updateObject(String cname, Object ob, int scale)
    throws SQLException
public void updateShort(int index, short s)
    throws SQLException
public void updateShort(String cname, short s)
    throws SQLException
public void updateString(int index, String str)
    throws SQLException
public void updateString(String cname, String str)
    throws SQLException
public void updateTime(int index, Time t)
    throws SQLException
public void updateTime(String cname, Time t)
    throws SQLException
public void updateTimestamp(int index, Timestamp ts)
    throws SQLException
public void updateTimestamp(String cname, Timestamp ts)
    throws SQLException
```

Description

These methods update a column in the current row of your result set as long as your result set supports updating. Once you are done modifying the row, you can call insertRow() or updateRow() to save the changes to the database.

updateRow()

```
public void updateRow() throws SQLException
```

Description

This method updates changes made to the current row to the database.

wasNull()

```
public boolean wasNull() throws SQLException
```

Description

This method returns true if the last column read was null; otherwise it returns false.

ResultSetMetaData

Synopsis

Interface Name:	java.sql.ResultSetMetaData
Superclass:	None
Immediate Subclasses:	None
Interfaces Implemented:	None
Availability:	JDK 1.1

Description

This class provides meta-information about the types and properties of the columns in a ResultSet instance.

Class Summary

```
public interface ResultSetMetaData {
    static public final int columnNoNulls;
    static public final int columnNullable;
    static public final int columnNullableUnknown;
    String getCatalogName(int index)
        throws SQLException;
    String getColumnClassName(int index)
        throws SQLException;
    public int getColumnCount() throws SQLException;
    public int getColumnDisplaySize(int index)
```

```
          throws SQLException;
    public String getColumnLabel(int index)
          throws SQLException;
    public String getColumnName(int index)
          throws SQLException;
    public int getColumnType(int index) throws SQLException;
    public String getColumnTypeName(int index)
          throws SQLException;
    public int getPrecision(int index) throws SQLException;
    public int getScale(int index) throws SQLException;
    public String getSchemaName(int index)
          throws SQLException;
    public String getTableName(int index)
          throws SQLException;
    public boolean isAutoIncrement(int index)
          throws SQLException;
    public isCaseSensitive(int index)
          throws SQLException;
    public boolean isCurrency(int index)
          throws SQLException;
    public boolean isDefinitelyWritable(int index)
          throws SQLException;
    public int isNullable(int index) throws SQLException;
    public boolean isReadOnly(int index)
          throws SQLException;
    public boolean isSearchable(int index)
          throws SQLException;
    public boolean isSigned(int index) throws SQLException;
    public boolean isWritable(int index)
          throws SQLException;
}
```

Class Attributes

columnNoNulls

    static public final int columnNoNulls

Description

The column in question does not allow null values.

columnNullable

    static public final int columnNullable

Description

The column in question allows null values.

columnNullableUnknown

    static public final int columnNullableUnknown

Description

It is not known if the column in question can accept null values.

Object Methods

getCatalogName()

```
public String getCatalogName(int index) throws SQLException
```

Description

This method provides the catalog name associated with the specified column's table.

getColumnClassName()

```
public String getColumnClassName(int index)
    throws SQLException
```

Description

This method provides the fully qualified name of the Java class that will be instantiated by a call to ResultSet.getObject() for this column.

getColumnCount()

```
public int getColumnCount() throws SQLException
```

Description

This method returns the number of columns in the result set.

getColumnDisplaySize()

```
public int getColumnDisplaySize(int column)
    throws SQLException
```

Description

This method returns the maximum width for displaying the column's values.

getColumnLabel()

```
public String getColumnLabel(int column) throws SQLException
```

Description

This method returns the display name for the column.

getColumnName()

```
public String getcname(int column) throws SQLException
```

Description

This method returns the database name for the column.

getColumnType()

```
public int getColumnType(int column) throws SQLException
```

Description

This method returns the SQL type for the specified column as a value from java.sql.Types.

getColumnTypeName()

> public String getColumnTypeName(int column)
>   throws SQLException

Description

> This method returns the name of the SQL type for the specified column.

getPrecision()

> public int getPrecision(int column) throws SQLException

Description

> This method returns the number of decimal digits for the specified column.

getScale()

> public int getScale(int column) throws SQLException

Description

> This method returns the number of digits to the right of the decimal for this column.

getSchemaName()

> public String getSchemaName(int column) throws SQLException

Description

> This method returns the schema for the table of the specified column.

getTableName()

> public String getTableName(int column) throws SQLException

Description

> This method returns the name of the table for the specified column.

isAutoIncrement()

> public boolean isAutoIncrement(int column) throws SQLException

Description

> This method returns true if the column is automatically numbered and therefore read-only.

isCaseSensitive()

> public boolean isCaseSensitive(int column) throws SQLException

Description

> This method returns true if the column's case is important.

isCurrency()

> public boolean isCurrency(int column) throws SQLException

Description

> This method returns true if the value for the specified column represents a currency value.

isDefinitelyWritable()

```
public boolean isDefinitelyWritable(int column)
    throws SQLException
```

Description

This method returns true if a write operation on the column will definitely succeed.

isNullable()

```
public int isNullable(int column) throws SQLException
```

Description

This method returns true if null values are allowed for the column.

isReadOnly()

```
public boolean isReadOnly(int column) throws SQLException
```

Description

This method returns true if the column is read-only.

isSearchable()

```
public boolean isSearchable(int column) throws SQLException
```

Description

This method returns true if the column may be used in a where clause.

isSigned()

```
public boolean isSigned(int column) throws SQLException
```

Description

This method returns true if the column contains a signed number.

isWritable()

```
public boolean isWritable(int column) throws SQLException
```

Description

This method returns true if it is possible for a write on a column to succeed.

SQLData

Synopsis

Interface Name:	java.sql.SQLData
Superclass:	None
Immediate Subclasses:	None
Interfaces Implemented:	None
Availability:	New as of JDK 1.2

Description

This interface is implemented by custom Java objects designed to be stored as Java objects in a Java-relational database. Any Java class registered in a type mapping must implement this interface. Programmers should never make direct calls to these methods.

Class Summary

```
public interface SQLData {
    String getSQLTypeName() throws SQLException;
    void readSQL(SQLInput input, String tname)
      throws SQLException;
    void writeSQL(SQLOutput output) throws SQLException;
}
```

Object Methods

getSQLTypeName()

```
public String getSQLTypeName() throws SQLException;
```

Description

> This method provides the name of the SQL user-defined type to which this implementation of SQLData maps.

void readSQL()

```
public void readSQL(SQLInput input, String tname)
  throws SQLException;
```

Description

> Using data of the relational database from the input stream, this method assigns values to the object's attributes. This method reads values from the input stream by calling the appropriate readXXX() methods in the SQLInput instance.

void writeSQL()

```
public void writeSQL(SQLOutput output) throws SQLException;
```

Description

> This method writes the attributes of this object to the specified output stream using the writeXXX() methods of the SQLOutput instance.

SQLInput

Synopsis

Interface Name: `java.sql.SQLInput`
Superclass: None
Immediate Subclasses: None
Interfaces Implemented: None
Availability: New as of JDK 1.2

Description

This interface represents a stream of data coming from a relational database. In this respect, it is very similar to an `ObjectInputStream` class. Programmers should never use this class, as it exists purely for drivers in supporting Java-relational type mapping.

Class Summary

```
public interface SQLInput {
    Array readArray() throws SQLException;
    InputStream readAsciiStream() throws SQLException;
    java.math.BigDecimal readBigDecimal()
      throws SQLException;
    InputStream readBinaryStream() throws SQLException;
    Blob readBlob() throws SQLException;
    boolean readBoolean() throws SQLException;
    byte readByte() throws SQLException;
    byte[] readBytes() throws SQLException;
    Reader readCharacterStream() throws SQLException;
    Clob readClob() throws SQLException;
    Date readDate() throws SQLException;
    double readDouble() throws SQLException;
    float readFloat() throws SQLException;
    int readInt() throws SQLException;
    long readLong() throws SQLException;
    Object readObject() throws SQLException;
    Ref readRef() throws SQLException;
    short readShort() throws SQLException;
    String readString() throws SQLException;
    Time readTime() throws SQLException;
    Timestamp readTimestamp() throws SQLException;
    boolean wasNull() throws SQLException;
}
```

Object Methods

readArray(), readAsciiStream(), readBigDecimal(), readBinryStream(), readBlob(), readBoolean(), readByte(), readBytes(), readCharacterStream(), readClob(), readDate(), readDouble(), readFloat(), readInt(), readLong(), readObject(), readRef(), readShort(), readString(), readTime(), and **readTimestamp()**

```
public Array readArray() throws SQLException;
public InputStream readAsciiStream() throws SQLException;
public java.math.BigDecimal readBigDecimal()
    throws SQLException;
public InputStream readBinaryStream() throws SQLException;
public Blob readBlob() throws SQLException;
public boolean readBoolean() throws SQLException;
public byte readByte() throws SQLException;
public byte[] readBytes() throws SQLException;
public Reader readCharacterStream() throws SQLException;
public Clob readClob() throws SQLException;
public Date readDate() throws SQLException;
public double readDouble() throws SQLException;
public float readFloat() throws SQLException;
public int readInt() throws SQLException;
public long readLong() throws SQLException;
public Object readObject() throws SQLException;
public Ref readRef() throws SQLException;
public short readShort() throws SQLException;
public String readString() throws SQLException;
public Time readTime() throws SQLException;
public Timestamp readTimestamp() throws SQLException;
```

Description

These methods read the next object off the stream as the datatype matching the method call. The readDate() method, for example, reads the next method as a java.sql.Date object.

wasNull()

```
public boolean wasNull() throws SQLException
```

Description

This method returns true if the last object read from the stream was a null value.

SQLOutput

Synopsis

Interface Name: java.sql.SQLOutput
Superclass: None

Immediate Subclasses:	None
Interfaces Implemented:	None
Availability:	New as of JDK 1.2

Description

This interface represents a stream of data sent to a relational database. This interface is used by JDBC drivers and should never be used directly by a programmer.

Class Summary

```
public interface SQLOutput {
    void writeArray(Array arr) throws SQLException;
    void writeAsciiStream(InputStream is) throws SQLException;
    void writeBigDecimal(java.math.BigDecimal bd)
        throws SQLException;
    void writeBinaryStream(InputStream is) throws SQLException;
    void writeBlob(Blob bl) throws SQLException;
    void writeBoolean(boolean b) throws SQLException;
    void writeByte(byte b) throws SQLException;
    void writeBytes(byte[] data) throws SQLException;
    void writeCharacterStream(Reader rdr) throws SQLException;
    void writeClob(Clob cl) throws SQLException;
    void writeDate(Date d) throws SQLException;
    void writeDouble(double d) throws SQLException;
    void writeFloat(float f) throws SQLException;
    void writeInt(int i) throws SQLException;
    void writeLong(long l) throws SQLException;
    void writeObject(Object ob) throws SQLException;
    void writeRef(Ref ref) throws SQLException;
    void writeShort(short s) throws SQLException;
    void writeString(String str) throws SQLException;
    void writeStruct(Struct s) throws SQLException;
    void writeTime(Time t) throws SQLException;
    void writeTimestamp(Timestamp ts) throws SQLException;
}
```

Object Methods

writeArray(), writeAsciiStream(), writeBigDecimal(), writeBinaryStream(), writeBlob(), writeBoolean(), writeByte(), writeBytes(), writeCharacterStream(), writeClob(), writeDate(), writeDouble(), writeFloat(), writeInt(), writeLong(), writeObject(), writeRef(), writeShort(), writeString(), writeStruct(), writeTime(), and **writeTimestamp()**

```
public void writeArray(Array arr) throws SQLException;
public void writeAsciiStream(InputStream is) throws SQLException;
public void writeBigDecimal(java.math.BigDecimal bd)
```

```
        throws SQLException;
    public void writeBinaryStream(InputStream is) throws SQLException;
    public void writeBlob(Blob bl) throws SQLException;
    public void writeBoolean(boolean b) throws SQLException;
    public void writeByte(byte b) throws SQLException;
    public void writeBytes(byte[] data) throws SQLException;
    public void writeCharacterStream(Reader rdr) throws SQLException;
    public void writeClob(Clob cl) throws SQLException;
    public void writeDate(Date d) throws SQLException;
    public void writeDouble(double d) throws SQLException;
    public void writeFloat(float f) throws SQLException;
    public void writeInt(int i) throws SQLException;
    public void writeLong(long l) throws SQLException;
    public void writeObject(Object ob) throws SQLException;
    public void writeRef(Ref ref) throws SQLException;
    public void writeShort(short s) throws SQLException;
    public void writeString(String str) throws SQLException;
    public void writeStruct(Struct s) throws SQLException;
    public void writeTime(Time t) throws SQLException;
    public void writeTimestamp(Timestamp ts) throws SQLException;
```

Description

These methods write the specified object to the output stream for storage in a relational database.

Statement

Synopsis

Interface Name:	`java.sql.Statement`
Superclass:	None
Immediate Subclasses:	`java.sql.PreparedStatement`
Interfaces Implemented:	None
Availability:	JDK 1.1

Description

This class represents an embedded SQL statement and is used by an application to perform database access. Closing a `Statement` automatically closes any open `ResultSet` associated with the `Statement`.

Class Summary

```
public interface Statement {
    void addBatch(String sql) throws SQLException;
    void cancel() throws SQLException;
```

```
    void clearBatch() throws SQLException;
    void clearWarnings() throws SQLException;
    void close() throws SQLException;
    boolean execute(String sql) throws SQLException;
    int[] executeBatch() throws SQLException;
    ResultSet executeQuery(String sql)
        throws SQLException;
    int executeUpdate(String sql) throws SQLException;
    Connection getConnection() throws SQLException;
    int getFetchDirection() throws SQLException;
    int getFetchSize() throws SQLException;
    int getMaxFieldSize() throws SQLException;
    int getMaxRows() throws SQLException;
    boolean getMoreResults() throws SQLException;
    int getQueryTimeout() throws SQLException;
    ResultSet getResultSet() throws SQLException;
    int getResultSetConcurrency() throws SQLException;
    int getResultSetType() throws SQLException;
    int getUpdateCount() throws SQLException;
    SQLWarning getWarnings() throws SQLException;
    void setCursorName(String name) throws SQLException;
    void setEscapeProcessing(boolean enable)
        throws SQLException;
    void setFetchDirection(int dir) throws SQLException;
    void setFetchSize(int rows) throws SQLException;
    void setMaxFieldSize(int max) throws SQLException;
    void setMaxRows(int max) throws SQLException;
    void setQueryTimeout(int seconds)
        throws SQLException;
}
```

Object Methods

addBatch()

```
public void addBatch(String sql) throws SQLException
```

Description

This method adds the specified SQL statement to the current set of batch commands.

cancel()

```
public void cancel() throws SQLException
```

Description

In a multithreaded environment, you can use this method to flag that processing for this Statement in another thread should be canceled. In this respect, it is similar to the stop() method for Thread objects.

clearBatch()

```
public void clearBatch() throws SQLException
```

Description

This method clears out any batch statements.

clearWarnings() and getWarnings()

```
public void clearWarnings() throws SQLException
public SQLWarning getWarnings() throws SQLException
```

Description

The clearWarnings() method allows you to clear all warnings from the warning chain associated with this class. The getWarnings() method retrieves the first warning on the chain. You can retrieve any subsequent warnings on the chain using that first warning.

close()

```
public void close() throws SQLException
```

Description

This method manually closes the Statement. It is generally not required because a Statement is automatically closed whenever the Connection associated with it is closed.

execute(), executeQuery(), and executeUpdate()

```
public boolean execute(String sql) throws SQLException
public ResultSet executeQuery(String sql) throws SQLException
public int executeUpdate(String sql) throws SQLException
```

Description

These methods execute the Statement by passing the specified SQL to the database. The first method, execute(), allows you to execute the Statement when you do not know if it is a query or an update. It will return true if the statement has result sets to process. The executeQuery() method is used for executing queries. It returns a result set for processing. The executeUpdate() statement is used for executing updates. It returns the number of rows affected by the update.

executeBatch()

```
public int[] executeBatch(String sql) throws SQLException
```

Description

This method submits the batched list of SQL statements to the database for execution. The return value is an array of numbers that describe the number of rows affected by each SQL statement.

getConnection()

`public Connection getConnection() throws SQLException`

Description

This method returns the Connection object associated with this Statement.

getFetchDirection(), setFetchDirection(), getFetchSize(), and setFetchSize()

`public int getFetchDirection() throws SQLException`
`public void setFetchDirection(int dir) throws SQLException`
`public int getFetchSize() throws SQLException`
`public void setFetchSize(int rows) throws SQLException`

Description

These methods provide optimization hints for the driver, which the driver is free to ignore. The fetch size is the suggested number of rows the driver should prefetch each time it grabs data from the database. The direction is a hint to the driver about the direction in which you intend to work.

getMaxFieldSize() and setMaxFieldize()

`public int getMaxFieldSize() throws SQLException`
`public void setMaxFieldSize(int max) throws SQLException`

Description

These methods support the maximum field size attribute that determines the maximum amount of data for any BINARY, VARBINARY, LONGVARBINARY, CHAR, VARCHAR, and LONGVARCHAR column value. If the limit is exceeded, the excess is silently discarded.

getMaxRows() and setMaxRows()

`public int getMaxRows() throws SQLException`
`public void setMaxRows(int max) throws SQLException`

Description

These attributes represent the maximum number of rows a ResultSet can contain. If this number is exceeded, then any excess rows are silently discarded.

getMoreResults()

`public boolean getMoreResults() throws SQLException`

Description

This method moves to the next result and returns true if that result is a ResultSet. Any previously open ResultSet for this Statement is then implicitly closed. If the next result is not a ResultSet, or if there are no more results, this method will return false. You can test explicitly for no more results using:

`(!getMoreResults() && (getUpdateCount() == -1)`

getQueryTimeout() and setQueryTimeout()

```
public int getQueryTimeout() throws SQLException
public void setQueryTimeout(int seconds) throws SQLException
```

Description

This attribute is the amount of time a driver will wait for a Statement to execute. If the limit is exceeded, a SQLException is thrown.

getResultSet()

```
public ResultSet getResultSet() throws SQLException
```

Description

This method returns the current ResultSet. You should call this method only once per result. You never need to call it for executeQuery() calls that return a single result.

getResultSetConcurrency()

```
public int getResultSetConcurrency() throws SQLException
```

Description

This method returns the concurrency for result sets generated by this Statement.

getResultSetType()

```
public int getResultSetType() throws SQLException
```

Description

This method returns the result set type for result sets generated by this Statement.

getUpdateCount()

```
public int getUpdateCount() throws SQLException
```

Description

If the current result was an update, this method returns the number of rows affected by the update. If the result is a ResultSet or if there are no more results, –1 is returned. As with getResultSet(), this method should only be called once per result.

getWarnings()

```
public SQLWarning getWarnings() throws SQLException
```

Description

This method retrieves the first warning associated with the object.

setCursorName()

```
public void setCursorName(String name) throws SQLException
```

Description

This method specifies the cursor name to be used by subsequent Statement executions. For databases that support positioned updates and deletes, you can then use this cursor name in coordination with any ResultSet objects returned by your execute() or executeQuery() calls to identify the current row for a positioned update or delete. You must use a different Statement object to perform those updates or deletes. This method does nothing for databases that do not support positioned updates or deletes.

setEscapeProcessing()

```
public void setEscapeProcessing(boolean enable)
      throws SQLException
```

Description

Escape processing is on by default. When enabled, the driver performs escape substitution before sending SQL to the database.

Struct

Synopsis

Interface Name:	java.sql.Struct
Superclass:	None
Immediate Subclasses:	None
Interfaces Implemented:	None
Availability:	New as of JDK 1.2

Description

This class maps to a SQL3 structured type. An Struct instance has values that map to each of the attributes in its associated structured value in the database.

Class Summary

```
public interface Struct {
    Object[] getAttributes() throws SQLException;
    Object[] getAttributes(Map map) throws SQLException;
    String getSQLTypeName() throws SQLException;
}
```

Object Methods

getAttributes()

```
public Object[] getAttributes() throws SQLException
public Object[] getAttributes(Map map) throws SQLException
```

Description

This method provides the values for the attributes in the SQL structured type in order. If you pass a type map, it will use that type map to construct the Java values.

getSQLTypeName()

```
public String getSQLTypeName() throws SQLException
```

Description

This method provides the SQL type name for this structured type.

Time

Synopsis

Class Name: `java.sql.Time`
Superclass: `java.util.Date`
Immediate Subclasses: None
Interfaces Implemented: None
Availability: JDK 1.1

Description

This version of the `java.util.Date` class maps to a SQL TIME datatype.

Class Summary

```
public class Time extends java.util.Date {
    static public Time valueOf(String s);
    public Time(int hour, int minute, int second);
    public Time(long time);
    #public int getDate();
    #public int getDay();
    #public int getMonth();
    #public int getYear();
    #public int setDate(int i);
    #public int setMonth(int i);
    public void setTime(long time);
    #public void setYear(int i);
    public String toString();
}
```

Object Constructors

Time()

```
public Time(int hour, int minute, intsecond)
public Time(long time)
```

Description

> This constructor creates a new Time object. The first prototype constructs a Time for the hour, minute, and seconds specified. The second constructs one based on the number of seconds since January 1, 1970 12:00:00 GMT.

Object Methods

getDate(), setDate(), getDay(), getMonth(), setMonth(), getYear(), and setYear()

- ◆public int getDate()
- ◆public int getDay()
- ◆public int getMonth()
- ◆public int getYear()
- ◆public int setDate(int i)
- ◆public int setMonth(int i)
- ◆public void setYear(int i)

Description

> These attributes represent the individual segments of a Time object.

setTime()

    public void setTime(long time)

Description

> This method sets the Time object to the specified time as the number of seconds since January 1, 1970, 12:00:00 GMT.

toString()

    public String toString()

Description

> This method formats the Time into a String in the form of hh:mm:ss.

valueOf()

    static public Timestamp valueOf(String s)

Description

> This method creates a new Time based on a String in the form of hh: mm:ss.

Timestamp

Synopsis

Class Name:	java.sql.Timestamp
Superclass:	java.util.Date
Immediate Subclasses:	None

Interfaces Implemented: None
Availability: JDK 1.1

Description

This class serves as a SQL representation of the Java Date class specifically designed to serve as a SQL TIMESTAMP. It also provides the ability to hold nanoseconds as required by SQL TIMESTAMP values. You should keep in mind that this class uses the java.util.Date version of hashcode(). This means that two timestamps that differ only by nanoseconds will have identical hashcode() return values.

Class Summary

```
public class Timestamp extends java.util.Date {
    static public Timestamp valueOf(String s);
    #public Timestamp(int year, int month, int date,
        int hour, int minute, int second, int nano);
    public Timestamp(long time);
    public boolean after(Timestamp t);
    public boolean before(Timestamp t);
    public boolean equals(Timestamp t);
    public int getNanos();
    public void setNanos(int n);
    public String toString();
}
```

Object Constructors

Timestamp()

```
◆public Timestamp(int year, int month, int date, int hour, int minute,
        int second, int nano)
public Timestamp(long time)
```

Description

This constructor creates a new Timestamp object. The first prototype constructs a Timestamp for the year, month, date, hour, minute, second, and nanosecond specified. The second prototype constructs one based on the number of seconds since January 1, 1970, 12:00:00 GMT.

Object Methods

after()

```
public boolean after(Timestamp t)
```

Description

This method returns true if this Timestamp is later than the argument.

before()

```
public boolean before(Timestamp t)
```

Description

This method returns true if this Timestamp is earlier than the argument.

equals()

```
public boolean equals(Timestamp t)
```

Description

This method returns true if the two timestamps are equivalent.

getNanos() and setNanos()

```
public int getNanos()
public void setNanos(int n)
```

Description

This attribute represents the number of nanoseconds for this Timestamp.

toString()

```
public String toString()
```

Description

This method formats the Timestamp into a String in the form of yyyy-mm-dd hh:mm:ss.fffffffff.

valueOf()

```
static public Timestamp valueOf(String s)
```

Description

This method creates a new Timestamp based on a String in the form of yyyy-mm-dd hh:mm:ss.fffffffff.

Types

Synopsis

Class Name:	java.sql.Types
Superclass:	None
Immediate Subclasses:	None
Interfaces Implemented:	None
Availability:	JDK 1.1

Description

This class holds static attributes representing SQL datatypes. These values are the actual constant values defined in the XOPEN specification.

Class Summary

```
public class Types {
    static public final int ARRAY;
    static public final int BIGINT;
    static public final int BINARY;
    static public final int BIT;
    static public final int BLOB;
    static public final int CHAR;
    static public final int CLOB;
    static public final int DATE;
    static public final int DECIMAL;
    static public final int DISTINCT;
    static public final int DOUBLE;
    static public final int FLOAT;
    static public final int INTEGER;
    static public final int JAVA_OBJECT;
    static public final int LONGVARBINARY;
    static public final int LONGVARCHAR;
    static public final int NULL;
    static public final int NUMERIC;
    static public final int OTHER;
    static public final int REAL;
    static public final int REF;
    static public final int SMALLINT;
    static public final int STRUCT;
    static public final int TIME;
    static public final int TIMESTAMP;
    static public final int TINYINT;
    static public final int VARBINARY;
    static public final int VARCHAR;
}
```

12

The JDBC Optional Package Reference

The JDBC Optional Package is a new extension to the JDBC API. Its purpose is to provide nonessential, but useful database access features without bogging down the core API. Because it is in the `javax` namespace, this package does not come with the JDK. Certain vendors may, of course, choose to include this package with their virtual machines. If yours does not include the JDBC Optional Package, you can download it from *http://java.sun.com/products/jdbc*.

You may notice that a number of the interfaces and classes in this reference section are not discussed anywhere else in the book. While the JDBC Optional Package does specify their existence, they are not used by application developers. They are instead used by driver implementors. Figure 12-1 shows all of the classes and interfaces in the JDBC Optional Package.

ConnectionEvent

Synopsis

Class Name: `javax.sql.ConnectionEvent`
Superclass: `java.util.EventObject`
Immediate Subclasses: None
Interfaces Implemented: None
Availability: New as of JDK 1.2

Description

This class is used by the connection pooling subsystem to provide information about connection events, including `SQLException` being thrown.

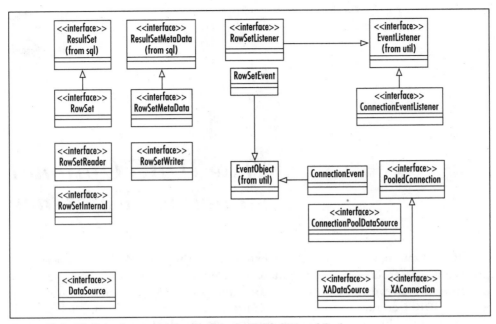

Figure 12-1. All of the classes and interfaces in the JDBC Optional Package

Class Summary

```
public class ConnectionEvent extends java.util.EventObject {
    public ConnectionEvent(PooledConnection conn);
    public ConnectionEvent(PooledConnection conn,
                        java.sql.SQLException ex);
    public java.sql.SQLException getSQLException();
}
```

Object Constructors

ConnectionEvent()

```
public ConnectionEvent(PooledConnection conn);
public ConnectionEvent(PooledConnection conn,
                    java.sql.SQLException ex);
```

Description

This constructor creates a ConnectionEvent instance tied to the specified pooled connection having the specified SQLException.

Object Methods

getSQLException();

```
public java.sql.SQLException getSQLException();
```

Description

> This method provides the SQLException associated with this event. This value can be null.

ConnectionEventListener

Synopsis

Interface Name:	javax.sql.ConnectionEventListener
Superclass:	java.util.EventListener
Immediate Subclasses:	None
Interfaces Implemented:	None
Availability:	New as of JDK 1.2

Description

This interface is implemented by classes wishing to know about events happening to pooled connections. A JDBC driver vendor implements this interface to be notified when a given connection has closed or thrown an exception.

Class Summary

```
public interface ConnectionEventListener
extends java.util.EventListener {
    void connectionClosed(ConnectionEvent evt);
    void connectionErrorOccurred(ConnectionEvent evt);
}
```

Object Methods

connectionClosed()

```
public void connectionClosed(ConnectionEvent evt);
```

Description

> This method is called by a pooled connection when the close() method has been called.

connectionErrorOccurred()

```
public void connectionErrorOccurred(ConnectionEvent evt);
```

Description

> This method is called by a pooled connection whenever a fatal error occurs during communications with a database. For example, if the server goes down, the connection needs to notify the pool to discard this connection from the pool and attempt a reconnect.

ConnectionPoolDataSource

Synopsis

Interface Name:	`javax.sql.ConnectionPoolDataSource`
Superclass:	None
Immediate Subclasses:	None
Interfaces Implemented:	None
Availability:	New as of JDK 1.2

Description

Implementors of this interface act as factories for providing `PooledConnection` instances. As with the `DataSource` interface, this class is designed to be registered with a JNDI directory service for applications to look up by name.

Class Summary

```
public interface ConnectionPoolDataSource {
    int getLoginTimeout() throws java.sql.SQLException;
    java.io.PrintWriter getLogWriter()
      throws java.sql.SQLException;
    PooledConnection getPooledConnection()
      throws java.sql.SQLException;
    PooledConnection getPooledConnection(String uid, String pw)
      throws java.sql.SQLException;
    void setLoginTimeout(int sec)
      throws java.sql.SQLException;
    void setLogWriter(java.io.PrintWriter lw)
      throws java.sql.SQLException;
}
```

Object Methods

getLoginTimeout() and **setLoginTimeout()**

```
public int getLoginTimeout() throws java.sql.SQLException;
public void setLoginTimeout(int sec)
  throws java.sql.SQLException;
```

Description

This method gets and sets the interval that the system waits to establish a connection before giving up. This value is an interval in seconds. A value of zero directs the data source to depend on the default timeout for the underlying system.

getLogWriter() and **setLogWriter()**

```
public java.io.PrintWriter getLogWriter()
  throws java.sql.SQLException;
```

```
public void setLogWriter(java.io.PrintWriter pw)
   throws java.sql.SQLException;
```

Description

> This method gets and sets the print writer for use in logging events. The character stream is used by all methods in this data source and all methods in objects constructucted by this data source.

getPooledConnection()

```
public PooledConnection getPooledConnection()
   throws java.sql.SQLException;
public PooledConnection getPooledConnection(String uid, String pw)
   throws java.sql.SQLException;
```

Description

> This is a factory method for creating a pooled connection to a database.

DataSource

Synopsis

Interface Name:	javax.sql.DataSource
Superclass:	None
Immediate Subclasses:	None
Interfaces Implemented:	None
Availability:	New as of JDK 1.2

Description

This class provides access to a database via JNDI. To get a JDBC connection, you can look up a data source in a JNDI naming or directory service and then grab a connection from that data source.

Class Summary

```
public interface DataSource {
    java.sql.Connection getConnection()
      throws java.sql.SQLException;
    java.sql.Connection getConnection(String uid, String pw)
      throws java.sql.SQLException;
    int getLoginTimeout() throws java.sql.SQLException;
    java.io.PrintWriter getLogWriter()
      throws java.sql.SQLException;
    void setLoginTimeout(int sec) throws java.sql.SQLException;
    void setLogWriter(java.io.PrintWriter pw)
      throws java.sql.SQLException;
}
```

Object Methods

getConnection()

```
public java.sql.Connection getConnection()
  throws java.sql.SQLException;
public java.sql.Connection getConnection(String uid, String pw)
  throws java.sql.SQLException;
```

Description

These are factory methods for the allocation of a connection to a database from a connection pool.

getLoginTimeout() and setLoginTimeout()

```
public int getLoginTimeout() throws java.sql.SQLException;
public void setLoginTimeout(int sec)
  throws java.sql.SQLException;
```

Description

These methods get and set a connection for the interval that the system waits to establish before giving up. This value is an interval in seconds. A value of zero directs the data source to depend on the default timeout for the underlying system.

getLogWriter() and setLogWriter()

```
public java.io.PrintWriter getLogWriter()
  throws java.sql.SQLException;
public void setLogWriter(java.io.PrintWriter pw)
  throws java.sql.SQLException;
```

Description

These methods get and set the print writer for use in logging events. The character stream is used by all methods in this data source and all methods in objects constructucted by this data source.

PooledConnection

Synopsis

Interface Name:	`javax.sql.PooledConnection`
Superclass:	None
Immediate Subclasses:	`javax.sql.XAConnection`
Interfaces Implemented:	None
Availability:	New as of JDK 1.2

Description

A PooledConnection represents a physical connection to a data source. An application uses a PooledConnection to grab a specific JDBC connection object from the connection pool for use in talking to a database.

Class Summary

```
public interface PooledConnection {
    void addConnectionEventListener(ConnectionEventListener l)
      throws java.sql.SQLException;
    void close() throws java.sql.SQLException;
    java.sql.Connection getConnection()
      throws java.sql.SQLException;
    void removeConnectionEventListener(ConnectionEventListener l)
      throws java.sql.SQLException;
}
```

Object Methods

addConnectionEventListener() and removeConnectionEventListener()

```
public void addConnectionEventListener(ConnectionEventListener l)
  throws java.sql.SQLException;
public void removeConnectionEventListener(ConnectionEventListener l)
  throws java.sql.SQLException;
```

Description

These two methods manage the addition and removal of objects listening for connection events generated by this pooled connection.

close()

```
public void close() throws java.sql.SQLException;
```

Description

This method will close all resources for the underlying connection to the database held by this pooled connection.

getConnection()

```
public java.sql.Connection getConnection()
  throws java.sql.SQLException;
```

Description

The getConnection() method provides temporary access to a pooled, physical connection to the database. That connection is returned to the pool when the application attempts to close it or encounters a fatal error.

RowSet

Synopsis

Interface Name:	`javax.sql.RowSet`
Superclass:	`java.sql.ResultSet`
Immediate Subclasses:	None
Interfaces Implemented:	None
Availability:	New as of JDK 1.2

Description

Implementation of this class provides a JavaBeans frontend to a JDBC result set. The key advantage of a RowSet is its ability to be configured at design time and executed at runtime.

Class Summary

```
public interface RowSet extends java.sql.ResultSet {
    void addRowSetListener(RowSetListener l);
    void clearParameters() throws java.sql.SQLException;
    void execute() throws java.sql.SQLException;
    String getCommand();
    String getDataSourceName();
    boolean getEscapeProcessing() throws java.sql.SQLException;
    int getMaxFieldSize() throws java.sql.SQLException;
    int getMaxRows() throws java.sql.SQLException;
    String getPassword();
    int getQueryTimeout() throws java.sql.SQLException;
    int getTransactionIsolation();
    java.util.Map getTypeMap() throws java.sql.SQLException;
    String getUrl() throws java.sql.SQLException;
    String getUserName();
    boolean isReadOnly();
    void removeRowSetListener(RowSetListener l);
    void setArray(int col, java.sql.Array arr)
      throws java.sql.SQLException;
    void setAsciiStream(int col, java.io.InputStream is,
                        int len) throws java.sql.SQLException;
    void setBigDecimal(int col, java.math.BigDecimal bd)
      throws java.sql.SQLException;
    void setBinaryStream(int col, java.io.InputStream is,
                         int len) throws java.sql.SQLException;
    void setBlob(int col, java.sql.Blob bl)
      throws java.sql.SQLException;
    void setBoolean(int col, boolean tf) throws java.sql.SQLException;
    void setByte(int col, byte b) throws java.sql.SQLException;
    void setBytes(int col, byte[] b) throws java.sql.SQLException;
```

```
void setCharacterStream(int col, Reader rdr, int len)
  throws java.sql.SQLException;
void setClob(int col, java.sql.Clob cl)
  throws java.sql.SQLException;
void setCommand(String sql) throws java.sql.SQLException;
void setConcurrency(int cncr) throws java.sql.SQLException;
void setDataSourceName(String dsn)
  throws java.sql.SQLException;
void setDate(int col, java.sql.Date d)
  throws java.sql.SQLException;
void setDate(int col, java.sql.Date d, java.util.Calendar cal)
  throws java.sql.SQLException;
void setDouble(int col, double d) throws java.sql.SQLException;
void setEscapeProcessing(boolean ep)
  throws java.sql.SQLException;
void setFloat(int col, float f) throws java.sql.SQLException;
void setInt(int col, int x) throws java.sql.SQLException;
void setLong(int col, long l) throws java.sql.SQLException;
void setMaxFieldSize(int max) throws java.sql.SQLException;
void setMaxRows(int max) throws java.sql.SQLException;
void setNull(int col, int stype) throws java.sql.SQLException;
void setNull(int col, int stype, String tname)
  throws java.sql.SQLException;
void setObject(int col, Object ob)
  throws java.sql.SQLException;
void setObject(int col, Object ob, int stype)
  throws java.sql.SQLException;
void setObject(int col, Object ob, int stype, int scale)
  throws java.sql.SQLException;
void setPassword(String pw) throws java.sql.SQLException;
void setQueryTimeout(int sec) throws java.sql.SQLException;
void setReadOnly(boolean ro) throws java.sql.SQLException;
void setRef(int col, java.sql.Ref ref)
  throws java.sql.SQLException;
void setShort(int col, short s) throws java.sql.SQLException;
void setString(int col, String str)
  throws java.sql.SQLException;
void setTime(int col, java.sql.Time t)
  throws java.sql.SQLException;
void setTime(int col, java.sql.Time t, java.util.Calendar cal)
  throws java.sql.SQLException;
void setTimestamp(int col, java.sql.Timestamp ts)
  throws java.sql.SQLException;
void setTimestamp(int col, java.sql.Timestamp ts,
                  java.util.Calendar cal)
  throws java.sql.SQLException;
void setTransactionIsolation(int ti)
  throws java.sql.SQLException;
void setType(int t) throws java.sql.SQLException;
```

```
      void setTypeMap(java.util.Map map) throws java.sql.SQLException;
      void setUrl(String url) throws java.sql.SQLException;
      void setUsername(String uid) throws java.sql.SQLException;
}
```

Object Methods

setArray(), **setAsciiStream()**, **setBigDecimal()**, **setBinaryStream()**, **setBlob()**, **setBoolean()**, **setByte()**, **setBytes()**, **setCharacter-Stream()**, **setClob()**, **setDate()**, **setDouble()**, **setFloat()**, **setInt()**, **setLong()**, **setNull()**, **setObject()**, **setRef()**, **setShort()**, **setString()**, **setTime()**, and **setTimestamp()**

```
    public void setArray(int col, java.sql.Array arr)
      throws java.sql.SQLException
    public void setAsciiStream(int col, java.io.InputStream is,
                               int length)
      throws java.sql.SQLException
    public void setBigDecimal(int col, java.math.BigDecimal d)
      throws java.sql.SQLException
    public void setBinaryStream(int col, java.io.InputStream is,
                                int length)
      throws java.sql.SQLException;
    public void setBlob(int col, java.sql.Blob b)
      throws java.sql.SQLException
    public void setBoolean(int col, boolean b)
      throws java.sql.SQLException
    public void setByte(int col, byte b)
      throws java.sql.SQLException
    public void setBytes(int col, byte[] bts)
      throws java.sql.SQLException
    public void setCharacterStream(int col, java.io.Reader rdr,
                                   int len)
      throws java.sql.SQLException
    public void setClob(int col, java.sql.Clob c)
      throws java.sql.SQLException
    public void setDate(int col, java.sql.Date d)
      throws java.sql.SQLException
    public void setDate(int col, java.sql.Date d,
                        java.util.Calendar cal)
      throws java.sql.SQLException
    public void setDouble(int col, double d)
      throws java.sql.SQLException
    public void setFloat(int col, float f)
      throws java.sql.SQLException
    public void setInt(int col, int x)
      throws java.sql.SQLException
    public void setLong(int col, long x)
      throws java.sql.SQLException
    public void setNull(int col, int type)
```

```
   throws java.sql.SQLException
public void setNull(int col, int type, String tname)
   throws java.sql.SQLException
public void setObject(int col, Object ob)
   throws java.sql.SQLException
public void setObject(int col, Object ob, int type)
   throws java.sql.SQLException
public void setObject(int col, Object ob, int type,
    int scale) throws SQLException
public void setRef(int col, java.sql.Ref ref)
   throws java.sql.SQLException
public void setShort(int col, short s)
   throws java.sql.SQLException
public void setString(int col, String str)
   throws java.sql.SQLException
public void setTime(int col, java.sql.Time t)
   throws java.sql.SQLException
public void setTime(int col, Time t, Calendar cal)
   throws java.sql.SQLException
public void setTimestamp(int col, Timestamp ts)
   throws java.sql.SQLException
public void setTimestamp(int col, Timestamp ts,
    Calendar cal) throws SQLException
```

Description

These methods bind a value to the specified parameter. The bindings may be saved as part of a rowset configuration.

addRowSetListener() and removeRowSetListener()

```
public void addRowSetListener(RowSetListener l);
public void removeRowSetListener(RowSetListener l);
```

Description

These methods support maintenance of the list of objects listening to the rowset for special events. Any object interested in such events registers its interest via addRowSetListener().

clearParameters()

```
public void clearParameters() throws java.sql.SQLException;
```

Description

This method clears out settings for the currently bound parameters so that the rowset may be reused with new parameters.

execute()

```
public void execute() throws java.sql.SQLException;
```

Description

This method executes the currently stored SQL command with the current set of bindings.

getCommand() and setCommand()

```
public String getCommand();
public void setCommand(String sql) throws java.sql.SQLException;
```

Description

These methods manage the SQL command used by this rowset to generate its results. The command must be a SQL that will generate results, such as a SELECT statement.

getDataSourceName() and setDataSourceName()

```
public String getDataSourceName();
public void setDataSourceName(String dsn)
  throws java.sql.SQLException;
```

Description

These methods enable you to manage a data source name at design time so that a rowset knows where to get its results at runtime.

getEscapeProcessing() and setEscapeProcessing()

```
public boolean getEscapeProcessing() throws java.sql.SQLException;
public void setEscapeProcessing(boolean ep)
  throws java.sql.SQLException;
```

Description

These methods control whether the driver performs escape processing on SQL before sending it to the database. The default is for escape processing to be on.

getMaxFieldSize() and setMaxFieldSize()

```
public int getMaxFieldSize() throws java.sql.SQLException;
public void setMaxFieldSize(int fs)
  throws java.sql.SQLException;
```

Description

These methods manage the maximum amount of data that can be returned for any column value. This limitation can only apply to BINARY, VARBINARY, LONGVARBINARY, CHAR, VARCHAR, and LONGVARCHAR columns.

getMaxRows() and setMaxRows()

```
public int getMaxRows() throws java.sql.SQLException;
public void setMaxRows(int mr) throws java.sql.SQLException;
```

Description

These methods manage the maximum number of rows that can appear in a rowset. If the actual results for the execution of its SQL command contain more rows than the value for max rows, those rows are silently dropped.

getPassword() and setPassword()

```
public String getPassword();
public void setPassword(String pw) throws java.sql.SQLException;
```

Description

These methods manage the password used to authenticate this rowset with its data source.

getQueryTimeout() and setQueryTimeout()

```
public int getQueryTimeout() throws java.sql.SQLException;
public void setQueryTimeout(int to)
  throws java.sql.SQLException;
```

Description

These methods enable you to control how long a rowset waits before its SQL executes. If the timeout is exceeded, the execution aborts.

getTransactionIsolation() and setTransactionIsolation()

```
public int getTransactionIsolation() throws java.sql.SQLException;
public void setTransactionIsolation int ti)
  throws java.sql.SQLException;
```

Description

These methods control the transaction isolation level of the result set behind this rowset. A full discussion of transaction isolation levels occurs in Chapter 4, *Advanced JDBC*.

getTypeMap() and setTypeMap()

```
public java.util.Map getTypeMap() throws java.sql.SQLException;
public void setTypeMap(java.util.Map map)
  throws java.sql.SQLException;
```

Description

These methods enable you to control how the JDBC maps user-defined SQL types to Java classes.

getUrl() and setUrl()

```
public String getUrl();
public void setUrl(String url) throws java.sql.SQLException;
```

Description

These methods control the JDBC URL used for making a connection to the database. This method is only necessary if you are not using JNDI to make connections.

getUsername() and setUsername()

```
public String getUsername();
public void setUsername(String uid)
  throws java.sql.SQLException;
```

Description

> These methods manage the user ID the rowset should use for making its database connections.

isReadOnly() and setReadOnly()

```
public boolean isReadOnly();
public void setReadOnly(boolean ro)
  throws java.sql.SQLException;
```

Description

> These methods enable you to control whether or not this rowset should be read-only.

setConcurrency

```
public void setConcurrency(int cncr)
  throws java.sql.SQLException;
```

Description

> This method assigns a concurrency value to the rowset.

RowSetEvent

Synopsis

Class Name:	`javax.sql.RowSetEvent`
Superclass:	`java.util.EventObject`
Immediate Subclasses:	None
Interfaces Implemented:	None
Availability:	New as of JDK 1.2

Description

Rowset events occur whenever something of interest happens in a `RowSet` instance. Examples of such events include column value changes and cursor movements.

Class Summary

```
public class RowSetEvent extends java.util.EventObject {
    public RowSetEvent(RowSet src);
}
```

Object Constructors

RowSetEvent()

```
public RowSetEvent(RowSet evt);
```

Description

> This constructor creates a new rowset event.

RowSetInternal

Synopsis

Interface Name:	javax.sql.RowSetInternal
Superclass:	None
Immediate Subclasses:	None
Interfaces Implemented:	None
Availability:	New as of JDK 1.2

Description

RowSet instances present themselves to a reader or writer as an instance of the RowSetInternal interface. The RowSetInternal interface contains methods that enable a reader or writer to access the internal state of a RowSet.

Class Summary

```
public interface RowSetInternal {
    java.sql.Connection getConnection()
      throws java.sql.SQLException;
    java.sql.ResultSet getOriginal() throws java.sql.SQLException;
    java.sql.ResultSet getOriginalRow()
      throws java.sql.SQLException;
    Object[] getParams() throws java.sql.SQLException;
    void setMetaData(RowSetMetaData rsmd)
      throws java.sql.SQLException;
}
```

Object Methods

getConnection()

```
public java.sql.Connection getConnection()
  throws java.sql.SQLException;
```

Description

This method provides the connection used by the rowset.

getOriginal()

```
public java.sql.ResultSet getOriginal() throws java.sql.SQLException;
```

Description

This method provides the original result set underlying the rowset.

getOriginalRow()

```
public java.sql.ResultSet getOriginalRow()
  throws java.sql.SQLException;
```

Description

> This method provides a result set that contains data only from the current rowset row. It throws an exception if there is no current row.

getParams()

```
public Object[] getParams() throws java.sql.SQLException;
```

Description

> This method provides the parameters that were bound to generate the current results.

setMetaData()

```
public void setMetaData(RowSetMetaData rsmd)
  throws java.sql.SQLException;
```

Description

> This method assigns a rowset's meta-data.

RowSetListener

Synopsis

Interface Name:	`javax.sql.RowSetListener`
Superclass:	`java.util.EventListener`
Immediate Subclasses:	None
Interfaces Implemented:	None
Availability:	New as of JDK 1.2

Description

Objects wanting to know when rowset events occur in a `RowSet` instance implement this interface to be notified of those events.

Class Summary

```
public interface RowSetListener extends java.util.EventListener {
    void cursorMoved(RowSetEvent evt);
    void rowChanged(RowSetEvent evt);
    void rowSetChanged(RowSetEvent evt);
}
```

Object Methods

cursorMoved()

```
public void cursorMoved(RowSetEvent evt);
```

Description

> This method is called whenever the cursor for the rowset being monitored by the implementor of this interface has moved.

rowChanged()

```
public void rowChanged(RowSetEvent evt);
```

Description

This method is called whenever a change has occurred to a row in the rowset being monitored by this object.

rowSetChanged()

```
public void rowSetChanged(RowSetEvent evt);
```

Description

This method is called whenever a change has occurred that affects the rowset as a whole.

RowSetMetaData

Synopsis

Interface Name:	`javax.sql.RowSetMetaData`
Superclass:	`java.sql.ResultSetMetaData`
Immediate Subclasses:	None
Interfaces Implemented:	None
Availability:	New as of JDK 1.2

Description

RowSetMetaData provides meta-data for RowSet instances.

Class Summary

```
public interface RowSetMetaData
extends java.sql.ResultSetMetaData {
    void setAutoIncrement(int col, boolean ai)
      thows java.sql.SQLException;
    void setCaseSensitive(int col, boolean cs)
      throws java.sql.SQLException;
    void setCatalogName(int col, String cname)
      throws java.sql.SQLException;
    void setColumnCount(int cc) throws java.sql.SQLException;
    void setColumnDisplaySize(int col, int sz)
      throws java.sql.SQLException;
    void setColumnLabel(int col, String lbl)
      throws java.sql.SQLException;
    void setColumnName(int col, String nom)
      throws java.sql.SQLException;
    void setColumnType(int col, int stype)
      throws java.sql.SQLException;
    void setColumnTypeName(int col, String tname)
```

```
        throws java.sql.SQLException;
    void setCurrency(int col, boolean b)
        throws java.sql.SQLException;
    void setNullable(int col, int nllbl)
        throws java.sql.SQLException;
    void setPrecision(int col, int prec)
        throws java.sql.SQLException;
    void setScale(int col, int sc) throws java.sql.SQLException;
    void setSchemaName(int col, String sname)
        throws java.sql.SQLException;
    void setSearchable(int col, boolean s)
        throws java.sql.SQLException;
    void setSigned(int col, boolean s)
        throws java.sql.SQLException;
    void setTableName(int col, String tname)
        throws java.sql.SQLException;
}
```

Object Methods

setAutoIncrement()

```
public void setAutoIncrement(int col, boolean ai)
    throws java.sql.SQLException;
```

Description

This method specifies whether or not the column is automatically numbered and thus read-only.

setCaseSensitive()

```
public void setCaseSensitive(int col, boolean cs)
    throws java.sql.SQLException;
```

Description

This method specifies whether or not the column is case-sensitive.

setCatalogName()

```
public void setCatalogName(int col, String cname)
    throws java.sql.SQLException;
```

Description

This method specifies the column's catalog name, if any.

setColumnCount()

```
public void setColumnCount(int cc)
    throws java.sql.SQLException;
```

Description

This method specifies the rowset's column count.

setColumnDisplaySize()

```
public void setColumnDisplaySize(int col, int sz)
   throws java.sql.SQLException;
```

Description

This method specifies the column's normal maximum width in characters.

setColumnLabel()

```
public void setColumnLabel(int col, String lbl)
   throws java.sql.SQLException;
```

Description

This method specifies a suggested display label for the column.

setColumnName()

```
public void setColumnName(int col, String cname)
   throws java.sql.SQLException;
```

Description

This method specifies the name of the column.

setColumnType()

```
public void setColumnType(int col, int ctype)
   throws java.sql.SQLException;
```

Description

This method specifies the SQL datatype of the column.

setColumnTypeName()

```
public void setColumnTypeName(int col, String tname)
   throws java.sql.SQLException;
```

Description

This method specifies the database-engine specific type name of the column's SQL type.

setCurrency()

```
public void setCurrency(int col, boolean cur)
   throws java.sql.SQLException;
```

Description

This method specifies whether or not the column represents currency data.

setNullable()

```
public void setNullable(int col, boolean nlbl)
   throws java.sql.SQLException;
```

Description

This method specifies whether or not the column is nullable.

setPrecision()

```
public void setPrecision(int col, int p)
    throws java.sql.SQLException;
```

Description

This method specifies the column's maximum number of decimal digits.

setScale()

```
public void setScale(int col, int scale)
    throws java.sql.SQLException;
```

Description

This method specifies the number of digits to the right of the decimal for numeric column values.

setSchemaName()

```
public void setSchemaName(int col, String sname)
    throws java.sql.SQLException;
```

Description

This method specifies the name of the schema represented by the column.

setSearchable()

```
public void setSearchable(int col, boolean s)
    throws java.sql.SQLException;
```

Description

This method specifies whether or not the column can appear in a WHERE clause.

setSigned()

```
public void setSigned(int col, boolean s)
    throws java.sql.SQLException;
```

Description

This method specifies whether or not the column is a signed value.

setTableName()

```
public void setTableName(int col, String tname)
    throws java.sql.SQLException;
```

Description

This method specifies the name of the table supporting the column.

RowSetReader

Synopsis

Interface Name: javax.sql.RowSetReader
Superclass: None
Immediate Subclasses: None
Interfaces Implemented: None
Availability: New as of JDK 1.2

Description

A class implementing the RowSetReader interface registers itself with a RowSet object that supports the reader/writer paradigm. A RowSet then calls the RowSetReader to produce a new set of rows that will become the contents of the RowSet.

Class Summary

```
public interface RowSetReader {
    void readData(RowSetInternal rsi) throws java.sql.SQLException;
}
```

Object Methods

readData()

```
public void readData(RowSetInternal rsi)
  throws java.sql.SQLException;
```

Description

This method reads the new contents of a rowset. The execute() method in a rowset calls this method for rowsets that support the reader/writer paradigm.

RowSetWriter

Synopsis

Interface Name: javax.sql.RowSetWriter
Superclass: None
Immediate Subclasses: None
Interfaces Implemented: None
Availability: New as of JDK 1.2

Description

A class implementing the RowSetWriter interface registers itself with a RowSet object that supports the reader/writer paradigm. A RowSet then calls the RowSetWriter to write the contents of the RowSet to the database.

Class Summary

```
public interface RowSetWriter {
    boolean writeData(RowSetInternal rsi)
      throws java.sql.SQLException;
}
```

Object Methods

writeData()

```
public void writeData(RowSetInternal rsi)
  throws java.sql.SQLException;
```

Description

This method writes data back to the data source behind the rowset.

XAConnection

Synopsis

Interface Name:	javax.sql.XAConnection
Superclass:	javax.sql.PooledConnection
Immediate Subclasses:	None
Interfaces Implemented:	None
Availability:	New as of JDK 1.2

Description

This class represents a connection in a distributed transaction. An XAConnection instance is enlisted in a distributed transaction via a javax.transaction.xa. XAResource object.

Class Summary

```
public interface XAConnection {
    javax.transaction.xa.XAResource getXAResource()
      throws java.sql.SQLException;
}
```

Object Methods

getXAResource()

```
public javax.transaction.xa.XARResource getXAResource()
  throws java.sql.SQLException;
```

Description

This method provides the XA resource behind this connection.

XADataSource

Synopsis

Interface Name:	javax.sql.XADataSource
Superclass:	None
Immediate Subclasses:	None
Interfaces Implemented:	None
Availability:	New as of JDK 1.2

Description

The XADataSource interface is implemented by classes that provide a JNDI gateway into distributed connections.

Class Summary

```
public interface XADataSource {
    int getLoginTimeout() throws java.sql.SQLException;
    java.io.PrintWriter getLogWriter()
      throws java.sql.SQLException;
    XAConnection getXAConnection()
      throws java.sql.SQLException;
    XAConnection getXAConnection(String uid, String pw)
      throws java.sql.SQLException;
    void setLoginTimeout(int sec)
      throws java.sql.SQLException;
    void setLogWriter(java.io.PrintWriter lw)
      throws java.sql.SQLException;
}
```

Object Methods

getLoginTimeout() and setLoginTimeout()

```
public int getLoginTimeout() throws java.sql.SQLException;
public void setLoginTimeout(int sec)
  throws java.sql.SQLException;
```

Description

These methods get and set a connection for the interval that the system will wait to establish before giving up. This value is an interval in seconds. A value of zero directs the data source to depend on the default timeout for the underlying system.

getLogWriter() and **setLogWriter()**

```
public java.io.PrintWriter getLogWriter()
  throws java.sql.SQLException;
public void setLogWriter(java.io.PrintWriter pw)
  throws java.sql.SQLException;
```

Description

These methods get and set the print writer to be used for logging events. This character stream is used by all methods in this data source and all methods in objects constructed by this data source.

getXAConnection()

```
public XAConnection getXAConnection()
  throws java.sql.SQLException;
public XAConnection getXAConnection(String uid, String pw)
  throws java.sql.SQLException;
```

Description

These are factory methods for the creation of a distributed database connection.

Index

About the Author

George Reese has taken an unusual path into business software development. After earning a B.A. in philosophy from Bates College in Lewiston, Maine, George went off to Hollywood where he worked on television shows such as *The People's Court* and ESPN's *Up Close*. The L.A. riots convinced him to return to Maine, where he finally became involved with software development and the Internet. George has since specialized in the development of Internet-oriented Java enterprise systems. He is the author of *Database Programming with JDBC and Java* and the world's first JDBC driver, the mSQL-JDBC driver for mSQL. He currently lives in Minneapolis, Minnesota with his wife Monique and three cats, Misty, Gypsy, and Tia. He makes his living as a senior architect for Imaginet, LLC.

Colophon

Our look is the result of reader comments, our own experimentation, and feedback from distribution channels. Distinctive covers complement our distinctive approach to technical topics, breathing personality and life into potentially dry subjects.

Ann Schirmer was the copyeditor and interior compositor for *Database Programming with JDBC™ and Java™, Second Edition*. Catherine Morris, Claire Cloutier, and Jane Ellin performed quality control reviews. Mary Anne Weeks Mayo proofread the book. Judy Hoer wrote the index.

Edie Freedman designed the cover of this book. The image of a jacks game on the cover of *Database Programming with JDBC™ and Java™, Second Edition* is from the CMCD PhotoCD Collection. The cover image was manipulated by Edie Freedman using Adobe Photoshop 3.0 and Adobe Gallery Effects filters. Emma Colby produced the cover layout with QuarkXPress 4.1 using the Bodoni Black font from URW Software and the BT Bodoni Bold Italic font from Bitstream.

Alicia Cech and David Futato designed the interior layout based on a series design by Nancy Priest. Mike Sierra implemented the design in FrameMaker 5.5.6. The heading font is Bodoni BT; the text font is New Baskerville. The illustrations that appear in the book were produced by Robert Romano and Rhon Porter using Macromedia Freehand 8 and Adobe Photoshop 5.

Whenever possible, our books use a durable and flexible lay-flat binding. If the page count exceeds this binding's limit, perfect binding is used.

Java

Java Servlet Programming

By Jason Hunter with William Crawford
1st Edition November 1998
528 pages, ISBN 1-56592-391-X

Java servlets offer a fast, powerful, portable replacement for CGI scripts. *Java Servlet Programming* covers everything you need to know to write effective servlets. Topics include: serving dynamic Web content, maintaining state information, session tracking, database connectivity using JDBC, and applet-servlet communication.

JavaServer Pages

By Hans Bergsten
1st Edition November 2000
450 pages, ISBN 1-56592-746-X

JavaServer Pages shows how to develop Java-based web applications without having to be a hardcore programmer. The author provides an overview of JSP concepts and illuminates how JSP fits into the larger picture of web applications. There are chapters for web authors on generating dynamic content, handling session information, and accessing databases, as well as material for Java programmers on creating Java components and custom JSP tags for web authors to use in JSP pages.

Enterprise JavaBeans, 2nd Edition

By Richard Monson-Haefel
2nd Edition March 2000
492 pages, ISBN 1-56592-869-5

Enterprise JavaBeans, 2nd Edition provides a thorough introduction to EJB 1.1 and 1.0 for the enterprise software developer. It shows you how to develop enterprise Beans to model your business objects and processes. The EJB architecture provides a highly flexible system in which components can easily be reused, and which can be changed to suit your needs without upsetting other parts of the system. *Enterprise JavaBeans* teaches you how to take advantage of the flexibility and simplicity that this powerful new architecture provides.

Java and XML

By Brett McLaughlin
1st Edition June 2000
498 pages, ISBN 0-596-00016-2

Java revolutionized the programming world by providing a platform-independent programming language. XML takes the revolution a step further with platform-independent language for interchanging data. *Java and XML* shows how to put the two together, building real-world applications in which both the code and the data are truly portable.

The Java Enterprise CD Bookshelf

By O'Reilly & Associates, Inc.
1st Edition November 2000
622 pages, Features CD-ROM
ISBN 1-56592-850-4

The Java Enterprise CD Bookshelf contains a powerhouse of books from O'Reilly: both electronic and print versions of *Java Enterprise in a Nutshell*, plus electronic versions of *Java in a Nutshell, 3rd Edition*; *Java Foundation Classes in a Nutshell*; *Enterprise JavaBeans, 2nd Edition*; *Java Servlet Programming*; *Java Security*; and *Java Distributed Computing*.

Java Message Service

By Richard Monson-Haefel & David Chappell
1st Edition December 2000
240 pages, ISBN 0-596-00068-5

This book is a thorough introduction to Java Message Service (JMS) from Sun Microsystems. It shows how to build applications using the point-to-point and publish-and-subscribe models; use features like transactions and durable subscriptions to make applications reliable; and use messaging within Enterprise JavaBeans. It also introduces a new EJB type, the MessageDrivenBean, that is part of EJB 2.0, and discusses integration of messaging into J2EE.

How to stay in touch with O'Reilly

1. Visit Our Award-Winning Web Site

http://www.oreilly.com/

★ "Top 100 Sites on the Web" —*PC Magazine*
★ "Top 5% Web sites" —*Point Communications*
★ "3-Star site" —*The McKinley Group*

Our web site contains a library of comprehensive product information (including book excerpts and tables of contents), downloadable software, background articles, interviews with technology leaders, links to relevant sites, book cover art, and more. File us in your Bookmarks or Hotlist!

2. Join Our Email Mailing Lists

New Product Releases

To receive automatic email with brief descriptions of all new O'Reilly products as they are released, send email to:
listproc@online.oreilly.com
Put the following information in the first line of your message (*not* in the Subject field):
subscribe oreilly-news

O'Reilly Events

If you'd also like us to send information about trade show events, special promotions, and other O'Reilly events, send email to:
listproc@online.oreilly.com
Put the following information in the first line of your message (*not* in the Subject field):
subscribe oreilly-events

3. Get Examples from Our Books via FTP

There are two ways to access an archive of example files from our books:

Regular FTP

- ftp to:
  ftp.oreilly.com
  (login: anonymous
  password: your email address)
- Point your web browser to:
  ftp://ftp.oreilly.com/

FTPMAIL

- Send an email message to:
  ftpmail@online.oreilly.com
  (Write "help" in the message body)

4. Contact Us via Email

order@oreilly.com
To place a book or software order online. Good for North American and international customers.

subscriptions@oreilly.com
To place an order for any of our newsletters or periodicals.

books@oreilly.com
General questions about any of our books.

software@oreilly.com
For general questions and product information about our software. Check out O'Reilly Software Online at **http://software.oreilly.com/** for software and technical support information. Registered O'Reilly software users send your questions to: **website-support@oreilly.com**

cs@oreilly.com
For answers to problems regarding your order or our products.

booktech@oreilly.com
For book content technical questions or corrections.

proposals@oreilly.com
To submit new book or software proposals to our editors and product managers.

international@oreilly.com
For information about our international distributors or translation queries. For a list of our distributors outside of North America check out:
http://www.oreilly.com/www/order/country.html

5. Work with Us

Check out our website for current employment opportunites:
www.jobs@oreilly.com
Click on "Work with Us"

O'Reilly & Associates, Inc.
101 Morris Street, Sebastopol, CA 95472 USA
TEL   707-829-0515 or 800-998-9938
           (6am to 5pm PST)
FAX   707-829-0104

International Distributors

http://international.oreilly.com/distributors.html

UK, EUROPE, MIDDLE EAST AND AFRICA (EXCEPT FRANCE, GERMANY, AUSTRIA, SWITZERLAND, LUXEMBOURG, AND LIECHTENSTEIN)

INQUIRIES
O'Reilly UK Limited
4 Castle Street
Farnham
Surrey, GU9 7HS
United Kingdom
Telephone: 44-1252-711776
Fax: 44-1252-734211
Email: information@oreilly.co.uk

ORDERS
Wiley Distribution Services Ltd.
1 Oldlands Way
Bognor Regis
West Sussex PO22 9SA
United Kingdom
Telephone: 44-1243-843294
UK Freephone: 0800-243207
Fax: 44-1243-843302 (Europe/EU orders)
or 44-1243-843274 (Middle East/Africa)
Email: cs-books@wiley.co.uk

FRANCE

INQUIRIES & ORDERS
Éditions O'Reilly
18 rue Séguier
75006 Paris, France
Tel: 33-1-40-51-52-30
Fax: 33-1-40-51-52-31
Email: france@oreilly.fr

GERMANY, SWITZERLAND, AUSTRIA, LUXEMBOURG, AND LIECHTENSTEIN

INQUIRIES & ORDERS
O'Reilly Verlag
Balthasarstr. 81
D-50670 Köln, Germany
Telephone: 49-221-973160-91
Fax: 49-221-973160-8
Email: anfragen@oreilly.de (inquiries)
Email: order@oreilly.de (orders)

CANADA (FRENCH LANGUAGE BOOKS)
Les Éditions Flammarion ltée
375, Avenue Laurier Ouest
Montréal (Québec) H2V 2K3
Tel: 00-1-514-277-8807
Fax: 00-1-514-278-2085
Email: info@flammarion.qc.ca

HONG KONG
City Discount Subscription Service, Ltd.
Unit A, 6th Floor, Yan's Tower
27 Wong Chuk Hang Road
Aberdeen, Hong Kong
Tel: 852-2580-3539
Fax: 852-2580-6463
Email: citydis@ppn.com.hk

KOREA
Hanbit Media, Inc.
Chungmu Bldg. 210
Yonnam-dong 568-33
Mapo-gu
Seoul, Korea
Tel: 822-325-0397
Fax: 822-325-9697
Email: hant93@chollian.dacom.co.kr

PHILIPPINES
Global Publishing
G/F Benavides Garden
1186 Benavides Street
Manila, Philippines
Tel: 632-254-8949/632-252-2582
Fax: 632-734-5060/632-252-2733
Email: globalp@pacific.net.ph

TAIWAN
O'Reilly Taiwan
1st Floor, No. 21, Lane 295
Section 1, Fu-Shing South Road
Taipei, 106 Taiwan
Tel: 886-2-27099669
Fax: 886-2-27038802
Email: mori@oreilly.com

INDIA
Shroff Publishers & Distributors Pvt. Ltd.
12, "Roseland", 2nd Floor
180, Waterfield Road, Bandra (West)
Mumbai 400 050
Tel: 91-22-641-1800/643-9910
Fax: 91-22-643-2422
Email: spd@vsnl.com

CHINA
O'Reilly Beijing
SIGMA Building, Suite B809
No. 49 Zhichun Road
Haidian District
Beijing, China PR 100080
Tel: 86-10-8809-7475
Fax: 86-10-8809-7463
Email: beijing@oreilly.com

JAPAN
O'Reilly Japan, Inc.
Yotsuya Y's Building
7 Banch 6, Honshio-cho
Shinjuku-ku
Tokyo 160-0003 Japan
Tel: 81-3-3356-5227
Fax: 81-3-3356-5261
Email: japan@oreilly.com

THAILAND
TransQuest Publishers (Thailand)
535/49 Kasemsuk Yaek 5
Soi Pracharat-Bampen 15
Huay Kwang, Bangkok
Thailand 10310
Tel: 662-6910421 or 6910638
Fax: 662-6902235
Email: puripat@.inet.co.th

ALL OTHER ASIAN COUNTRIES
O'Reilly & Associates, Inc.
101 Morris Street
Sebastopol, CA 95472 USA
Tel: 707-829-0515
Fax: 707-829-0104
Email: order@oreilly.com

AUSTRALIA
Woodslane Pty., Ltd.
7/5 Vuko Place
Warriewood NSW 2102
Australia
Tel: 61-2-9970-5111
Fax: 61-2-9970-5002
Email: info@woodslane.com.au

NEW ZEALAND
Woodslane New Zealand, Ltd.
21 Cooks Street (P.O. Box 575)
Waganui, New Zealand
Tel: 64-6-347-6543
Fax: 64-6-345-4840
Email: info@woodslane.com.au

ARGENTINA
Distribuidora Cuspide
Suipacha 764
1008 Buenos Aires
Argentina
Phone: 5411-4322-8868
Fax: 5411-4322-3456
Email: libros@cuspide.com

O'REILLY®

O'REILLY®

O'Reilly & Associates, Inc.
101 Morris Street
Sebastopol, CA 95472-9902
1-800-998-9938

Visit us online at:
www.oreilly.com
order@oreilly.com

O'REILLY WOULD LIKE TO HEAR FROM YOU

Which book did this card come from?

_____

Where did you buy this book?
- ❏ Bookstore   ❏ Computer Store
- ❏ Direct from O'Reilly   ❏ Class/seminar
- ❏ Bundled with hardware/software
- ❏ Other _____

What operating system do you use?
- ❏ UNIX   ❏ Macintosh
- ❏ Windows NT   ❏ PC(Windows/DOS)
- ❏ Other _____

What is your job description?
- ❏ System Administrator   ❏ Programmer
- ❏ Network Administrator   ❏ Educator/Teacher
- ❏ Web Developer
- ❏ Other _____

❏ Please send me O'Reilly's catalog, containing
a complete listing of O'Reilly books and
software.

Name	Company/Organization
Address	
City State	Zip/Postal Code Country
Telephone	Internet or other email address (specify network)

Nineteenth century wood engraving
of a bear from the O'Reilly &
Associates Nutshell Handbook®
Using & Managing UUCP.

POST CARD

BUSINESS REPLY MAIL

FIRST CLASS MAIL   PERMIT NO. 80   SEBASTOPOL, CA

Postage will be paid by addressee

O'Reilly & Associates, Inc.
101 Morris Street
Sebastopol, CA 95472-9902